THE SECRETS
—— OF ——
MODERN ARCHERY

THE SECRETS
— OF —
MODERN
ARCHERY

JAKE VEIT

ARCHWAY PUBLISHING

Archway Publishing books may be ordered through booksellers or by contacting:

Archway Publishing
1663 Liberty Drive
Bloomington, IN 47403
www.archwaypublishing.com
844-669-3957

Because of the dynamic nature of the Internet, any web addresses or links contained in this book may have changed since publication and may no longer be valid. The views expressed in this work are solely those of the author and do not necessarily reflect the views of the publisher, and the publisher hereby disclaims any responsibility for them.

Any people depicted in stock imagery provided by Getty Images are models, and such images are being used for illustrative purposes only. Certain stock imagery © Getty Images.

ISBN: 978-1-6657-0140-2 (sc)
ISBN: 978-1-6657-0141-9 (e)

Library of Congress Control Number: 2021900358

Print information available on the last page.

Archway Publishing rev. date: 01/26/2021

ORGANIZED ARCHERY HISTORY

Over the years shooting and teaching archery all around the US I have
met dedicated archers working at the local and or the state level
They are organized archery to the public
I found most don't know the full scope of Modern Archery
or how it was formulated over time
That is what this book is for

**This book is to the Unsung and Unknown
promoters of our sport of Archery**

I WISH TO THANK MY WIFE DIANE
WHO PUT UP WITH ME AND ARCHERY
for these many years

Resources: Listening and participating in archery for 65 years+
I used the LOC - Archery Hall of Fame
Robert Rhode's books on the NAA
the NFAA History - Archery Bowhunters Hall of Fame
and the US Patent office
Plus George Ryals III & George Ryals IV

CHAPTER 1

The Secrets of Modern Archery
(were did we come from in the US)

No one knows where or when the first Bow & Arrow was made and used. There are archery artifacts found on every continuant except on Antarctica. Many date back thousands of years. There are cave drawings showing man hunting with his bow & arrow dating back some 20,000 years. I feel the first bow & arrow was used to obtain food just for survival. It seems man developed into cultural groups or tribes with a common interest for companionship and survival all around the world. Because of mans' nature he found a comfortable existence in surroundings within his group or tribe, some more desirable then others. An outside groups or tribe would desire things another group had, so they tried to take it? The other group had to defend themselves. If seems easier to take and destroy, it is much harder to build something. Archery became a weapon of war. Archery has changed the development and direction of man over time. You can find the history of archery within the history of every outstanding civilizations or culture up to some 3000 years ago. Archery history by itself is hard to find.

Archery was outmoded in warfare by gun power, used with the cannon, not the rifle or pistol until much later. Many nations out of tradition and respect for the bow & arrow continued it's use within their social events as a competition. There have been archery competitions in Europe and England for some five hundred years. Many isolated groups or tribes around the world still use the bow & arrow today. In America the Indians' used their bow & arrows to hunt with, there are some one hundred different designed bows from the American Indian tribes. The English officers brought their archery with the longbow as part of their society and culture.

When you first think of archery does the American Indian come to mind, thanks to movies. Archery has a history going back before man knew how to write. Our form of archery came from the English. The English officers brought their archery with them as a social event along with tennis and other traditions. There is no record of them hunting with their archery equipment but it was a unified sport shot under traditional rules, mostly practice for warfare that they didn't use in war.

The English pride in their archery equipment from hundreds of years used in warfare could not be abandoned. When archery was discarded in warfare for the canon the English nobility kept the traditional long distance archery practice as one of their events for noble social gatherings. This is what came to the Americas with the English officers along with a written description of how the make and used such archery equipment. There had to be individuals or small groups here and there other then the English to keep archery alive. The first organized archery club shooting old English rounds was the United Bowmen of Philadelphia in 1845.

Our archery started with two brothers, Maurice and Will Thompson in Georgia, ex-confederate soldiers. They had to surrender their arms before going home, the war was over. They had hunted with the bow & arrow as youth, they took it up again I think to survive. In the 1870's they moved to Indiana. Maurice was a lawyer and writer who wrote short stories about their hunting with the bow & arrow and other subjects, published in magazines and local newspapers. Maurice wrote "The Witchery of Archery" in 1876 plus several other non-archery books. Archery clubs from around the country contacted him with an interest in promoting archery, in 1879 they advertised an Archery Convention in Jan. at Crawfordsville, Indiana to any club interested in promoting Archery. There where eight archery clubs from six states that formed the National Archery Association and electing Maurice Thompson as the first NAA Chairman or president. The NAA purpose was stated as to encourage foster and promote the practice of Archery in the US under one general management and head (standard set of rules). They scheduled and held their First Grand National Archery Meet in August of 1879 in Chicago. With the ladies shooting a Double Columbia Round with 20 participants'. The men shoot a Double York Round with 54 participants'. The attendance was considered large and composed of ladies and gentlemen of the highest social standing and connection. Will Thompson was the first National NAA Champion. The brothers love of archery was obvious and finding others was a bust to their shooting of the bow & arrow.

The NAA accepted only three archery rounds as official NAA competition for their members. The York Round shooting 144 arrows; 72 arrows at 100 yds, 48 arrows at 80 yds. and 24 arrows at 60 yds. The American round with the same distances shot today 60, 50 & 40 yds. shooting 30 arrows from each distance and the Columbia Round shooting 72 arrows; 24 arrows at 50 yds, 24 arrows at 40 yds and 24 arrows at 30 yds for the ladies. Only the York and Columbia Rounds would be shoot for National NAA Awards. The NAA has held their national championship every year since, except 1917/18. The National Archery Assoc. was the only national archery organization in the US with the old English archery equipment being shot. The results of the meeting and first national competition was published in "Forest and Steam". Remembering that "The Witchery of Archery" which started it all was a book about bowhunting. Archery was fascinating then as it is today.

NAA dues of $1 was paid to their home club before they where eligible to shoot in the annual Grand Meeting (their national championship). There were 14 affiliated archery clubs with 10 of them attending the second meeting. Dues were paid as an archery club to affiliate with the NAA. A new application for membership must be signed by the NAA President and Secretary of the NAA. A new application shell be voted upon at the annual business meeting by a written ballot marked "For" or "Against". Two ballots "Against" shall be sufficient to exclude the applicant. A double round will be shot for the Grand Annual Meet for the National Archery Championship. A description of one arrow shot for competition: Nock the arrow and as you raise the bow begin to draw the bowstring. When your bow-hand has reached the proper elevation for aiming, the arrow should be at least three-fourths drawn up. Here the aim is fixed if necessary a slight pause in the draw is allowable and then the draw is finished by a steady even pull to the chin, where the loose is accomplished without a further pause. There was no mention of a visual aiming system or sight being used at this time.

A peep-sight was ruled illegal for NAA in competition in 1880, plus money prizes were rejected. A peep-sight was a visual reference to put on the target for aiming. They didn't give a description of their peep-sight but I assume it was not what we think of today. I figure it was a sight mounted on the bow to peep through at the target? The 1880 Meeting and tournament results were printed in "The Bicycling World" and "Forest and Stream". The Champion shall be the member with the highest number of points and hits earned during the competition. That was using the English points system for most hits and gross score from each distance in the rounds shot, not the highest gross score at the end of the competition. The Ladies Champion is determined on the Double National and Double Columbia rounds. The Male Champion is determined on the Double York and Double American rounds. The posted scores must of included other rounds because their total scores shown were more then the above round totals. Manufactures at the time The Granger Archery - W. N. Granger & Co. and A. Mahan, Cortland NY (fine bows).

"Archery and Tennis News" was listed as the official magazine in 1882/83 out of New York City. In 1884 the NAA started accepting individual members not just archery club members; the NAA called clubs "Archery Societies". The NAA Championship Medals won were returned after a year to be competed for again. The procedure for such return of won medals was formalized in 1884. It also described how the targets belonging to the NAA were to be sent to the next location of the next national meeting. The NAA obviously owned targets to help promote new locations for their annual national championships. In 1887 NAA archers competed against the Third Artillery revolver team, the revolvers won. A comment about participation in Archery saying it is indispensable to the success of a pastime, so wholesome, exhilarating and health giving as is Archery.

A communication was read at the NAA 10th Annual Business Meeting 1888:"To the President of the NAA, the Dayton Lawn Tennis Club desire to, herewith extend to the visiting and local Archers now in our City a very cordial invitation to visit our courts at any time and view the games." A motion the communication was received and ordered spread upon the minutes and by vote the courtesy was reciprocated. Also at that meeting it was decided that the Association would give tokens to all retiring NAA Championship Medal Holders who had surrendered their medals to the Association, this to include all those of past years as well as those of the future. Starting in 1888 Lewis Marson won nine NAA National Championships and 14 NAA Flight Championships, he was NAA Secy. for four years, good job.

It was stated in 1889 that the Thompson brothers were largely responsible for the birth and growth of the NAA for the 1st ten years of its existence. Maurice Thompson said in 1879 "But it remained to be seen whether our people would as suddenly fling down archery as they had suddenly taken it up." That is what happened! even today. Some of the National tournaments were little more than a club shoot. A local archer may feel they are the only archers in the whole country until they get involved in an organized archery group. Archery clubs feel isolated until they are affiliated with a larger archery group. There are reasons why archery is hard to promote. First archery is inherently difficult to master and there are many forms of archery. Archery discourages many who lack the persistence necessary to acquire the skill. Another reason is the difficulty of getting satisfactory equipment at a reasonable price, plus the upkeep of the equipment. There are a lot of activities in the public eye that seem to be easier to do and more readily available. Archery locations are far apart and time is an important consideration because spare time is limited.

In 1892 there where 23 qualified representatives at the NAA Annual Meeting, some growth in 14 yrs., but the NAA was running a deficit most years. In 1893 the NAA defined a club team as bona fide members of the club as one who has shot as club members for at least 1 month prior to the national meet. Some clubs were bring in ringers! There were about $2000 worth of medals distributed to the winners of individual and team competitions. They awarded medals for the total score per distance plus the most hits of each distance shot and for the total score and most hits for each round shot plus a flight round competition and sometimes the Wand round. In 1899 it was the only time a husband and wife had won their individual NAA championships the same year. Mr. M.C. Howell and Mrs. M.C. Howell. Mrs. Howell went on to compete in 20 NAA Championships, winning 17 of them.

In1900 at Avondale, Ohio the 22nd NAA National Meet, there were 6 Ladies and 13 gentlemen shooting. In the minutes of the 1901 meeting stating this resolution about the passing of Mr. Maurice Thompson: "Whereas: in the providence of God, Mr. Maurice Thompson, the Father of Archery in America, has been translated to another world, Therefore; be it resolved by the National Association: First-that in the death of Mr. Thompson every lover of the Royal Sport has lost a friend, and the world of literature has lost a shining light: Maurice was a prolific writter in his life."   In 1902 the United States was selected by a congress of delegates representing all nations of the World as the site for this quadremiral International Olympian Games for 1904 to take place in the city of Chicago, Ill. The NAA pledges total support and cooperation in promoting interest in the said games. (It was not all the nations of the world and it ended up at the St. Louis World Fair). Archery was added to the Olympic venue in 1900. The NAA will use its best efforts to secure the attendance of its members and also arrange for participation in prize and World's championship contest in archery during the program of the International **Olympian Games of the 1904** National was a landmark tournament in that it was the start of the 2nd quarter century of the NAA. It was the 1st time the NAA brought Archery into the Olympic Games and was only the 2nd time Archery was in the Olympics.

This tournament brought many new archers into the NAA. The Olympic Games were held in conjunction with the World's Fair in St. Louis in Sept of 1904. I would like to point out that they kept total hits as well as total score as an NAA norm. There where no international archery rules. The winning man shoot 192 hits out of 288 shots on the Double York Round. He did much better on the Double American Round with 176 hits out of 180 shots. Of all the competitors in the so called Olympic Games very few foreign competitors entered the Games with no foreigners in the Archery at all. It was interesting to me that when the NAA ran a deficit for the year they added a so called assessment to the gentleman's fee the next year, got to keep things moving.

Also to show the steadfast support the NAA generated. Mr. A.G. Spalding; publisher of the "Spalding's Athletic Library" out of New York, donated two gold Special Medal's for the Women and Man who shot the most "Gold's". Ladies on the Double National Round and Gentlemen on the Double York Round. Each medal to remain the property of the NAA, but to be held by the winners until the succeeding Annual Meet. At that time they shall be returned to the President of the NAA to be competed for again. Also stated by Spalding in this donation in 1905, "In the event the NAA ceasing to exist or an indifferent towards the sport of Archery and fails to hold its annual public competition meet of archery, then these two medals are to revert to the donor. With over 40 archers at there 1905 contest this showed a further advance but a slow revival of Archery competition in the US. Spalding had attended the formation of the NAA meeting in 1879.

In 1907 the NAA had established some kind of a Handicap classes of shooting because they awarded 4 handicap awards in addition to their other awards. In the NAA minutes of the 1907 meeting Mr. Will H. Thompson (one of the original brothers) stated the duty of archers was to interest others into the sport of archery. Archery is in a sense an aristocratic sport (there concept). An outfit of bows & arrows may cost as high as $150 but sets could be as low as $3. Let no one stay away because their scores will not be the best. The best shots do not always have the best time shooting. The NAA was communicating with English archers to standardize their scoring. The interest in Archery was spreading throughout the US, small clubs are organizing in scattered locations and many country clubs are establishing archery ranges and encouraging their members to take up archery. Few of the new archers feel they have sufficient skill to attend our National meets. They were using the "Archery Review" to communicate with their members.

An NAA member placed third in the 1908 Olympic Games in Archery held in England. It was in 1909 that the NAA amended Article VII to read "Any archer having an arrow rebound, or pass through a target, may shoot another arrow, in place of such arrow rebounding from or passing through the target." Up until this time I assume that an arrow rebounding or passing through a target didn't count as score? This is a good time to express my confusion as to all the NAA National Archery Awards. They awarded a medal for the most hits and another medal for the highest score for each distance shot in a round. Then an award for the highest score for the round. There was to be a point system for most hits and total score for each distance shot for each medal won? I couldn't seem to find how these points were used in determining a National Champion? until in 1913! The point system was actually used to establish the NAA National Champion, not the total score shot. Most of the time total points accumulated and total score were the same to determine a national champion but not always. This was the controversy stated in 1913 about the point system.

Quite from a National Champion George Phillips Bryant; "I have long been of the opinion that the point system is unfortunate, and in some cases unfair. On the other hand I would not like to see any change that would affect the fair comparison of modern scores and the long line of past performance. I should like to see total score win, and in case of tied scores then total hits to win, and in case of both hits and score being tied, then settle it by points as now."

Quite from a National Champion Dr. Robert P. Elmer; "In my opinion championships should be decided on score alone with hits counted only in case of ties. This is an arbitrary opinion which I cannot base on any reasonable demonstration."

Quite from a National Champion H.R. Richardson; " There is no advantage, and much disadvantage, in the point method of scoring.

Whatever may be the official rule in England concerning the use of the point system, it was not enforced in 1908, the year I was there. the match was decided on the highest score. When I got one more then Brooks-King, there was no discussion of the points won."

Quite from past NAA President Dr. Wm. Carver Williams; " Replying to your recent note of inquiry about the use of the point system of scoring at tournaments of the NAA, I can tell you what I think of it in a very few words. It is antiquated and preposterous, and is retained through a sentimental loyalty to a supposed tradition. If its origin were to be investigated, I doubt whether there would be even that ground for its existence."

Quite from Will Thompson; " I am sorry to know that you are thinking of reviving the old controversy over the point system, as it can do no possible good, and can do much harm." In 1913 Mr. Thompson had placed 2nd even thou he had the highest score.

In England they wrangled over it for thirty years and finally abandoned it for two years in favor of gross score, and then came back to it gladly, and have ever since clung to it. We abandoned it for one year in 1880 at Buffalo, when Peddinghous won a gross score, though I should have won on points, having hits and score at 100 yards, hits and score at 60 yards and gross hits, 6 points in all, to his 4 points. The NAA changed back to points by unanimous vote, after the most elaborate discussion.

But what matters it? It gives all the same chance. Archery is an old game. The halo of age is about it. Its history is half its glory. Its old usages for life. The British have kept it alive through years and years of cannon and musket. Why not stay with them in all these little details that do no one wrong? But stability is best of all. We are at one with the English in this old, old pastime in all things save one. and in that they are right and we wrong, and that is in shooting both ways at targets. "There is nothing to be gained, such little, annoying things as the loss by rebounding arrows are far more important."

The point system for men shooting the York Round: 2 points are given the archer making the most number of hits for that round and 2 points to the one making the most score; 1 point for the most hits at 100 yards and 1 point for the highest score at 100 yards, 1 point for the most hits at 80 yards and 1 point for the highest score at 80 yards,1 point for most hits at 60 yards and 1 point for highest score at 60 yards; 10 points being perfect. The point system for the ladies shooting the National Round; 2 points are given the archer making the most number of hits for that round and 2 points to the one making the most score; 1 point for the most hits at 60 yards and 1 point for the highest score at 60 yards; 1point for the most hits at 50 yards and 1 point for the highest score at 50 yards; 8 points being perfect. The NAA awarded medals for the best score in the Double Columbia and Double National Rounds for the ladies and medals for the best score in the Double York and Double American Rounds for the men.

Then there was a National Champion for overall score for the men and ladies (that is a lot of awards but only for male and female, no styles of shooting).

This is the most divisive subject with the most discussion I've ever come across in the NAA to this point. At this time Will Thompson influence won the day and the points system was continued for a time. We have to remember that the archery of today is different from the archery of the past. The point system was given up for gross points alone to determine the NAA National Champion (don't know the year). The sport of archery is old and full of traditions even today. When we look back in a comparing of the scores as printed in the past we consider 1st the total score with just a glance at the number of hits, the point system is never shown. In 1911 the NAA awarded the Elmer Wooden Spoon an award for the lowest score shot, this was an annual award after that year. Most NAA Annual Business Meetings were to establish a location for the next years meet and elect new officers for that location.

Rounds normally shot for the Ladies: Double National Round - 96 arrows at 60 yards and 48 arrows at 50 yards plus a Double Columbia Round - 48 arrows at 50, 40 & 30 years. The Ladies Team Round was 96 arrows at 50 yards with a Flight Competition of 3 arrows shot. For the Gentlemen: Double York Round - 192 arrows at 100 yards, 96 arrows at 80 yards and 48 arrows at 60 yards plus a Double American Round - 60 arrows at 60, 50 & 40 yards. The Men's Team was 96 arrows at 60 yards with A Flight Competition of 3 arrows shot. They did not allow Crossbows at that time.

Did you know that in 1914 the Arrow Head flower or Sagittarius became the official flower of the NAA. In 1915 the NAA budget had a surplus. It was decided that the male archer with the highest total, adding hits and score will be the winner of the Double York Round. The female archer with the highest total, adding hits and score will be the winner of the Double National Round. A new membership to the NAA could be admitted if recommended by a member in good standing and approved by the President and Secretary/Treasurer. The membership fee was $3, the annual renewal fee is to be $2. There was a $3 target fee per shooter to participate in the Annual Tournament. It was stated that an arrow rebounding or passing through the scoring area of the face of the target shall count as one hit and score 5 points. In 1916 the NAA printed and distributed a hand book the "Manual of Archery" which included instructions and a history. I could not locate a copy.

In 1917 it was stated; the unexpected entry of the US into the war has upset many plans. There will be a postponement of the National Archery Tournament. The NAA National Archery Meet wasn't held until 1919. In 1920 on behalf of Dr. Harold G. Goldbery of Philadelphia, who presented to the NAA a silver medal of the United Bowmen of Philadelphia. This rare trophy was first presented in July of 1853. Its history is recorded by the Pennsylvanian History Society. It was presented to the NAA as a perpetual trophy to be awarded annually.

A occasional publication called "Archery" was distributed by Mr. Samuel G. McMeen of Columbus, Ohio. His purpose was to forward the interest of Archery in the US and particularly to give needed publicity of the NAA's activities. Mr. McMeen obtained a list of some 500 people interested in archery around the country and mailed copies at his own expense to that list from 1919 to 1926. A considerable volume of correspondence was the result by archers all over the US. It was recognized that there is some difficulty in obtaining suitable archery equipment, this is a serious obstacle to the growth of archery. A catalog company Wright and Didson contacted the NAA to express their willingness to carry a stock of archery goods. The NAA refer all inquiries for archery equipment to that company and included the companies name in all NAA mailings.

It was stated in 1920 that forty years is a great age for an athletic organization; never very strong and yet never in danger of death. At the 1921 National Meet the entertainment included a moving picture of the Eastern Archery Assoc's meet in Deerfield one night. Another night a lantern slide show was presented by Mr. Saxton Pope of San Francisco about Ishi. Dr. Pope was a welcome addition for the archers at the tournament. It was regrettable that Mr. Young and Mr. Compton could not be present. Dr. Saxton Pope was the NAA Flight Champion in 1921/22. All of the NAA National Meets included social events with the awards given at a banquet after the last day of shooting. Two examples of archeries status at that time; Douglas Fairbanks donated a special Trophy to the NAA to shoot a Robin Hood Contest and the Wand Round (a wood strip 2" wide and 6' high at 100 yards). James Fennimore Cooper donated a special Trophy to the NAA and the NAA Meet was held on his old home "Fynmere", this shows the status of archery at the time! The Field Captain always denied himself the pleasure of participation in that competition, as our judges do today.

The first mention of a Clout Shoot was in 1922. From 1922 to 1948 the official NAA publication was the "NAA Bulletin" published by Louis Smith. The Clout Round was added to the NAA Constitution in 1925. In the year 1926 the first time a Junior shooter is described as under 16 years of age. This being the 45th in 1924 NAA Annual Meet, it was held in conjunction with the US Sesquicentennial Sports Committee archery competition. The Sesquicentennial championship was open to all archers but the NAA championship was only open to NAA Members, separate awards were given. This duel archery tournament brought out 31 ladies and 73 gentlemen and 11 Junior shooters. The Sesquicentennial Sports Committee awarded medals for 1st, 2nd and 3rd highest score. The Sesquicentennial Sports Committee hosted youth archers from the Boy Scouts & Girl Scouts as Sesquicentennial Champions. The NAA used their usual awards protocol. This was the only tournament were Will J. Compton was mentioned as shooting in an NAA national tournament. He traveling some 3000 miles from Ca. He placed 2nd in the 1st York Round but not winning overall. The NAA listed 39 archery clubs and associations in the US not all affiliated with the NAA.

The "Ye Sylvan Archer" was published from 1927 to 1943. In 1927 the Intermediate shooting division was established as 16, 17 & 18 years shooting a separate division from the senior adult division. This was the year sights on the bow were discussed and determined that there was no rule prohibiting such a device. It was felt that the sight on the bow was a convenience, that an archer could make just as good a score without a sight. **The first Six Gold** was shoot and recorded at the 1928 Annual Tournament at 40 yards. That is six arrows for one end in the gold counting nine points each, there were only five color rings scoring 9, 7, 5, 3 &1 from the center out. After this discussion one of the top shooters removed his sight and on the 2nd York Round shot about the same score. On one evening of the tournament Art Young's "Alaskan Adventures" was shown (a moving picture). On another Mrs. H.S.C. Cummings described her husband and her attending the Grand National Archery Tournament in England. They shot on a field with targets at both ends of the field. They inquired about the use of a sight on the bow and were informed there was no rule prohibiting there use in England, but none where used. You have to take into consideration they were shooting longbows and wood arrows.

1929 was the first time the **NAA Annual Meet was held on the West Coast of the US**. Of the 110 archery clubs identified in 1929 only 27 where affiliated with the NAA. Of the 8 archery clubs identified in Canada only one was affiliated with the NAA. In 1930 there was a pursuant to have sections of National Forest Reserves set aside for bowhunting only because at the time there was only one hunting season in which gun and bow hunted together, not good. There was also a resolution to study having Archery as part of the Olympic Games; it is desirable to take whatever action that may be necessary to have archery become one of the Olympic Games sports. 1930 was the NAA's Jubilee Tournament. The **first Six Gold** was shot by a lady at 30 yards in a sanctioned tournament. It was noted that archery was one of a few sports that had been organized with active participation for 50 years. This was the first time a moving picture was shown at the Banquette of that tournament just attended. Printing the results of this 50th annual tournament the hits would not be added to the total scores. In 1931 it was decided that ties would be decided by the highest score shot at the longest distance. That the Team members would be limited to affiliated club members only. The male junior archers will shoot the Junior American round and the lady Junior archers will shoot the Junior Columbia round for their annual championship.

It is an unfortunate fact that a good many archers join the NAA for the purpose of entering one annual national tournament. Unfortunately they do not renew their NAA membership if they are not going to compete in the follow year. Paying members is an important factor to the NAA to be a greater service to archers in general. The NAA started keeping track of National, Regional, Sectional and State Archery Associations tournaments and archers scores. At the 1931 Annual Meeting there was a secret ballet taken for the first time to establish next years Annual Meet location. It was established that substitutions during the Annual Team Competition would be allowed at anytime, even during the competition. Even with the NAA membership being around 300 the NAA Financial Report showed over $3000 on hand as of Dec. 1931. The NAA acknowledged some NAA record score as World records. As I understand the NAA form of archery, it was only shot in the US and England? In 1932 an NAA committee was appointed to standardize rules for Archery Golf within the NAA. It was established that membership in the Six Gold Club be earned only at an official NAA tournament. NAA affiliated clubs could register 4 tournaments as official NAA tournaments for their organization. An American archer at the International Archery Federation was not an NAA member but was authorized to represent the NAA as an observer only. There seems to be a rapid growth in Archery, establishing scattered archery clubs and associations like the NAA but the understanding was with NAA had jurisdiction over the US.

There were **other archery associations** like the Eastern Archery Association, the Mid-Western Archery Association, the Western Archery association, the Pacific Northwest Archery Association, the Pacific Archery Association, the Channell Archery Association, the Southern Archery Association, the Missouri Valley Archery Association, Mound City District Archery Association with State Archery Associations in Maine, Connecticut, New York, New Jersey,

Pennsylvania, Ohio, Indiana, Illinois, Michigan, Wisconsin, Arizona, Oklahoma, Washington, Oregon and Utah all having jurisdiction over their regions. It was the purpose of the NAA to host an Annual National Archery tournament, the NAA must now keep in touch with all present archery activities and help and advise to archery organizations and new archery clubs as requested, this was becoming a full time job.

The annual 1932 Women's Intercollegiate Telegraphic Archery Tournament included 65 colleges with 560 individual archers, most not NAA members. It was voted to establish a committee of three to confer with representatives of the Archery Associations of other countries. It was proposed to the NAA to issue a certification of proficiency to persons wishing to coach archery- that was tabled. At the annual meeting of 1932 the Financial Report showed a dificent of some $582. The results of an NAA request of known US archery associations and state associations were: 17 Regional and District Archery Associations with 265 state associations and local archery clubs. With 71 having archery fields on public land with 31 of the affiliated with the NAA. 72 of all archery organizations found were affiliated with the NAA.

It was suggested to place flags behind the targets to help gauge the wind, no mention of a vote. There was a mention of an International Archery tournament in London, England; they didn't mention under who's authority. But the Federation Internationale De Tir A L'arc, FITA held their 2nd world tournament in England that year. It was voted that any Archery Golf tournament be played under the rules laid down by the sponsoring group, the NAA didn't want to get involved. They voted on a rule that no archer shall leave their ground quiver on the shooting line, it was voted down. There was an affirmation of NAA activities, to encourage membership, for members to adopt, interpret and enforce NAA rules for the practice of archery, for the NAA to hold an annual tournament to determine national champions. In general to act as the supreme governing body in all matters that pertain to archery in the US. They had just rejected Archery Golf? There will be an annual questionnaire sent to all known archery clubs for information about their activities with a self-addressed postcard.

When the NAA was formed there was the Eastern Archery Association already active. At present there is hardly a state in the US that doesn't boast of some archery. The NAA felt in 1933 it must take up the matter of a change in it's operation of the NAA. The change is sure to come while now we can do so without any outside influence. It was estimated that there is some 40,000 archers in the US, most not affiliated with the NAA. There was also the question about Amateur and Pro shooters? The making of two divisions could do nothing but hurt the NAA. That resolution didn't come until 1960 with International rules forced the NAA to comply. Being a little slow in reading all this, this is a good time to mention that at the NAA Annual Meet's they voted for the location of next years location was first voted on and then the NAA president was elected from that area every year. The NAA officers changed every year. The Inter-Club Team Shoot was established in 1934 with scores from 30 teams entering from affiliated NAA clubs, again most if the participants were not NAA members. The US was divided for the NAA sanctioned tournaments into Atlantic Region, Central Region and Pacific Region with the location of the annual meet rotating each year. It took only 5 of the 10

NAA Board members to make a quorum. At this time it was allowed for board members not present to vote by mail within six days of the meeting.

In 1935 there was a proposal to elect the NAA president for a 3 year term, it was rejected. Each of the 3 regions shell elect 3 delegates to the NAA Board; 1 for one year, 1 for two years and 1 for three years. After that one delegate is elected for a three years term each year for each region. The Secretary/Treasurer, weather 1 or 2 persons, shall be appointed by the NAA Board of Governors. There will be a First Vice-President and a Second Vice-President elected from the Board members. At this 1935 annual meeting it stated, to qualify for the Six Gold Club the perfect end must be shot in a major tournament. If an NAA club hosts more then four tournament per year, only four of their tournaments may be designated as major tournaments so their archers may qualify for the Six Gold Club in these tournaments. With individual membership being about 350, there was discussion about why archers don't join the NAA? with no results. The NAA office received 8 to 10 letters per day showing interest in archery. The membership has increased but very slowly. The Six Gold Club furnishes an important connection between the NAA and various archery clubs. Many NAA members feel that a magazine like the Archery Review with the NAA Bulletin free would establish and maintain an official connection to help every NAA member maintain their membership. Just for the information on archery but this would be expensive, something the NAA may not afford? If work had to be paid for it would amount to a tidy sum each year. It was expressed that archers shooting flight have done more to improve archery equipment and shooting overall than any other single activity in archery.

The NAA fiscal year became Sept. 1 to Aug 31 in 1936. In the flight shooting it was discussed if a bow should be weighted before or after the flight competition. If weighted before it may effect the bow. It was determined that only 1st, 2nd and 3rd places would be weighted after the shooting. This would save the weighing of every bow. The bow would be weighed only with the owner present. Decided that the York Round shooting lanes will be 5 yards wide, with the targets being set at 100 yards. Lanes cut with a mower and may have some white material as a marker. Mowing does not hurt the grass but if lime is used it can kill the grass for over a year. The mowed lanes were tried on the ladies field and compared with the white lanes on the men's field were found to be better. There should be a line 3 ft. from the target placement stakes toward the shooting line and parallel to the shooting line. On this 3 ft. line the legs of the NAA target stand should be placed for a consistent distance from the shooting line. The slant of the target with these stands will place the gold exactly over the target distance line. There should be lines parallel to the shooting line towards the targets at ten, twenty and forty yards. The twenty and forty yard line can be used by archers to practice the 80 and 60 yards distances. The targets will be moved forward during the competition.

There will be a Practice Field Captain in charge of all practice. The Practice Field Captain will see that the longest distance is the last practice round. Then when the Field Captain takes over for the competition the archers are ready to start. Only registered archers are allowed on the shooting field. All participants are encouraged to pre-register. It takes the income of four shooters to a target for the meet to pay for itself. They had in the past charged more and placed only three to a target to speed thing up. With three to a target the fee was $5 with the fee being only $4 with four to a target. The NAA Meets were becoming larger and there was concern about finding a large enough location. They considered increasing fees to bring the number of shooters down. If the archer has the time and money they will come. The Michigan Archery Assoc. has some 80 members in their state but only 29 attended the 1936 Meet.

The cost of this tournament was roughly 1/3 for targets, 1/3 for shade and the rest for medals, help, programs and other details. It was an advantage to have a Field Captain and a Lady Paramount who have experience in handling archers. They must be respected by the archers, such people are hard to find. Make sure the field of shooting has good water available and a first aid kit always handy. The Wand shoot is not being held this year and Archery Golf is better out of the NAA, just too much discussion as to how it is to be shot. The Art Young round was to be shot as a series of targets at unknown distances. By vote there will be no archery displays at the NAA tournament; this is a shoot not a convention. It was suggested to include Field Archery, didn't happen. The NAA Bulletin will continue in a reduced size. The Women's Intercollegiate Telegraphic Archery Tournament after seven years had 99 teams entered from 77 colleges. The entrance fee of $1 per team is sufficient to cover any cost. The NAA sent out information out to some 300 archery clubs and archery associations with but still less then 400 members. There were nearly 200 archery tournaments around the US on the NAA calendar for 1936. The Inter-Club Team tournament by mail was continued shooting the American Round.

A Bow Machine was purchased from Fred Bear for weighing bows for Flight Competition. There was scheduled an International shoot between Japanese and US archers in Oct. of 1937. I could not find the results of that tournament. During the York Round at the Annual Meet the men shot the 100 yard distance and then had lunch. The tradition of practice arrows at 80 yards came into question with no results at the time. The NAA contacted different museums that might be interested in an archery exhibit to see if the NAA could help add to their collection. It was recommended that exhibits of archery equipment, gadgets and accessories be displayed at the 1938 Annual Meet, to benefit archers attending. This was approved but left to the Tournament Committee. There was an expression about a lack of growth but the NAA is a venerable institution enjoying 60 years of uninterrupted existence. The NAA must introspective and severely critical of itself as an organization. 60 years has been ineffective in fostering the practice of archery that the average person still thinks of the bow & arrow as a child's toy. Archers are looking for a tangible asset for their membership money. Most seem to decide they are not getting a full value. What is needed: an increased knowledge of our sport to the public, there is a lack of permanent range facilities, a lack of competent instruction, a lack of promotional spirit among our archers and a lack of adequate funds to promote archery activities (sound familiar). The NAA originated a Family Membership plan where other family members can join at a minimal fee of $1. The NAA established a list of Leading Archers of the country, the top 100 through scores submitted through the mail-in Interclub Team Tournaments. New blood is continually coming in with new ideas. The Rules Committee recommends any new idea to be tried over a period of time and then accepted if popular with our archers. A report from the NAA Field Committee suggested pursuant of state legislation and game commissions to take action for areas to be established for the exclusive use by archers to bowhunt.

A letter from Howard Hill on Field Archery being included as part of the Annual NAA Meet 1937. I look at archery like the Olympic Games in that there are many sports with some of the sports having different branches. All contestants work at winning in their respective events for the general good for all but impossible for any one athlete to participate in all events. I look at the NAA archery with many branches and you have to make a choose between Target archery, game shooting in the field (Roving), flight, clout or any other event. It is all archery and each branch should help the other branch and aid in building up the sport as a whole. There has been insufficient time allotted for each division to be adequately presented. Put someone in charge of Field Archery so the Field is shot while the target is being shot. It would then be left up to the individual as to whether they shot target or field. The Field program could be arranged so that contestants in field could also compete in flight and clout (if this is his interest). I am certain that so long as we try to allow all archers to enter all events we will fall short of time. In having a separate field and shooing fee for the field event would cover the cost and add to the NAA. In the 1938 NAA Nationals would be a suitable time and place to try Field out. I will donate a cup for 1st place for the highest total Field score (it didn't happen).

The problem of the NAA Publicity Committee is really of educating the public. Unless funds to develop a program of this sort is a catch-as-catch can will continue. Information distributed for a good public relations job is expensive. The 1937 National NAA Lancaster Meet had a lot of publicity with local newspapers, the Associated Press, Life and the Newsreels present during the week. The NAA is a member of the International Archery Federation to expand archery world wide. The NAA published a list in the NAA Bulletin #215 of the top 100 scores of archers shoot in official NAA local archery tournaments from 1937. The NAA had 86 affiliated archery clubs at the beginning of 1938. The NAA Bulletin was sent to affiliated and known affiliated clubs and associations at no cost to keep members and archers informed regarding NAA activities. The NAA itself has around a 30% turn over in it's membership annually. Concern was shown that there was little participation at the Annual Meet by Jr. Archers. Remarks as to how to give the NAA Jr. Champion some real meaning. If there was less then 6 juniors competing that Jr. National Championship should be decided on the bases of scores shot in the National, Regional and State championship tournaments (really!) It was left to the NAA Board of Governors to approve, no results. The NAA rented space to commercial exhibits of archery tackle be placed only at the tournament headquarters. The exhibits are only open to NAA members and there will be no soliciting on the tournament field. It was voted and passed that if a round is broken for any reason that a practice may be permitted before resuming the round. At the 1938 NAA Annual Meet the 1st day included the rising of the US flag and the singing of the Star Spangled Banner.

For the first time in NAA history **the concerns of women** in archery is a matter of official consideration. The inclusion of ladies shooting the double American round in the Annual Meet is progress toward an international standard and a step in introducing archery into the Olympic games. Up to now the ladies and men shot different round for their championships. The NAA business is conducted by the Board of Governors composed of 9 men. Women should be represented in the NAA management of the organization. The problem of professionalism is creeping into the women's field as well. The question is do we discriminate against members who are commercial tackle makers? Tradition is worth maintaining and changing rounds for the championship loses a comparison with past records. Will the change encourage more archers or discourage participation? Perhaps an international standard should be the goal of our change? It would be better to gather information from other countries that shoot archery in hopes of forming common international rules (this is 1938).

In 1939 about 3/4 of NAA archery clubs are located on public property. These ranges were maintained by there public authority or city. It was only a few years ago that most archery club ranges were on private property. The NAA had 72 affiliated clubs in 1939. Public property is seen as an advantage to archery clubs and the NAA. Each club can register four tournaments for their members to earn a place in the Six Gold Club. Individual archers of affiliated clubs could join the NAA with no initiation fee. A Recognition certificate can be issued from the NAA to affiliated club champions. The die was made for the 1ˢᵗ **Maurice Thompson Medal of Honor** to be awarded sparingly to outstanding contribution to the NAA. The 1ˢᵗ Maurice Thompson Medal was presented to Dr. Paul Ernest Klopsteg of Chicago. Most new archers to the Annual Meet are impressed in which the tournament is run in such a business like manner because of the experience of the Field Officers and proficient organization of their work. This is indeed fortunate to all contestants because there is nothing more discouraging as confusion and uncertainty at a poorly run national event. You will learn for yourself that all archers develop a fellowship among their contestants in a common interest. You learn that the top shooters consider each novice, no matter their skill, in a fellowship because of their love of archery. It was felt a courteous and respect to all making the contest a pleasure. At a major archery tournament you learn things about bows, arrows and accessories to help you improve your shooting. It has been said the British Empire owes its crown to archery. The sport of archery bubbles with tradition and as you draw the bow, your imagination goes back to the days of Robinhood. Standing side by side with other archers there is s link in history, weather you miss or hit the wrong target, makes you think of the love of archery.

NAA affiliated clubs was 120 in 1940. Archery seems definitely on the up swing. An analysis only 30% of existing archery clubs are affiliated with the NAA. The NAA offered a free scholastic Membership to one individual in any camp program, schools and colleges that they had a list of. The NAA lowered membership fees for camps, school and colleges to $3. The NAA voted the award for Junior National Title to be based on State, Sectional, Regional and National scores. The NAA approved that the Archery Manufacturer's Assoc. be in charge of the Exhibition of Archery Tackle for display at the Amherst Annual Meet. The NAA voted to allow more then four Six Gold meets per club or archery organization with a payment of a $3 fee per event. Voted to make the "American Bowmen Review" the official publication of the NAA and provide a subscription to all NAA members. After exchanging letters with leading exponents of Field Archery it was concluded that the NAA could best help by cooperating with those interested to form the National Field Archery Association. The NAA will continue the regular Team competition with Open and State Teams in the event. Voted and passed that if any NAA member keeps up their membership for 20 years, they shall be elected as a

Life Member at a one time fee of $40. The NAA established a committee to look at various classification systems for the Annual Meet. It was stated that the NAA can't expect admiration and respect of outsiders until we give that respect to our sport of archery. Let us remember that we are judged by our appearance to others. The NAA was very conscience of it's image, they were a social group.

This is from the 1941 NAA Annual Report: The NAA forming back in 1879 was the first national sport before organizations like baseball, golf or tennis had been organized, it was before the radio and airplane were perfected, now it is 1941 62 years later. It was in 1928 that the NAA determined to rotate its national meet within its three regions and this has encouraged archery development throughout the US. In 1941 the American Bowman-Review was established as the official NAA monthly paper with distribution to all members. This paper had an "English Supplement" in it to inform our archers of English archery. There were 155 clubs and 115 schools and college groups active within the NAA. This year the NAA affiliated with the Olympic Bowmen's League to have **an Indoor Archery Program** offered to its members. The Olympic Bowmen's League has been shooting indoor archery for some 14 years. 64 teams took part in a series of ten matches, which involved over 500 archers. It was hoped that every NAA club would participate in next winter's series. In an effort to unify all archers Mr. W. Burton Wescott of Dover, Mass. created a patch called "Bowmen's Emblem" and made it available to anyone requesting it at no charge. The NAA established a Team competition in each of the three regions based on the Team Round shooting 90 arrows at 60 yards. There will be playoff matches conducted in the regions for "The Challenge Trophy" Wescott had donated. Also a new trophy will be presented to a lower bracket archer that shows humor & sportsmanship called "Good Sportsmanship Trophy" for there natural loveable personality. This may be given to a women, junior or man.

The NAA followed the progress of the NFAA and have given them our complete morel support and encouragement for their 500 members. The NAA is happy to see Field Archery promoted to its fullest extent and whenever possible we will lend all possible aid. I feel that including Field archery upset or was changing the NAA mind set or atmosphere from Target archery. They could of increased our membership but it didn't feel right. Instead of including this new form of archery the NAA felt better just helping it. For the first time the NAA sent an affiliated archery club a Membership Certificate. They wanted something tangible as evidence of affiliation for the club members to see. Few archers know of the amount of work that goes into the planning, correspondence and execution of a national meet. To try to please every archer to make the meet successful financially, socially and competitively well done. Now in 1941 the Women's Committee decided to move the archers and not the target butts when changing distances during a competition, for them not the men.

From 1942 to 1945 the NAA's Annual Meet was not held at just one location, travel was harder during World War II. In 1942 the NAA hosted an a Nationwide Mail Match with score divisions Women shooting a double National and double Columbia Rounds between August 1 thru the 16th. Men shooting a double York and a double American Rounds. Junior archers shot score on four Junior American Rounds. This competition used A, B, C, D and E classes for the adults. I'm only listing the first place winners in each class.

Women's Class A (over 950 points) National Champ Mrs. S. R. Robert Leaman of Pa., Class B (850 to 949) winner Mrs. E. C. Pilgrim of Okla., Class C (750 to 849) Jane Lewis of Ca., Class D (600 to 749) Alice Mericourt of Ca., Class E (below 600) Elva Herdman of Del.

Men's Class A (over 1300 points) National Champ C. J. Weese of NJ, Class B (110 to 1299) winner Harold Rainier of Ind., Class C (900 to 1099) Gilbert Frey of Va., Class D (700 to 899) John W. Adams of NJ., Class E (below 700) Wayne Dye of Ca.

Jr. Girls - Maryellen Bramlet of Ill., Jr. Boys - John Mahoney of Ca.

Women's Team - Cleveland Archery Club of Ohio

Men's Team - Elysian Archers of Ca.

They also included a Mail In Flight competition only listing Class 1 winners and for Women-Millie Hill shot 344yds 2ft &6ins. Men-Homer Prouty shot 455 yds., Jr. Boy- Charles Henderson shot 355 yds. 1ft., a Freestyle- Mike Humbert shot 524yds. 2ft. there were no states given for flight. There were 384 women, 491 men, 23 Jr. girls and 53 Jr. boys competing. I didn't include the team members and flight shooter, many archers shoot many disciplines of archery.

In 1943 the NAA Nationwide Mail Match again the Women shooting a double National and a double Columbia Rounds. The Men shooting a double York and a double American Rounds, Junior archers shooting four Junior American Rounds.

Women's Class A (over 950) National Champ Mrs. S. Robert Leaman of Pa., Class B (850 to 949) winner Bettie Stanley of Ohio, Class C (750 to 849) Mrs. Code of Pa., Class D (600 to 749) Mrs. T. W. Kirkwood of Ark., Class E (below 699) Ann Brebber of Wis.

Men's Class A (over 1300) National Champ Carl J. Weese of NJ, Class B (1100 to 1299) winner Harold P. Black of Mass., Class C (900 to 1099) J. F. Burshears of Colo., Class D (700 to 899) Carson Wallon of NY, Class E (below 700) L. M. Jackson of Ca.

Jr. Girls - Marilyn Reinecke of Ill., Jr. Boys - John Mahoney of Ca.

Women's Team - Milwaukee Archers of Wis., Men's Team - Pasadena Archery Club of Ca.

Again a flight competition held Oct. 1 thru 24 again only listing the Class 1 winners. Women - Babe Bitzenburger of Ca. shot 380 yds. 1ins., Men - Charles Henderson of Ind. shot 455yds. 1 ft. 5ins., Jr. Boys - Charles Henderson of Ind. shot 377yds 1 ft. There were 283 women, 395 men, 14 Jr. Girls and 65 Jr. boys participating, again I didn't count team member and flight shooters.

In 1944 the NAA Nationwide Mail Match shooting the same rounds in August 5 thru 20.

Women's Class A - National Champ Verna G. Leaman of Pa., Class B - Phyllis Garner of Ca., Class C - Bernice Doebler of NY, Class D - Eva Kern of Ohio, Class E - Bertha Olson of Conn.

Men's Class A - National Champ Larry Hughes of Ca., Class B winner - Lee A. Pollard of Fl., Class C - Albert Jones of Ca., Class D - Manly Tinkler of Ca. Class E - Stanley Presnall of Conn. There was an Oldster's Division (no age given) Harold A. Titcomb of Maine

Jr. Girls - Rita Dispenziere of NJ, Jr.Boys - John Mahoney of Ca.

Women's Team - The Bronx Arcehrs of NY, Men's Team - Madison Long Bows of NJ.

Flight winner of Class 1 Flight competition was Oct 1 thru 22nd - Women Babe Bitzenburger of Ca. shot 383yds 2ft., Men Minte Hammer of Ca. shot 486yds 1 in., Jr. Girls - Marylin Strandwold of Wash. shot 256yds 4ins., Jr. Boys - Donald C. Kunz of Ohio shot 318yds 2ft 3ins. There were 273 women, 491 men, 7 Oldsters, 14 Jr. Girls and 70 Jr. Boys competing. I didn't list the team member or flight shooters.

In 1945 the NAA Nationwide Mail Match shooting the same rounds in August 4 thru 19.

Women's Class A - National Champ Verna G. Leaman of Pa., Class B - Tress Galbraith of Pa., Class C - Anne P. Code of Pa., Class D - Blanche Mulvaney of Ill., Class E - Audery Hanson of Wash.

Men's Class A - National Champ W. J. Everman of Ohio, Class B - Edward Marker of NY, Class C - Charles E. Fish of Mass., Class D - George Helwig of Ohio, Class E - Nick Carter of Mass.

Oldster Division (over 70) Harold A. Titcaomb of Maine

Jr. Girls - Marilyn Reinecke of Ill., Jr. Boys - John Mahoney of Ca.

Women's Team - The Bronx Archers of NY, Men's Team - Madison Long Bows of NJ. I'm only listing Class 1 in flight held Sept 1 thru 30th.

Women - Mrs. Verne Trittin of Utah shot 452yds 1ft., Men - Michael Humbert of Ohio shot 468yds 2ft 4ins., Jr. Girls - Peggy Dunaway of Ohio shot 347yds 1ft 11ins., Jr. Boys - Lawrence Tucker of Colo. shot 319yds. There were 268 women, 464 men, 14 Jr. girls and 655 Jr. Boys.

This is a summery of the NAA activities up thru 1945, we will continue later. But for your consumption I'm listing the NAA Annual Meet locations and winners up thru 1941.

NAA NATIONAL RESULTS

	Women	Men
1879 Chicago, Ill.	Mrs. Spalding Brown	Mr. W. H. Thompson
	74 contestants	
1880 Buffalo, NY	Mrs. T. Davis	L.L. Peddinghaus
	46 contestants Palace Hotel	
1881 Brooklyn, NY	Mrs. Gibbes	F.H. Walworth
	at Prospect Park	Pierrefront House
	77 contestants	
1882 Chicago, Ill.	Mrs. A.H. Gibbs	D.A. Nash
	at Lincoln Park	
	36 contestants	
1883 Cincinnati, Ohio	Mrs. M.C. Howell	Col. Robert Williams
	at Kennedy Heights	Burnet House Hotel
	68 contestants	
1884 Chicago, Ill	Mrs. H. Hall	R. Williams
	at Pullman, Ill	Hotel Florence
	15 contestants	
1885 Eaton, Ohio	Mrs. M.C. Howell	Robert Williams
	34 contestants	Raichel House Parlors
1886 Lake Chautauqua, NY	Mrs. M.C. Howell	Mr. W.A. Clark
	at Assembly Grounds	Hotel Athenaum
	20 contestants	
1887 Washington DC	Mrs. A.M. Phillips	W.A. Clark
	36 contestants	National Hotel
1888 Dayton, Ohio	Mrs. A.M. Phillips	L.W. Maxson
	at National Soldiers Home	Phillips House
	54 contestants	
1889 Dayton, Ohio	Mrs. Phillips	L.W. Maxson
	at National Soldiers Home	Phillips House
	52 contestants	
1890 Norwood, Ohio	Mrs. M,C, Howell	Mr. L.W. Maxson
	at Hamilton Co.	32 contestants
1891 Natural Bridge, Va.	Mrs. M.C. Howell	Mr. L.W. Maxson
	28 contestants	
1892 Old Point Comfort, Va.	Mrs. M.C. Howell	Mr. L.W. Maxson

at Parade Grounds/ Fortress Monroe		Hygenia Hotel
	21 contestants	
1893 Dayton, Ohio	Mrs. M.C. Howell	Mr. L.W. Maxson
at National Soldiers Home/Battery Park		Phillips House
	30 contestants	
1894 Washington DC	Mrs. A. Kern	Mr. L.W. Maxson
	at Arsenal Grounds	Ebbitt House
	19 contestants	
1895 Dayton, Ohio	Mrs. M.C. Howell	Mr. W.B. Robinson
	at National Soldiers Home	Hotel Atlas
	24 contestants	
1896 White Sulphur Springs, WV		Grand Hotel Greenbriar
	11 contestants	
1897 Old Point Comfort, Va.	Mrs. J.S. Barker	W.A. Clark
	at Parade Ground	Hygeia Hotel
	11 contestants	
1898 Wyoming, Ohio	Mrs. M.C. Howell	Mr. L.W. Maxson
	20 contestants	
1899 Norwood, Ohio	Mrs. M.C. Howell	M.C. Howell
	near Cincinnati	11 contestants
1900 Cincinnati, Ohio	Mrs. M.C. Howell	Mr. A.R. Clark
	at Avondale Athletic Grounds	19 contestants
1901 Cincinnati, Ohio	Mrs. C.E. Woodruff	Mr. W.H. Thompson
	at Avondale Athletic Grounds	21 contestants
1902 Mountain Lake Park, Md.	Mrs. M.C. Howell	Mr. Will Thompson
	at Lock Lynn Heights	Lock Lynn Hotel
	17 contestants	
1903 Niagara Falls, NY	Mrs. M.C. Howell	Mr. W.H. Thompson
	at Niagara Falls Country Club	Temperance Hotel
	21 contestants	
1904 St. Louis, Mo.	Mrs. M.C. Howell	Mr. G.P. Bryant
	at St. Louis World's Fair	Louisiana Exposition
	27 contestants	
1905 Chicago, Ill.	Mrs. M.C. Howell	Mr. G.P. Brant
	at Washington Park Great	Northern Hotel
	33 contestants	
1906 Boston, Mass.	Mrs. E.C. Cooke	Mr. H.B. Richardson

	at Soldier's Field	16 contestants _____
1907 Chicago, Ill.	Mrs. M.C. Howell	Mr. H.B. Richardson
	at Washington Park	Lexington Hotel
	35 contestants _____	
1908 Chicago, Ill.	Miss. Harriet Case	Mr. W.H. Thompson
	at Washington Park	Lexington Hotel
	28 contestants _____	
1909 Chicago, Ill.	Miss Harriet Case	Mr. George Bryant
	at Washington Park	Lexington Hotel
	37 contestants _____	
1910 Chicago, Ill.	Miss J.V. Sullivan	Mr. H.B. Richardson
	at Washington Park	Refectory
	38 contestants _____	
1911 Chicago, Ill.	Mrs. J.S. Taylor	Dr. R.P. Elmer
	at Washington Park	Vendome Hotel
	34 contestants _____	
1912 Boston, Mass.	Mrs. Witwer Taylor	G.P. Bryant
	at Soldier's Field	Stadium of Soldier's Field
	34 contestants _____	
1913 Boston, Mass.	Mrs. P. Fletcher	G.P. Bryant
	at Soldier's Field	Hotel Bellevue
	36 contestants _____	
1914 Haverford, Pa.	Mrs. B.P. Gray	R.P. Elmer
	Jr. Male & Female - Dorothy Smith	
	at Merion Cricket Club	Waynewood Hotel
	52 contestants _____	
1915 Chicago, Ill.	Cynthia Wesson	Dr. Robert Elmer
	at Washington Park	Auditorium Hotel
	28 contestants _____	
1916 Jersey City, NJ	Miss Cynthia Wesson	Dr. R.P. Elmer
	at Fairmount Grounds	Fairmount Hotel
	26 contestants _____	
WORLD WAR I _____		
1919 Cambridge, Mass.	Miss Dorothy Smith	Dr. R.P. Elmer
	at Soldier's Field	Hotel Thorndike
	38 contestants _____	
1920 Wayne, Pa.	Miss C.M. Wesson	Dr. R.P. Elmer

	at Athletic Field of St. Luke's	Princeton Club
	30 contestants	
1921 Cambridge, Mass.	Miss D.D. Smith	Mr. J.S. Jiles
	at Crecy & Agincourt Field	Boston Art Club
	46 contestants	
1922 Cooperstown, NY	Miss. Dorothy Smith	Dr. R.P. Elmer
	at Polo Grounds on Clark Estate	Hotel Otasaga
	44 contestants	
1923 Chicago, Ill.	Miss Norma L. Pierce	W.H. Palmer
	at Grant Park	27 contestants
1924 Deerfield, Mass.	Miss Dorothy Smith	Mr. J.S. Jiles
	at Deerfield Academy	44 contestants
1925 Rome, NY	Miss Dorothy Smith	Paul Crouch
	at Central NY Scholl of the Deaf	
	61 contestants	
1926 Bryn Mawr, Pa.	Miss Dorothy Smith	S.F. Spencer
	Jr. Champ - Donald MacKenzie	
	at St. Luke's School	Teugega Country Club
	115 contestants	
1927 Boston, Mass.	Mrs. Robert Johnson	Dr. Paul Crouch
	Jr. Male - Ware Lynch	
	at Soldier's Field	93 contestants
1928 Rye, NY	Mrs. Beatrice Hodgson	W.H. Palmer
Intermediate	Miss V. Douglas	Donald MacKenzie
Junior	Miss Rosamund MasKenzie	Lowell Comme
	at Westchester-Biltmore Country Club	
	94 contestants	
1929 Santa Barbara, Ca.	Mrs. E.D. Grubbs	Dusty Roberts
Intermediate	Betty Gene Hunt	Jack Selby
Junior	Kathleen Thornxurn	B. McCrew Jr.
	at Hope Ranch Club Polo Field	Chamber Commerce Building
	112 contestants	
1930 Chicago, Ill. 50th	Mrs. Audrey Grubbs	Russell Hoogerhyde
Intermediate	Miss Betty Gene Hunt	Roy Case Jr.
Junior	Margherita Childs	E. Hodgson
	at Grant Park	Stevens Hotel/Tower Bell Room
	117 contestants	

1931 Canadaigua, NY	Mrs. Dorothy Cummings	Russ Hoogerhyde
Intermediate	Miss Elsie Mache	Dale Hallett
Junior	Madaline Taylor	Gordon Schopfer
	at Canadaigua Country Club	Hotel Canadaigua
	155 contestants _____	_____
1932 Seattle, Wa.	Ilda Hanchette	Russ Hoogerhyde
Intermediate	Natalie Seifert	Shirley Peterson
Junior		John Hobson
		Hotel Edmund Meany
	86 contestants _____	_____
1933 St. Louis, Missouri	Miss. M. Taylor	R. Miller
Intermediate	Marie Klopsteg	Richard Collings
Junior	Anna May King	Walter Houry
	at Forest Park	Hotel Chase
	71 contestants _____	_____
1934 Storrs, Conn.	Mrs. Desales Mudd	Russ Hoogerhyde
Junior	Patricia Flynn	Kenneth Bradley
	at Connecticut State College	
	188 contestants _____	_____
1935 Los Angeles, Ca.	Ruth Hodgert	Gilman Keasey
Junior	Bessie Gubb	Hullis Hanchett
	at University of Ca.	148 contestants _____
1936 Battle Creek, Mich.	Gladys M. Hammer	Gilman Keasey
Junior	Marian Sturm	Richard Weber
	at Battle Creek Country Club	
	164 contestants _____	_____
1937 Lancaster, Pa.	Jean Tenney	Russ Hoogerhyde
Junior	Marian Sturm	Robert Goldich
	at Franklin & Marchall College	
	178 contestants _____	_____
1938 San Francisco, Ca.	Jean A, Tenney	Pat Chambers
Junior	Merta Langley	Sunny Johns
	at a Stadium	Hotel Bellevue
	147 contestants _____	_____
1939 Minniapolis-St. Paul	Belvia Carter	Pat Chambers
Junior	Jean Schweitzer	Fred Fulberth
	at Minnesota State College	Auditorium

	188 contestants	
1940 Amherst, Mass.	Ann Weber	Russ Hoogerhyde
Junior	Mary Thompson	Freddie Folberth
	at Massachusetts State College Auditorium	
	253 contestants	
1941 Portland, Oregon	Ree Dillinger	Larry Hughes
Junior	Dorothy Axtelle	Billy West
	155 contestants	

CHAPTER 2

Olympic Games

The International Olympic Committee was formed in 1894. Two Americans were on the first International Olympic Committee, IOC to learn and organize the participation of the US athletes in the inaugural modern Olympic Games. They were held in 1896 in Athens, Greece and Archery was not included. The Olympic effort in the US was named American Olympic Association, AOA at the New York Athletic Club in 1921. This group was granted a nonprofit corporation as United States Olympic Assoc., USOA in 1945. The USOA was changed to the United States Olympic Committee in 1961. The Amateur Sports Act of 1978 a federal law appointed the USOC as the coordinating body for all athletic activity in the United States directly relating to international competition, including the sports on the programs of the Olympic, Paralympic, Pan American and Parapan American Games. The act included provisions for recognizing National Governing Bodies, NGB for the sports is about these organizations, the United States Archery Assoc., USAA (NAA) is a NGB. The USOC moved its headquarters from New York City to Colorado Springs, Co. on July 1, 1978.

Olympic Archery

Archery in the 1900 Olympic Games held in France.
    Au Cordon Dore at 50 Meters - Henri Herouin of France
    Au Cordon Dore at 35 Meters - Henri Herouin of France
    Au Chapelet at 50 Meters - Eugene Moigin of France
Sur la Perche a la Herse (no distance given) - Emmanuel Foulon of Belgium

Archery in the 1904 Olympic Games held in the US
    Men Double American 40,50 & 60 yds. - George Bryant of US
    Men Double York 60, 80 & 100 yds. - George Bryant of US
    Men Team - Potomic Archers - William Thompson
                        Robert Williams

Louis Maxson

Galen Spencer

Ladies Double Columbia 30, 40 & 50 yds.

Matilda Howell

Ladies Double National 50 & 0 yds - Matilda Howell

Ladies Team - no team name given - Matilda Howell

Jessie Pollock

Emily Woodrull

Leonie Taylor

Archery in the 1908 Olympic Games held in England

Men Continental Style 50 Meters - Eugene Grisot of France

Men Double York 60, 80 & 100 yds. - William Dod of Great Britian

Ladies Double National 50 & 60 yds - Queene Newwall GB

Archery in the 1920 Olympic Games held in Antwerp, Belgium

No Ladies and no Target Archery

Fixed Large Bird (no distance given) - Edmond Cloetens of Belgium

Team Fixed Large Bird

Fixed Small Bird (no distance given) - Edmond van Moer of Belgium

Team Fixed Small Bird

Moving Bird at 28 Meters - Hubert Van Innis of Belgium

Team Moving Bird at 28 Meters

Moving Bird at 33 Meters - Hubert Van Innis of Belgium

Team Moving Bird at 33 Meters

Moving Bird at 50 Meters - Julien Brule of France

Team Moving Bird at 50 Meters

The first modern Olympic Games was in 1896, archery was not in these first modern Olympic Games. Archery was in the next three Olympic Games; France, the US and then England. The forth time archery was in the modern Olympic Games was in Belgium in 1920. At this time it was noticed that the archery competition was always that of the host country. With archery's long history and independent development around the world it was a different form of archery each time, Olympia's archery was dropped after the 1920 Games. The **first International Archery Congress** was held in Lwow, Poland on Sept. 4, 1931. Seven countries were represented to elect Mr. Quentin of France it's first President and named the new international archery organization "Federation Internationale De Tir A L'arc" FITA. The US was one of these countries but as an observer. The first International Championship was held that same year in Lwow, Poland with 22 archers from four countries. Ladies & Gentlemen shot together. They had 4 countries that competed in the team championship. There were targets placed at both ends of the field.

The Polish Archery Union sent a circular to all known foreign countries Archery Associations proposing the creation of FITA and hosting the above International Archery competition.

Archers in England, Estonia, France, Peru, Sweden, Switzerland and Czechoslovakia responded. Archery Associations from the US, Holland, Hungary, and Italy expressed their interest. FITA's stated it's purpose was to foster international archery sporting events leading to participation in the Olympic Games. If there are several archery associations in one country each archery association may send delegates as members of FITA but each members country will have only one vote. Positions on the Board where reserved for delegates from counties in which the sport of archery has attained a generally recognized status. The first year on FITA a great deal of time was working out and standardization of regulations dealing with FITA archery competition.

First FITA World Championship was shot from 30, 40 & 50 Meters with 3 arrows ends. The target face scoring the five colors from center out 9, 7, 5, 3 & 1 with Michal Sawicki of Poland being the first FITA Champion. France having 5000 archers at home selected only five archers to participate. The Polish Archery Union sent out a circular to all known archery associations proposing the creation of FITA. Archers in England, Estonia, France, Peru, Sweden, Switzerland and Czechoslovakia approved that proposal. With the United States, Holland, Hungary and Italy expressing an interest. The 90 Meter event was added to the second FITA World Championship held in Warsaw.

The FITA Board authorized the Polish delegation to the Olympic Committee to make the motion to introduce archery into the program of the Olympics. It was not accepted. The 1932 international FITA rules stated that all accessories and marks on the bow be eliminated during shooting of the archery competition. The 90 meter event was optional for FITA archery competition locally. The FITA office sent the results of the 2nd International Archery competition and the minutes of the 2nd FITA Congress to all FITA members plus archery associations of countries practicing the sport of archery. FITA sent out a questionnaire to all known archery associations to determine the status, requesting literature of their shooting systems, results and records. The results established a voluble reference file but there was still no standard round for FITA competition for the Olympics.

FITA competitions and effort continued from 1931 thru 1939 with a brake for the 2nd World War. FITA World Archery picked up again in 1946. The US didn't really get involved with FITA competition until 1950 with the 1st Men's Team in Copenhagen. The US only had three members when other countries had four on the FITA score board. In 1952 the US Ladies Team won their 1st World Championship with the Men's Team placing 8th. The US had three ladies and five men participating. In 1955 FITA was officially invited to the IOC Meeting in Paris. The French and Belgian Archery Assoc.'s held an Archery Demonstration for the IOC using a Standard FITA round: Men 36 arrows from 90, 70, 50 & 30 meters. The Ladies shooting 36 arrows from 70, 60, 50 & 30 meters.

In 1957 pin-sights where standardized under FITA rules in Prague. The US won 1st place in both the Men's and Ladies Individual and Team competition using sights. All FITA Members in good standing may enter competitors but only amateur archers may compete under the rules of their respective National Archery Assoc.'s. Again in 1961 the US won the Men's and Ladies Individual and Team World Championships. FITA continued it's effort to reinstate Archery into the Olympic Games. It wasn't until 1972 when archery was accepted as a regular sport of the Modern Olympic Games with Men and Ladies competition, no team competition.

CHAPTER 3

Interest in Bowhunting in the US

To me it is obvious throughout the eons' the bow & arrow was used to hunt food. In 1911 a stone age Indian named "Ishi" came out the wood in Oroville, Ca. Locals called the sheriff as they held the wild man. "Ishi", he was expecting to be killed, he knew only that the white man murdered his tribe in the past. Many tried to talk to Ishi but neither understood the other. Two anthropologist from the University of California read the story and felt it was of some importance. They took responsibility for Ishi and took him back to the university in San Francisco. They tried every Indian dialect they knew of, Ishi responded to a dialect of Yahi. They still communicated with great difficulty. Anthropology was a department with a museum alongside the Medical School at the Berkeley campus. The attending physician to Ishi was Dr. Saxon Pope.

Ishi taught Dr Pope how to make archery equipment and hunt with it the Indian way. My favorite story is, Dr. Pope and Ishi were hunting and a deer came out of the brush, they both shot. The deer ran off and they followed. Dr. Pope found the animal and saw it was his arrow that had downed the deer. He was yelling, jumping up & down about his success. Then he noticed Ishi was ceremonially giving the deer food and drink to apologize for taking his life. That is respect for nature and life.

Some years earlier a young man named William John Compton, growing up hunting with the Sioux in Nebraska and Oklahoma he became an accomplished bowhunter. Compton migrated west to Origen being known as Chief Compton because he had been with the Sioux, here he worked with a bowyer for years making the longbow out of Yew wood. He had read about Ishi and migrated south into Ca. with as many Yew staves for longbows as he could transport. Compton looking up and met Dr. Pope and Ishi. Will Compton had harvested with a bow several deer, antelope, elk, bear and a buffalo by the age of 20. Will Compton was attending a Japanese Archery exposition and he meet another hunter interested in archery, Art Young. Art Young was a young hunter and explorer with a gun. Will Compton, Dr. Saxton Pope, Art Youth and Ishi bowhunted together. Ishi lived about five years after entering the modern world, he died of Tuberculosis in 1916. Saxton Pope, Art Young and Compton continued to bowhunt together. Compton showed Pope & Young how to make and use the

English Longbow. Pope & Young bowhunted all around the country and overseas gathering specimens for the museum of natural history back home under a contact to supply such. Chief Compton never left Ca. to bowhunt. He was 50 years old when he met Dr. Pope. Saxton Pope wrote "Hunting with the Bow and Arrow" in 1923. In 1926 Art Young made a motion picture short called "The Adventures of Art Young in Alaska" it showed him down every big game in Alaska with the Bow & Arrow. This film was shown all over the US in movie theaters creating a lot of interest in bowhunting.

Experimentation on a new archery round for bowhunting started in **1934 with an NAA archery club in Redlands, Ca.** A novelty field round was initiated by bowhunters around the country not content with the rounds shot by the NAA's, all long distances. Many NAA members that bowhunted were not target archers at heart but just wanted to bowhunt. About this time target archery clubs in Ohio, Michigan, Wisconsin, Oregon and other states shot an annual novelty round in the fall resembling Field Archery, more realistic unmarked distances for bowhunting. These tournaments encouraged the Redlands club to build a permanent Field like archery range. There were no strew butts so targets were just pinned to a pile of dirt or sand. Redlands started with a 20 target course set in rough terrain but through contact with other NAA clubs began to come up with a standard round.

This type of round grew shooting shorter distances but with ever target shot being a different unknown distance from 20 ft. to 80 yards. There was little similarity between these courses shot around the country for some time. Most shot four arrows per target scoring 5 points for a 1st arrow hit, 3 points for a 2nd arrow hit and 1 point each for the 3rd or 4th arrow hit. Most archers shot instinctive but one day a good Target shooter using a sight joined the game. He took so much time in setting his sight for each target! It slowed the shooting so much that sights were banned in field tournaments.

By 1936 members of the NAA were trying to tie the Field Archery round to met approval of the NAA. Remember the NAA target archery was the only game in town, it didn't work for most bowhunters. Exempts from the litter, members of the NAA field committee had written in early 1939.

"This NAA association is the organization that should be the logical one to start and organize field archery."

"an organization exists for the benefit of its membership NOT OUTSIDERS."

"That brings up two questions: Should the NAA do what the outsiders want done in order to enlarge its membership? Should it do what its membership wants it to do?"

There was no contacting with other Field shooters except through the NAA target archery clubs. With the help of several of the NAA officers helping the field groups. The NAA itself refused to acknowledge the right of a group of archers to organize except under the NAA. A letter between Field clubs: "After months of consideration the NAA Committee on Field Archery gave a report, the substance of which was that Field Archery should be organized by field archers with the NAA acting only as a good friend." The NAA will continue with its formal style of shooting target archery.

With the help and encouragement of several NAA officers a temporary constitution was written in 1939. With it's purpose to develop rounds and regulations for competitive field style shooting. To conduct championship tournaments using these rounds. In doing these things we shall not set our game up as being superior to other forms of archery but rather as a complement to them. It was stated in organizing Field Archery: "If such middle of the road games can be made the means of multiplying the number of instinctive shooters, we will have succeeded in greatly increasing the number of archery hunters. For that reason such games can and well be made the nucleus upon which a Field Association can be built." The NFAA organized with five states and members in 11 other states using a 28 target Field course almost the same as today, except with unmarked but standard distances. The NFAA was trying to develop field archery in a manner that would attract the hundreds of unorganized instinctive archers all round the US.

Field archers in Michigan promoted the new NFAA round for their state championship in 1939 with Instinctive and Free Style divisions with over 400 shooters. Fred Bear won the Instinctive class with a score of 460 points shooting 56 targets, besting the Free Style class winner by 152 points. In 1940 the NAA dropped their Committee on Field Archery. The NFAA formally organized in 1940 with the constitution written in 1939. Everything was temporary that first year. The only change was dropping the words "Instinctive Archer". Many archers in the Eastern US were sight shooters, it was felt if a state affiliating with the NFAA wishes to adopt Instinctive and Free Style divisions there was no objections but NFAA National Championships to be instinctive only for now. It was felt that after the Michigan experience it won't take them long to switch to instinctive shooting on a field course. The NFAA has never denied a club the right to organize the type of club felt most suited to its needs.

The first official NFAA tournament was a series of mail-in Field tournaments in 1940. This was the year the "Ye Sylvan Archer" becoming the official NFAA magazine for it's members. Together with receiving the magazine with the NFAA membership it was $1 per year. This was the year the Art Young Big Game Award was established. Also added to the NFAA Board was an Eastern, Mid-West and Western representatives. The Arrow & Stump logo was adopted in 1941 with the 20 pin for shooting a perfect target on the Field Round in 1942.

In a letter from the NFAA President in late 1942: "America is at war. Man cannot live alone by fighting, nor can he efficiently produce by working without rest day in and day out. There comes a time when fatigue, mental and physical, slows up production. To keep our minds and our bodies healthy and at peak of efficiency there must be periods of rest and recreation. Rest and recreation are to our minds and bodies what lubrication are to machinery. Without it they wear out and deteriorate. In war time, sports are necessary not only in the armed services but in the home front, to keep up morale, to take our minds for a moment from thoughts of war, to relax tired bodies and release stored up nervous tension. From our sports we can return to our work with renewed vigor and energy." I included this because it states a philosophy we can use and need today. It was also pointed out about this time that the archer who went out for the fun of it and didn't take his sport too seriously was the archer who had the most fun.

The **first Handbook** by the NFAA was printed and distributed in 1942 with 906 members nation wide. In 1943 the Flint Indoor Round was adopted and the first Indoor Mail-in Tournament was promoted. "Archery" magazine became the official NFAA magazine in 1944.

The NFAA came out of the war in 1945 with an Outdoor Field and an Indoor round with both a Big Game and Small Game awards program plus promoting their 20 pin for Field shooting but still only one shooting division, Instinctive. In 1946 a Southern Board Representative was added. Also that year the first outdoor National NFAA Field Championship was held with 4500 national members. In 1948 a Free Style division was established with much interest by the new members but with little participation. By 1953 the NFAA had over 10,000 national members. Field Archery is a uniquely American form of archery formed by bowhunters for bowhunters to practice before going afield to hunt. The NFAA is the only archery organization that has an archery representative in all 50 states today and promotes bowhunting awards program and competition. If you join the NFAA you are a member of their state affiliate archery organization in the state you live in. Within the NFAA's effort to promote bowhunting their members helped establish bowhunting only season around the US. This was not easy and it took years because they had to prove the bow & arrow (considered a primitive weapon) could harvest big game humanly. Today with our Archery only hunting season and it is easier to find archery equipment our bowhunters don't feel a need to help our national or local archery clubs and organizations.

The **first NFAA Compton Medal of Honor** was given at the Salt Lake City Field Nationals in 1947. This award was named in honor of W.J. "Chief" Compton, the man who taught Art Young & Saxton Pope to make and shoot the longbow. This award is not given annually by the NFAA but only when there is someone who deserves the honor. In 1950 NFAA officers were elected by mail ballot by the membership rather then by the NFAA Board of Governors. 1950 was the year NFAA members had some turmoil over having Instinctive and Free Style divisions, very divisive for awhile. In 1953 the NFAA formulated a Landowners Guarantee card for its bowhunter members to carry the card from the NFAA to show land owns you are a responsible archer. This guarantees any landowner that if an NFAA member caused any damage to his property the NFAA would make it right, this is so today. Today most bowhunters get a small group together and lease land to hunt on, in most states. In 1954 the NFAA started Chartering individual archery clubs within an affiliated state organization. In 1957 the NFAA started recording Big Game records in their Pope & Young program, not the Pope & Young club yet. 1958 was a crisis for the main office, it had to be moved. Their was a Building Fund advertised through the Archery magazine and got contributions from all around the US to buy the location for the badly needed office space. Al Van der Kogel donated his collection of archery equipment to display as a museum at the new office. In 1959 any record Big Game animal must be taken under the rules of fair chase to be accepted into the Pope & Young program. Also in 1959 Dr. Charles Grayson donated his collection of archery equipment to expand the new NFAA Archery Museum. In 1959 the NFAA eliminated the circular target kill area to an oval within the animal to better fit within the animal body's viral area plus they added a hair & hide cut off line on all animal targets.

The first NFAA Secretary/Treasurer John Vount kept all NFAA activity records in his bedroom starting in 1940. He and his wife Vera were active also in NAA Target archery. While secretary of the NFAA both Vera and John were awarded the NAA "Thompson Medal of Honor". Eventually Vera insisted all archery records be removed from the house and a barn was built outback. In 1958 Karl Palmatier was elected NFAA President, he was a Free Style target shooter and a member of the NAA. John Vount wished to keep Field Archery as it was, mostly Instinctive. He resigned his post and had the NFAA office material removed, they needed that new NFAA office. The NFAA office was moved to Redland, Ca. with Roy Hoff as secretary/treasurer. This request was run in "Archery" magazine for financial help for a Building Fund, over $16,000 was raised, The NFAA had a new home.

The NFAA was a sponsor for the 1st Las Vegas Open in 1962. In 1962 the NFAA started marking the distances of each target on the Field range, no standard distance change just marked it . The reason was because at National Field tournaments there were 8 to 10 - 28 Target Field courses to accommodate all the archers, one course shot each day for five days of the championship. Archers would record the distances on the course they shot. Check the course assignment for the next day and offer to sell the distances of that course to someone shooting that course to next day, go figure. In 1963 all eight Sectional Championships were standardized, also the NFAA had a financial crisis. The Archery Institute contributed $3000 to the NFAA and also loaned them $5000 which solved the temporary problem. It was in 1964 that Glenn St. Charles promoted Bowhunter Divisions that were added to the NFAA tournaments for competition. This was also the year the Instinctive class was change to Bare Bow. Instinctive archers were learning point of aim methods of shooting, not considered instinctive. The NFAA purchased and started printing the "Archery" magazine as it's own in 1969. The Pope & Young Club was formed as a separate entity with the help of Glenn St. Charles and the NFAA.

Now the NFAA was growing, to standardize they had an annual course inspection & approval for all archery club Field curses that re-affiliated or rejoined the NFAA annually. Every Field course in the US was consistent and by the rules of the time, this was and is a complex undertaking. The US was divided into 8 sections to help archers attend an NFAA Sectional Championship without having to travel all that far. The NFAA had a councilman for each section on their Executive Board. The Board of Directors was made up of NFAA Director from each state affiliate, they even had a director from Europe. In 1968 they **established a handicap system** for their tournament competition. They started a youth only membership and adopted a 20 pin for the Hunter round. In 1969 the NFAA adopted the PAA Outdoor Round and called it the International Round shot on their Field courses. This year the NFAA purchases and publishes Archery magazine. The magazine was provided with an NFAA membership even today. The NFAA become affiliated with the new International Field Archery Association, IFAA. The IFAA is using the NFAA rounds and rules. After the war US servicemen stationed around the world, shot the NFAA rounds locally. This with the help of the NFAA established the IFAA in 1969 and active today.

Struggles for NFAA had in the late 1960's and early 70's: How should a bow be shot, the problem was archers using a release aid. So how should an archer release the arrow. Release aids were allowed in Free Style only but not in bowhunter and barebow classes. What form should be used in instinctive aiming, some so called instinctive shooters had a single mark on the bow riser, not a real sight. This was made illegal but String Walking or three fingers under the arrow on the bowstring was allowed in barebow but not in bowhunter classes. Face walking or not just one single anchor point was allowed in Free Style and Barebow but not in Bowhunter classes. What type of bow should be legal or illegal? It was decided a bow must have two working limbs. The compound bow began appearing at some Field Tournaments with little objection at first. Until in 1970 at the National Field Championship the Free Style class was won with a compound bow. It was 1970 that the NFAA started it's Indoor League program around the US for local archery clubs to promote archery. This was a new Indoor Round. In 1971 the Compound Bow was accepted in all NFAA shooting divisions as a regular bow for their competitions. Compound and Recurve archers shooting fingers competed in the same classification, Freestyle Limited. In 1972 the NFAA National Bowhunter Defense Fund was created with a direct NFAA Bowhunter membership created to fund it. I know of the NFAA helping fund law suits against bowhunting to defend bowhunter rights. NFAA Bowhunter members were not eligible to compete in NFAA tournaments just the use of the NFAA bowhunter programs and awards. 1972 was the year **the NFAA Instructor School** was started to certify all new NFAA Archery Instructors with Mr. Cushman as the new NFAA Instructor Chairmen. This year the NFAA held their 1st National Bowhunter Rendezvous in Georgia.

The professional archers shooting for money wanted to shoot the best scores they could for competition. The existing professional group PAA at the time sided with the NAA and did not allow the compound bow in their competitions until 1993. The NFAA started their Professional division with the compound bow in 1973. The NFAA Pro shooters started at the Outdoor Field Nationals in Aurora with a purse of $2,800. Because of the release aid's popularity in 1974 the NFAA split their Freestyle shooters into Open and Freestyle Limited for finger shooters. Also in this year the NFAA established a flight system in their competitions. That is if there were 50 shooters in one class they divided it into five flights of ten shooters each. They gave awards of 1st, 2nd & 3rd in each flight but with the winner in the first flight being the national champion. The first IFAA World Field Championship was held in the US was in 1975 at Jay, Vt. along with the NFAA National Field Championship.

The **NFAA National Bowhunter Education Program, NBEP;** began in 1976 by Bill Wadsworth with encouragement for none NFAA members to attend and learn. It wasn't very many years until it went out on it's own under the name International Bowhunter Education Foundation, IBEF. At the 1977 NFAA Annual Board meeting there was a proposal to made all NFAA target faces and distances metric. There was a lot of excitement, this would made Field Archery more of an international game. The NFAA office was getting low on target faces. The NFAA Nationals was coming up and target faces had to be ordered. If they reordered the regular target faces and the motion passed, they couldn't be used. It was assumed this motion could pass and the new metric target faces were ordered. The motion to covert to metric failed, now what to do? The new metric target faces were made official for all NFAA competitions. The NFAA today uses metric target faces and shoots from yardage distances. Also that year the Bowhunter Freestyle class was established with a maximum of five fixed pins, or no movable sight, and one 12" stabilizer allowed, (continued later).

CHAPTER 4

Promoters that helped archery grow
(Manufactures, Bowhunters and Competitors)

J. Maurice (born 1844,died 1901) **and Will H.** (born 1848, died 1918)**Thompson** helped start the National Archery Association in 1879, all ready described. Both were ex-confederate solders that had their firearms confiscated after the Civil War before they went home to Georgia. They had hunted with the bow and arrow as youth and took archery up again after the Civil War. Maurice wrote articles about bowhunting and other things that were published in the New York Tribune, Atlantic Monthly and Harper's Monthly. Maurice's book "Witchery of Archery" stirred much interest to encourage the formation of a national archery organization, the NAA. The Witchery of Archery was his and his brothers bowhunting advertizes, both were lawyers by trade. Will Thompson competed in 18 NAA National Meets winning 5 also being the first NAA Champion in 1879. Maurice Thompson was inducted the first year the Archery Hall of Fame started 1972. Will Thompson was inducted to the Archery Hall of Fame in 1979.

Louis Carter Smith (born 1870, died 1961) he was the driving force to keep the NAA active through the early years. After the first several years archery seemed to not be a priority. Smith started new programs to bring new archers into the NAA. One being the NAA Inter-Collegiate Telegraphic Mail Matches. He continued this up through the great depression of the 1930's and World War II. Smith helped form the Newton Archers in Newton, Massachusetts in 1911. The only archery club in the area for years. Smith published "The Bulletin of the National Archery Association" from 1924 to 1948. In 1926 Smith went to Ca. to encourage archers to travel east to participate in the NAA National Meets with little success. In 1929 he succeeded in establishing three regions in the US for the NAA. Smith was Secretary/Treasurer for the NAA from 1919 to 1946. He received the NAA Thompson Metal of Honor in 1940 and is in the Archery Hall of Fame. Smith's daughter was Dorothy Smith Cummings inducted into the Archer Hall of Fame in 1974.

William John "Chief" Compton (born 1863, died 1938) is all ready described. Young Compton grow up around the Sioux in Nebraska. Compton was a bowyer, bowhunter and competitor.

Compton was in Montana when he heard of a Oregon bowyer and moved there in 1894. Then with 1000 fine yew billets or staves in 1913 he moved to California to meet "Ishi". Compton attended the Panama-Pacific Exposition in San Francisco in 1915 and met Art Young, the two men shared an interest in archery. Compton introduced Young to Dr. Pope & Ishi at the museum. Compton, Dr. Pope, Art Young and Ishi shot and hunted together for a year. Compton's friend Ray Hodgson wrote "Compton never went for publicity. He quietly went about helping others." Compton was inducted to the Archery Hall of Fame in 2010 and is also in the Bowhunters Hall of Fame. Born in Flint Michigan moved to Nebraska as a youth. Took his first deer at 14 in 1877. Chief Compton not only introduced Saxton Pope & Art Young but taught them how to make and use the longbow. Compton and Pope bowhunted with Ishi. Compton competed in the 1924 US Sesquicentennial Sports Archery. Will took 20 deer, 4Antelope, 2 elk and a bison before his 20th birthday. Will Compton was the last of the trio; Pope, Young and Compton to pass. Will Compton is in the Archery Hall of Fame and the Bowhunters Hall of Fame. The National Field Archery Association, NFAA created the Compton Medal of Honor in 1947. The Compton Traditional Bowhunters was formed in 1999.

Ishi's age was unknown, In Tehama County, Ca locals were puzzled by the disappearance of grain from mountain cabins. Sheep men were suffering losses and found obsidian arrow heads in dead sheep. Workmen putting in a drainage ditch for a Gold mine saw a naked Indian fishing with a spear. As they saw each other the Indian disappeared. Some time later near a butchers house near Oroville, Ca. they heard a dog barking in the yard outside. Investigating they found a naked Indian near the house. Ishi the wild man of Oroville came out of the wilderness in Aug. 1911.The people of Oroville called the sheriff. Ishi expected to be put to death, the rest of his tribe was gone many killed by the whites. The University of California sent anthropologists to investigate. Ishi was found to be from Yana Indian area but the southernmost lost tribe of Yahi. A Mr. Waterman from the university came, he was a student of dead languages. He tried out different Indian languages but none got a response from Ishi. After much communication the Indian Bureau in Washington gave permission to take Ishi to the University's museum for study and housed at Affiliated Colleges. At the hospital next door he was checked out by a Dr. Saxton Pope, they became fast friends. Ishi became a janitor in the Department of Anthropology. Ishi taught Dr. Pope his Indian ways and making bow and arrows. Ishi and Pope hunted up Deer Creek in Lassen County, Ishi's home territory. Ishi was proficient at knapping stone, making native bows and arrows. The California Motion Picture Corp. actually made some film of the Wild Man Ishi, but it was lost. There were many still pictures and more then one book written. Ishi died of TB in 1916, he had the grace of a visiting dignitary during those years. He was buried in an Italian cemetery in San Francisco, the last of the Yana Indians. Ishi was inducted into the Bowhunters Hall of Fame. Ishi's grave site is a Ca. Register Historical Land Mark # 809.

Dr. Saxton Temple Pope, (born 1875, died 1926); was the doctor to Ishi from 1911 to 1916. Pope was a military brat growing up in military camps and frontier towns. Pope tried archery, horsemanship, riflery and knife making shills, he was an outdoorsman. Dr. Saxton Pope was a surgeon, he became chief instructor at the medical school. Ishi taught Pope how to make an Indian bow and how to bowhunt with it. Later Chief Compton helped Pope make and use the longbow. Pope was NAA National Flight Champion in 1921 & 1922, placing 13th in the NAA Target Competition in 1921. Pope published "Hunting with a Bow and Arrow" in 1922. Pope bowhunted with Art Young all over the US and Africa. Pope & Young were contracted by the San Francisco Museum of Natural History to bring back a grizzly bear for the museum, it is still shown today at the California Academy of Sciences. Dr. Saxton Pope was inducted into the Archery Hall of Fame in 1973 and is in the Bowhunters Hall of Fame.

Art Young, (born 1883, died 1935); was a gun hunter and adventurer who meet Chief Compton at a Japanese Archery exposition in 1915. Chief Compton introduced Dr. Pope and Ishi to Young. Art Young worked for the San Francisco Call newspaper. Young and Pope took 6 grizzlies in Wyoming. Young was an accomplished writer. Young accompanied by cameraman Jack Robertson were in Alaska in 1922/23 to film bowhunting, neither carried a firearm. Their bowhunting in Alaska captured the harvesting on film a mountain sheep, mountain goat, moose and Alaskan brown bear on Kodiak Island it was released later as "Alaskan Adventure" shown all over the US. In 1925 Art Young, Saxton Pope and Steward White went to Mombasa, Africa; their Safari spawned 2 books and a series of articles in Field and Stream, 7 lions were taken with the bow. Young took both walrus and polar bear in Greenland. Young settled into a routine of lecturing around the US on bowhunting. Art Young was inducted into the Archery Hall of Fame 1973 and the Bowhunters Hall of Fame.

Dr. Robert P. Elmer, (born 1877 & died 1951), a competitor and author published "The Book of the Longbow", "American Archery" and "Target Archery". Won six NAA National Meets from 1911 to 1922. Was NAA National Flight Champion three times from 1911 to 1922. Dr. Elmer coined the term "Archery's Paradox" working with high speed filming with Dr. Hickman. Dr. Elmer was president of the NAA 1914 - 1920. Dr. Elmer was a recipient of the Thompson Medal of Honor in 1948 and was inducted into the Archery Hall of Fame 1973.

Dorothy Smith Cummings, (born 1903, died 1995), daughter of Louis Carter Smith started shooting archery when she was 10. Dorothy won her first NAA National Meet in 1919 as a Youth Shooter. She won six NAA National Meets as an adult, from 1921 to 1931. Cummings was the foremost US Lady archer for many years. She set a World archery record in 1931 that stood for 36 years and was inducted into the Archery Hall of Fame 1974.

Dr. Clarence H. Hickman, (born 1889, died 1981); considered the Father of Scientific Archery. From rural Indiana Hickman was noted for achievements in diverse and highly technical fields. He developed an early interest in archery, magic, photography, mathematics, physics, languages and music. Hickman was an associate of Dr. Robert Goddard. He had the patent on the recoilless rifle (the Bazooka), high velocity aircraft rockets and many more military patents. He had several patents in archery, he was using a high speed camera filming for the first time the "Archer's Paradox" working with Dr. Smith and Dr. Elmer. Hickman was given a new high speed camera will working for Bell Labs and asked to find a practical use for it. As an archer he filmed a friend shooting his bow and arrow. What they saw on film was the bending or oscillation of the arrow as it was propelled into free flight, the Archer's Paradox. Hickman worked for Bell Telephone Laboratories for 20 years and had some 30 patents with them. He developed the first portable Chronograph. Both Earl Hoyt and Fred Bear purchased one to analysis their equipments performance. He developed a radical bow design (never marketed) and prism sights for the longbow, built a mechanical shooting machine in 1927. He was Dean Emeritus at The World Archery Center, TWAC for over 50 yrs. Authored some 47 Historical Aspects on Archery, one was "The Dynamics of a Bow and Arrow". He was awarded the U.S. Medal of Honor by Harry Truman in 1948. He was awarded the NAA Thompson Medal of Honor in 1950 and was inducted into the Archery Hall of Fame 1977. He was awarded the Automatic Musical Instrument Collectors Honor in 1976, he was an influence in many fields archery was his love.

Dr. Paul Klopsteg, (born 1889, died 1991), all recurve composite bows made today are built from his scientific findings. Performed ballistics research during World War I which he applied to the study of archery. Had asteroid "3520 Klopsteg" named for him and the annual Klopsteg Memorial Award was founded in him memory. Paul was Chairmen of the NAA Board of Governors from 1935 to 1939. Received the NAA Thompson Medal of Honor in 1939 and received the NFAA Compton Medal of Honor in 1947. He was director of research at Northwestern University Technical Institution from 1951 to 1958 and was associate director of the National Science Foundation. He was president of the American Association for the Advancement of Science from 1958 through 1959. In 1979 he was awarded the Extraordinary Oersted Medal Award at the age of 90. He had published the "Turkish Archery" and "The Composite Bow" and was inducted into the Archery Hall of Fame 1976.

Ben Pearson, (born 1898, died 1971); is considered the Father of Modern Archery. Ben Pearson became interested in archery in 1925. He was a bowyer, bowhunter and competitive archer. By 1927 he was building bows and crafting wood arrows part time in his back yard workshop while working at the Arkansas Power Co. As sales increased he hired some part time help, this was in the great depression. Ben Pearson entered the Arkansas State Championship in 1926 and placed next to last and he was determined to improve his shooting. The following year he entered again and won the championship. Ben needed financing to grow, Carl Haun, an Oklahoma oilman, stopped by his shop to buy some arrows for his son. Haun was impressed by Pearson's operation and he offered to fiancé an expansion an incorporate into Pearson Archery Inc. in Pine Bluff. Ben designed and built the machinery needed to mass produce bows, arrows and accessories. He wanted the price of archery equipment to fall and distributed over a larger area of the US and even some foreign countries. By 1943 Ben Pearson Inc. employed 365 people in a plant covering 15 acres. Ben Pearson archery was the largest archery manufacturer for the better part of three decades. Ben Pearson gave exhibitions around the US, he never charges a fee or accepted expenses. Pearson archery promoted archery programs, tournaments, films and international bowhunts. Howard Hill shot for Ben Pearson Archery and make many short films about bowhunting. Pearson Archery published one of the first books on archery called "Archery" by Pat Chambers. The Ben Pearson Bowhunting Museum displays North American big game that include mounts of his Polar Bear and Grizzly Bear. He promoted the Professional Archers Association, PAA and the Archery Manufacturers Organization, AMO plus helped the NFAA in forming archery clubs around the US. He was awarded the NFAA Compton Medal of Honor and was inducted into the Archery Hall of Fame 1972 and is in the Bowhunters Hall of Fame. Ben Pearson and his archery equipment stood alone as an early achiever in supplying archery equipment to the public.

Fred Bear, (born 1902, died 1988); considered the Father of Modern Bowhunting. He was a bowhunter, competitor, manufacturer, author, TV appearances through the 1940's to the 1970's and world traveling bowhunting. He was on "The Tonight Show", the "Mike Douglas Show" and the "To Tell the Truth". In 1927 he saw Art Young's "Alaskan Adventures" and became interested in bowhunting. Bear met Art Young at a lector and his lifetime of bowhunting quest began in earnest. Fred began making bows, arrows and bowstrings in his basement workshop. Bear carved his first bow from an Osage orange stave he bought for $8. In 1933 Bear and Charles Piper gathered $600 to start Bear Products Co. mainly an advertising company. Fred was building archery equipment for his friends on the side. Fred won the Michigan State Archery Championship in 1934, 1937 and 1939. In 1939 Bear started Bear Archery Co. Fred barnstormed the sports show circuit with his shooting exhibitions around Chicago and St. Louis. Bear equipment was at many sports shows, he made many bowhunting films. He started a Bowhunting Museum in 1967 at Grayling. In 1970 Dick Lattimer organized the Fred Bear Sports Club working for Bear. Bear said he would never produce a compound bow and didn't until he sold interest in 1978 and they started producing the Whitetail Hunter, very successful. Bear and Glenn St. Charles pioneered the Pope & Young Club. In 1976 he was the recipient of the Winchester-Western "Outdoorsman of the Year". Bear Archery moved to Gainesville, Fl in 1978, his museum followed in 1985 to the Bear plant in Fl. The museum was sold to Bass Pro Shops in 2003 and moved to Springfield, Missouri, also the home of the Archery Hall of Fame (started 1972). He was inducted into the Sporting Goods Industry Hall of Fame receiving the "Lifetime Career Award", awarded the NAA Thompson Medal of Honor in 1977, the NFAA Compton Medal of Honor in 1964, the Safari Club International Hunting Hall of Fame in 1987. Fred Bear was inducted into the Archery Hall of Fame 1972 and is in the Bowhunters Hall of Fame. Ted Nugent even wrote a sang "Fred Bear" on his album Spirit of the Wild. Fred felt there was to much emphasis on the kill and not being in natures great outdoors. A quote from Fred "A downed animal is most certainly the object of a hunting trip, but it becomes an anti-climax when compared to the many pleasures of the hunt. A period of remorse is in order. Perhaps a few words of forgiveness for having taken a life. After this there is a self-satisfaction for having accomplished a successful stalk and made a good shot." "But a hunt based only on trophies taken falls short of what the ultimate goal should be. I have known many hunters who, returning empty-handed, have had nothing to say of the enjoyment of time spent in natures outdoors." Bear remained active in designing archery products and promoting the sport he loved until his death in 1988 at the age of 86. Bear was a member of the Explorer's Club, the

Boone & Crockett Club, the Safari Club International and the Outdoor Writer's Assoc. of America. Dick Lattimer wrote a book "Hunting with Fred Bear" and "Quote from Fred Bear ". Another Bear quote "Too many people are uncomfortable in the woods. They do not feel at home when they should be. The woods is a friendly place. Yes, the woods is a big place to get lost in, or to get into trouble in, but the main thing when outdoors is to use good judgment, stay out of trouble and have a good time." This is something that has to be learned. Fred Bear was cremated and his ashes spread near the AuSable River in Michigan where he hunted.

James Douglas "Doug" Easton, (born 1907,died 1974); in 1921 a hunting accident in which Doug was shot in both legs layed him up for some time. He was given Dr. Saxton Pope's book "Hunting with the Bow and Arrow" and he became fascinated with archery. In 1922 Easton was crafting custom bows and wood arrows in Watsonville, Ca. His footed wood arrow shafts were well known in a short time. In 1924 he was shooting at the San Francisco's Golden Gate Park Archery Range talking to an older man, Doug credited his craftsmanship to the book Hunting with the Bow and Arrow. He was talking to Saxton Pope his mentor. In 1927 in moved to Los Angeles where he made archery equipment in his garage. Doug helped organize the 1935 NAA National Championship tournament in LA. Doug was frustrated with inconsistency of wood shafts. Easton made his archery equipment part time for some years supporting himself by driving a delivery truck. During this time being in LA he became friends with Howard Hill and other Hollywood elite. Hill lived just a couple of blocks from Doug Easton. In 1939 he began manufacturing Aluminum arrows, in 1941 Larry Hughes won the NAA National Meet with his arrows. Doug Easton was buying aluminum tubing to experiment with to make his medal arrows, that was before World War II. The government commandeered all supplies of aluminum for the military. Doug in 1946 couldn't get the aluminum tubing he wanted so he began his own process. He designed and built extrusion machines to make the aluminum tubing he wanted for his arrows. His first aluminum arrow was a soft 24SRT but it worked, in shooting them you learned how to straighten them by hand as you shot from target to target. His alloys got better over time until you have the variety today. Easton stopped making his finished aluminum arrows, electing to manufacturing just the shaft to avoid competing with customers and friends. The XX75 came out in 1958 and the X7 in 1964. Doug Easton had worked with FITA in the effort to get archery back into the Olympic Games, which happened in 1972. Easton Aluminum was incorporated in 1953 as James D. Easton Archery. Easton's 24SRT was so successful that in 1957 he moved to Van Nuys into a new 10,000 SF building with fulltime employees. In 1964 Easton introduced aluminum ski pole shafts. In 1967 Easton used its expertise in precision tubing to make the thermal shroud for the seismometer used on the Apollo 11 moon landing in 1969. Easton makes tubing for all kinds of products, since 1972 Easton arrows have help win an Olympic Medal for many years. Easton developed a high-strength carbon fiber and aluminum alloy tubing for arrows and other produces. Easton grow from $13 million in 1977 to $90 million just 10 years later. Easton acquired Hoyt Archery in 1983 and acquired Curley Bates 2 years later. Easton Sports was formed in 1985 through acquisition with James Easton at its head. Easton Sports Canada was launched in 1986 to make mast & boom tubing for sailboards and bike frame tubing. Easton produced some 16 million aluminum arrow in 1992 which was 80 % of the market at that time but archery products where but 30% of Easton's total revenues. In the 1990's Easton developed a titanium softball bat that performed so well it was banned for professional play. Easton expanded externally in 1995 with the acquisition of Beman arrows. Doug Easton was inducted into the Archery Hall of Fame 1974 and is in the Bowhunters Hall of Fame.

James L. Easton (born 1935 -), Few people have had more of an impact on modern archery. Jim graduated from the University of California with a bachelor of science in 1959. He worked for Douglas Aircraft Co. until 1964. Joining his fathers company with brother Bob, they developed the first aluminum ski poles and then the first aluminum baseball bats, they affected many other sports. Jim became Chairman, Chief Executive Officer and President of Jas. D. Easton in 1973. Easton served as President of FITA (now World Archery Federation) form 1959 to 1964. From 1980 to 1984 Jim served as the Olympic Commissioner of Archery on the LA Olympic Organizing Committee and mayor of the Olympic Athletes Village for the 1984 LA Olympic Games. Jim Easton was elected President of FITA in 1989 and reelected in 1993. Easton has been a member of the IOC (International Olympic Committee) since 1994. Jim Easton helped developed the Olympic Round, OR Round for the Barcelona Olympics to make Archery more of a spectators sport. Jim Easton serves as the Chairman of the Easton Foundations a family philanthropic foundation. Jim was appointed to the Board of Trustees of the UCLA Foundation in 1985. Jim Easton was a recipient into The Archery Hall of Fame in 1997. Jim received the NFAA Compton Medal of Honor in 2002. He was the recipient of International Archery Federation Gold Plaquette. He was awarded the UCLA Medal in 2014 and serves on the Board of Visitors of the UCLA Anderson School of Management. Jim Easton has been approached many times to buy the company to take it public but he remained content to keep the business private.

Karl E. Palmatier, (born 1898,died 1988), his interest in archery started in 1927 when he helped start an archery class in a school he was teaching at. He became the secretary of the Michigan Archers Assoc. in 1928. He became an NAA member in 1935. When the NAA Annual Meet was held in Kalamazoo, Karl was elected NAA President in 1936. The same qualities displayed for the Michigan Archers became known throughout the archery community. He had learned the details of handling a major archery tournament. He was elected to the NAA Board of Governors in 1937. Karl had learned what archery had to offer, self-confidence and discipline in your effort at shooting, which helped personal development. This made him a prolific promoter of all archery. He received the NAA Thompson Medal of Honor in 1943. Karl was NFAA Tournament Director form 1940 to 1960. Served as NFAA President in 1959 & 1960. Was awarded the NFAA Compton Medal of Honor in 1952. Published a book called "Hunting Manual". Officiated at some 50+ NAA, NFAA & PAA Tournaments from 1936 to 1970. When the PAA started Karl served as Secy/Tres from 1962 to 1968. He was sought after for the US Indoor Open and the Ben Pearson Open Indoor to officiate, both some of the first large money archery tournaments. Karl was inducted into the Archery Hall of Fame in 1972 and they created the Karl E. Palmatier Award of Merit for the organizations highest honor.

Howard Hill, (born 1899, died 1975); unofficially referred to as the Worlds Greatest Archer. There can be no question that from 1930 to 1955 Hill was responsible for bringing more people into Archery than all other efforts combined. Howard Hill began shooting archery in the early 1920's in Florida. Hill bagged a Moose and deer in Canada in 1925. Hill won the NAA Flight competition in 1928 setting a record of 391 yds. 1 ft. and 11 in. That year he placed 40th in the target competition. Hill helped establish rules for archery golf in 1928. When you think of Howard Hill as a bowhunter and exhibition shooter. He was outstanding, he was a fine competitive field shooter. Early in his shooting in Fl. the won the Florida State Target Championship in 1928. In 1939 and 1940 he won 196 consecutive NFAA Field tournaments. Howard won the International Field Tournament in 1942. Hill shot for Ben Pearson Archery and made many short films to promote archery and bowhunting. Hunting with the bow appealed to Howard much more than did competitive archery. Hill's first role in Hollywood was as a strongman in the movie Laughing Boy. He performed with Johnny Weissmuller and had a supporting role in the movie Robin Hood, he instructed the actors in archery techniques and did the difficult shots for Errol Flynn. He split the arrow in the center for the target in that film, don't know how many takes. Errol Flynn was Hill's friend because of their love of hunting and the outdoors. After his first film he met movie producers Louis B. Mayer, Carl Laemmele and Jerry Fairbanks, he made connections. Howard shot archery in seven major films. He produced many short films on his own from bowhunting to trick shooting. He did over 23 movies and shorts for Warner Brothers. He stared in Tembo a 1951 film in which he downed an elephant with one shot, shooting a 115 lb. longbow with a 41 in. arrow, the first white man to do so. Hill shot exhibitions in three World Fair's. Howard travelled about the country putting on exhibitions for schools and the general public. Hill patented the lamination of bamboo onto a longbow limb. He and his brother ran Howard Hill archery equipment for years. Howard Hill bows are still sold today but by another company buying the name. Howard was recorded pulling a 172 lb. bow a World record at the time. One of his outstanding tricks was flipping a coin into the air and hitting it with the arrow. Someone would flip a silver dollar, a half-dollar, a quarter, a nickel and a dime; hitting them in succession without a miss, did it more then once. He wrote "Hunting the Hard Way" (1953) and "Wild Adventure" (1954). He received the NAA Thompson Medal of Honor in 1963. Was one of the first inductees into the Archery Hall of Fame and is in the Bowhunters Hall of Fame. Howard Hill was elected an Honorary Life Member of the PAA. in 1962. Hill at the age of 62 practiced with a 75 lb. longbow shooting for at least an hour, almost every day. Hill never used a sight and considered a recurve or compound bows ; they were something that detracted from the romance of the ancient sport of archery he would say. His remarkably success as a bowhunter is most distinguished with over some 2000 animals taken with the bow and arrow. Hill was inducted into the Archery Hall of Fame 1972 and is in the Bowhunters Hall of Fame.

Russ Hoogerhyde, (born 1906, died 1985), Russ tried to get hired at an indoor archery range in Grand Rapids to learn to shoot the bow in 1929, pestering the owner. He was hired and within a year he was managing 13 indoor archery ranges. In 1930 he won the NAA National Meet in Chicago. He won six NAA Nationals before 1940. Russ instructed for some 40 years at TWAC. He dominated Target Archery for a decade, yet he was always willing to help new archers. He gave Shooting demonstrations, lectures and made some move shorts. He loved archery and it showed. He was inducted into the Archery Hall of Fame in 1972.

Lura R. Wilson, (born 1914, died 1997), Known as the "Mother of Scholastic Archery" she had taught many college couches to start archery programs. Lura is Director of guidance at Greene Central School. Was a nominee for coach of the first US Archery Team to the 1972 Olympic Games. She is acting director of Teala Wooket Archery Camp later named The World Archery Center, TWAC. Was on the NAA Board for 4 terms. Has been an NAA Clout Champion 3 times. She graduated from Syracuse University. She did gradate work at Cornell, Colgate and the State University of New York Collages. Lura has taught physical education in Riverhead, Schenectady and Greene New York for 27 years. She distributed "Archery-The Little Known Olympic Sports", "First Lessons in Archery" and "A Psychobiological Study of Archery Performance". Lura is an honorary member of the Association of Women in Physical Education of New York State, Member of the New York State Lifetime Sports Hall of Fame, Member of the New York State Archery Hall of Fame and was inducted into the Archery Hall of Fame in 1979.

Roy Case, (born 1888, died 1986), Roy the Father of Wisconsin Bowhunting coined the word "Bowhunting" in 1930. He got a special permit in 1930 to hunt with a bow in Wisconsin. Being successful at harvesting a deer that year made him the first man to legally hunt and kill a deed with a bow & arrow with a license. Although the bow and arrow had been used for centuries to hunt with, it had not been recognized by any state as a legal method to hunted with. Roy was influenced by Saxton Pope's Book of 1923. He helped organize Wisconsin's first archery club in 1927. He was a member of the NAA and the Wisconsin Archery Assoc. Roy organized the Wisconsin Bow Hunters Assoc. as a first in 1941. It was the first organized bowhunter organization in the US. He designed, produced and marketed Broadhead hunting points from 1920 to 1950's. He and others worked at establishing the first Bowhunting season for Wisconsin in 1934 and helped other bowhunting groups establish seasons in their states by establishing Legal Broadhead Standards Nationwide. Bowhunting became a state wide season in 1948. Roy had many bowhunting stories published in Ye Sylvan Archer. The official NFAA magazine of the time from 1927 to 1943. The Wisconsin Bowhunters Assoc. created the Wisconsin Bowhunting Heritage Foundation in 2004 to preserve bowhunting history with a museum. Roy was awarded the NFAA Compton Medal of Honor in 1948 an inducted into the Archery Hall of Fame in 1988.

John Yount, (born 1895, died 1981); one of the founders of the National Field Archery Association in 1939. He dreamed about making Field Archery going beyond the NAA, field shooting in the woods was an established archery round. Bowhunters around the US took to Field Archery to shoot from unknown but more realistic distances then the NAA. John was NFAA Secretary/Treasurer from 1939 to 1958. Yount was NAA Field Captain for the NAA National Meet in 1935. Recipient of the NAA Thompson Medal of Honor in 1944. Created the 1st NFAA handbook and designed and used the NFAA stump & arrow logo. John know there had to be a better way to practice before going afield to bowhunt. He was inducted into the Archery Hall of Fame 1974 and is in the Bowhunters Hall of Fame.

Roy Hoff, (born 1903, died 1985); owner, edited and publish of "Archery" magazine the official magazine for the NFAA for over 20 years. Roy was the first President of the California Bowhunters in 1943 and promoted the NFAA from the start. Roy was a competitor and avid bowhunter. He was extensively involved in the formation and growth of the NFAA. His tireless promotion of archery and bowhunting extended for over 40 years. Roy was instrumental in establishing Archery only hunting seasons in Ca. and other western US states. The California Archery Assoc. called him the "Father of Organized Archery". Roy published many books and articles over the years. In 1962 he was awarded the NFAA Compton Medal of Honor. He was a tireless promoter of Archery and Bowhunting for more then 4 decades. He was inducted into the Archery Hall of Fame 1978 and is in the Bowhunters Hall of Fame.

Clayton B. Shenk, (born 1908, died 2000); Clayton pioneered commercial Archery Ranges in 1939. Clayton helped establish Pennsylvania bowhunting only seasons. Clayton was president of the NAA in 1937, 1950, 1960 and 1966. He received the NAA Thompson Medal of Honor in 1959. Clayton was Secretary/Treasurer of the Pennsylvania Archery Assoc. for 39 years. He was Executive Sectary of the NAA from 1967 thru 1979. Clayton was inducted into the Archery Hall of Fame in 1973. He received the NAA Junior Olympic Archery Development Award in 1989. Clayton was a tireless worker for archery, he worked with the PAA to establish the NAA Pro or Non-Amateur (Adult) Divisions.

Harry Eugene Drake, (born 1915, died 1997); Drake was an pioneer in developing and promoting the composite bow design for competition and flight shooting. Harry was a bow designer, developer and was a flight shooter extraordinaire. Harry was the first man to shoot an arrow over 1000 yds. in 1964. Drake broke the world record for the longest shot with a footbow on Oct. 24, 1971 shooting 2,028 yards at age 56. Drake's bows won many State and National championships but he will be remembered for his flight bows. Harry's bows have established more flight records than any other bowyer. Starting in 1947, Drake bows have held the Men's National Flight records for 29 years. Harry died after a motor bike accident. Harry was inducted into the Archery Hall of Fame 1974 and in is the Bowhunters Hall of Fame. He was the recipient of the NAA Thompson Medal of Honor in 1993.

Glenn St. Charles, (born 1911, died 2010); Glenn spent several summers as a youth in timber-cruising camps with his father in the Kaniksu National Forest of northern Idaho. This was the background for his understanding of animals behavior in remote regions and he developed a love of nature. Glenn helped establish Archery Only Hunting Seasons in the Pacific Northwest in the 1930's. Glenn felt there was a need for a bowhunter club, like the Boone and Crockett Club. He was the Pope & Young Club Founder and an emeritus member of the Boone and Crockett Club. Realizing bowhunting needed better credibility with the general public, NFAA

President at the time Karl E. Palmatier asked Glenn for help in making this possible within the NFAA. Glenn was a bowyer, bowhunter, lecturer and writer. Books published, "Billets to Bows" 1984, "Legends of the Longbow" 1993 and "Bows on the Little Delta" 1997. Owner of Northwest Archery LLC from 1949 to 2004 when his family took over. Worked with the NFAA to establish recondition for bowhunting harvest using the fair chase policy. Glenn helped develop the Big Game Record Keeping system for the NFAA. Awarded the NFAA Compton Medal of Honor in 1958. Founder and First President of the Pope and Young Club in 1961. Was awarded the Ishi Award from the Pope & Young Club in 1958 and the Karl E. Palmatier Award from the Archery Hall of Fame. Promoted bowhunting for over 70 years. Glenn St. Charles was inducted into the Archery Hall of Fame 1991 and the Bowhunters Hall of Fame.

Tom Jennings, (born 1924, died 2013); referred to as Mr. Compound Bow. In 1935 he shot his first bow with a buddies equipment, in 1936 was a bowyer making his first bow at 12. Jennings bought a lemonwood stave at Bitzenburger lumber to make his first longbow. With this first bow he earned his Boy Scout Merit Badge in Archery and harvested a jackrabbit. Tom saved $20 and went back to Bitzenburger lumber and bought a yew stave out of Oregon for his second bow. In1941 he worked in a Lockheed aircraft plant and joined the military after the war broke out. He later joined the Valley West Archery Club in 1948. Was Archery Technical editor for the Eastern Bowhunter 1962, Archers Magazine Technical editor in1967 and Archery World magazine after that. Partner at S&J Archery in Southern Ca. Pioneered cosmetic and functional improvements in Laminated Recurve bows in 1952. Everyone was looking for a better ultimate bow. Purchased the 1st license under the H. W. Allen patent to make and sell the compound bow in 1967. Introduced the first 2 and 4 wheel compounds shortly after. Always pushed for the acceptance of the compound bow in Target, Field and bowhunting. Jennings archery was purchased by Bear Archery in 1982, he was near bankruptcy because of the royalties owned the Allen patent. He pioneered the use of exotic hardwoods in bow risers. He took a deer with an aluminum bow he had bought, all the rest of the bows he used he built. He joined the Arm Air Corps in 1943 and was honorably discharged in 1947. Tom traded a $35 bow for flying lessons, he had a pilot's licenses for decades. He flew himself to a lot of archery events and to Catalina Island to bowhunt. Hollis Allen contacted The Archery Magazine for a technical report on his new bow design. The bow was sent to Tom and he tested it, he said I saw potential in the bow. He got a license and I immediately began improving the design and manufactured my compound bows. Tom Jennings was inducted into the Archery Hall of Fame 1999 and is in the Bowhunters Hall of Fame.

Gail Martin, (born 1923, died 2013); was a bowyer, bowhunter and competitor and at 14 in 1937 Gail first shot his brothers bow. He joined the Army Air Corps. during World War II, served for 3 years. Sold wooden arrows and accessories at local archery gatherings through a home business. He joined the Blue Mountain Archers in 1947. Purchased him first new bow from Damon Howatt in 1949. Gail and Eva Martin and Martin Archery began in 1948 with a single fletching jig and a desire to make quality arrows. Gail and his wife, Eva officially founded Martin Archery in 1951. Purchased Damon Howatt Archery in 1976. Gail developed a bowstring making machine and got a contract with Bear Archery, he made bowstrings for Browning, Wing, Jennings and Allen bows. Martin created a compound bow with one-cam with a draw stop in 1975, he holds some 24 archery related patents. After bowhunting all over the world his favorite animal and method is still hunting for deer. Gail was patriarch of the oldest one-owner archery company in the US. Appointed to the Washington Generals, a goodwill ambassador and trade association. Received the US Small Business Administration's Small Business Person of the Year in 1984. Awarded the Safari Club International Hall of Honor Award in 1998. Received a Lifetime Achievement Award from the Washington State Bowhunters in 2003. Senior Member of the Pope & Young Club, also an official measurer for Pope & Young and Boone and Crochet Club. Also supported and was a board member of the Archery Manufactures Organization, now Archery Trade Association, ATA. He was inducted into the Bowhunters Hall of Fame in 1995 and inducted into the Archery Hall of Fame in 2012.

Al Henderson, (born 1907, died 1989); the Coach. Al became interested in archery in 1937 taking up the sport for exercise. After moving to Arizona in 1946 he competent in Target and Field archery but his interest turned to coaching archery. In 1975 he was selected as the coach for the 1976 Olympic Archery Team after coaching 7 national champions, 5 western states regional champions and some 34 state champions plus 12 All-American champions. Al gives himself to his students, he could look you in the eye and convince you, this is what you need to do. Darrell Pace and Luann Ryon, members of the Montreal Olympics won Gold in Archery. Al received the NFAA Compton Medal of Honor in 1979 and was a life member of the Professional Archery Assoc. being on the PAA Board of Directors from 1964 to 1978. Al developed a shooting program for the blind in 1975, never caught on. Henderson was the Coaching Editor for Archery World from 1972 to 1982. He wrote "Understanding Winning Archery" and "Peak Performance Archery" considered the best for helping archers understand shooting archery. Al Henderson was inducted into the Archery Hall of Fame in 1982.

C. A. "Chuck" Saunders, (born 1913, died 1995); invented the Indian Cord Fiber Archery Target Matt developed in the early 1940's, a standard in major archery competitions for years. Chuck and Phyllis Sanders founded Saunders Archery from the basement of a Chicago apartment. Chuck helped the founding of "Bowhunters Who Care". Instrumental in forming the Archery Manufacturers Organization, AMO in 1953. Helped develop the "ABCs of Archery" distributed by the AMO. Chuck became an Honorary Life Board member of the AMO in 1982. Chuck wanting to make archery fun, he developed the Bow Bird Aerial Target, the Slingshot for arrows and Archery SACO Rounds. During Chucks 50 plus years in the archery industry he was always active in the archery sporting goods industry, Saunders earned the Spinks Award for Outstanding Contribution to the Sporting Goods Industry. Sanders pride was offering products exclusively made in the USA, has been their core value. Saunders Archery was a main source for archery equipment and accessories for years. Chuck and his son had some 55 patents in their name. Chuck was inducted into the Archery Hall of Fame in 1985 and is in the Bowhunters Hall of Fame.

Henry Bitzenburger, (born 1899, died 1973); a perfectionist patented the Professional Fletchmaster jig in the early 1940's. This fletching jig is used by layman to archery manufacturers all over the world, even today. Henry loved to travel and enjoyed teaching archery to anyone interested. He was the 1st to be awarded the American Archery Council's Medal of Honor. He was married to **Babe Bitzenburger**, a great shooter. She won the first four NFAA National Field Championships. She loved flight shooting. She was inducted into the Archery Hall of Fame in 1976. Henry was inducted into the Archery Hall of Fame in 1986.

Earl H. Hoyt Jr., (born 1911, died 2001); Bowyer, competitor and bowhunter. Hoyt Archery was founded in 1931 in St. Louis with Sr. & Jr. producing cedar arrows and bows. They read Saxton Pope's books and many archery articles. It is said the duo started an archery business in 1942, maybe so. Earl was a music lover and played the banjo. Earl developed the dynamic balance bow limbs and bow limbs of equal length in 1947. Earl developed a semi-pistol grip handle and in 1956 introduced the full pistol grip. Earl invented and patented the Stabilizer system in late 1961, he has other patents as well. Earl was one of three archers to competed in 25 NAA Annual Meets. When archery was reintroduced into the Olympic Games in 1972 the men shot 90 Meters. Hoyt bows were preferred because of their performance at that distance, even today. John Williams and Doreen Wilber won the first Gold medals for the US in 1972 using Hoyt Bows. Earl received the Karl E. Palmatier Award of Merit from the PAA. Earl sold Hoyt Archery to Easton Archery in 1989. My understanding is he had a non-compete clause with Easton for 5 years. He married **Ann Weber** in 1971, he use to watch her compete and in the 1960's they began dating. Ann is an Archery Hall of Fame member herself,1972. Ann was NAA Champion six times. Ann was International and World Archery Champion in 1959. I think Ann started Sky Archery in 1989 with Earl's help after he sold Hoyt Archery. She had been a bowyer with Wing Archery. Ann was the 1st women to win both the NAA Target Nationals shooting with a sight and won the NFAA National Field shooting barebow the same year. Ann was a member of the US Women's Archery Team winning 1st at Brussels in 1958, Ann placed second in individual competition. The US Women's Archery Team won again in Stockholm with Ann winning the World Championship. Ann was on 8 US Archery Teams and competed in over 70 NAA Annual Meets. Ann was an avid bowhunter. Earl received the NAA Thompson Medal of Honor in 1977, Ann received the NAA Thompson Medal of Honor in 1984. She was the US Olympic Archery Team manager in 1984. She was also a competitor and bowhunter involved in archery production, sales and management of archery produces for over 40 years. After Earl's death in 2001 she sold Sky Archery to Mathews Archery and donated $1,000,000 to the Archery Hall of Fame. Earl was inducted into the Archery Hall of Fame in 1977 and he is in the Bowhunters Hall of Fame.

Julia Heagey Body (born 1929,-) Julia shot archery at the age of 10.She has been involved in almost every phase of archery but her personal focus has been coaching and teaching. Her mentor was Clayton B. Shenk who encouraged her to help instruct archery. One of the NCAA recognition of a competitive sport was being in the Olympic Games. Julia began certifying college level coaches and instructors and has for over 50 years. In 1968 Julia taught the first

NAA Instructor's School in the continuing Ed Department of Penn State University. She not only taught the initial course but she constructed the curriculum. Her promotion of the NAA accredited archery course led to hundreds of qualified archery instructors and coaches at major colleges and universities around the US. Julia co-authored a chapter for the American Association of Health Physical Education and Recreation book in 1960. Julia was a co-author of the NAA Instructors Manual in 1976 which was reprinted in 8 languages. Julia was invited to teach archery classes in South Africa in 1976 and in Yugoslavia in 1992. Julia taught archery instructor courses from 1999 to 2006 at the Olympic Training Center at the Lake Placid center. She has taught archery classes in Squaw Valley, Colorado Springs and Chula Vista. Julia was the US Wheelchair Team Coach at the Pan Am Wheelchair Games and coached the 1987 US Wheelchair Team in Paris. In 1988 Julia was awarded College Coach of the Year. Julia is also a competitor winning 19 State and Regional championships plus 6 NAA National Meets. She was a member of the NAA US Olympic Archery Sport Committee from 1974 to 1976. You could say she was involved being on the NAA administration Board for 38 years. Julia was inducted into the Archery Hall of Fame in 2008.

Margaret Klann (born 1911, died 2000); Margaret helped found the Arizona State Archery Assoc. she was there first president. She was coach of the Arizona State University Archery from 1945 to 1976. Margaret was Program Director for the NAA College Division from 1960 to 1974. Margaret organized the US Intercollegiate Championships in 1967. She helped the selection of NAA All-American Collegiate Teams. Margaret was inducted into the Archery Hall of Fame in 2014.

Jean Lee Lombardo (born 1925, died 2010); Jean Lee started archery in an archery course at the University of Massachusetts in 1944. From 1946 to 1950 Jean attended Teela Wooket Archery when it was in Vermont, the course later was called The World Archery Center, TWAC. She started as a student and continued as a teacher. Jean's first major tournament was the 1947 NAA National Target held at Amherst, Mass. where she placed 15th. In 1948 she started a winning streak capturing four NAA National Target Championships braking many records. In 1950 Jean Lee traveled to Kobenhavn, Denmark to compete in the World Target. She shocked the archery world by winning by over 300 points, establishing a new set of World records. She won again in 1952. In 1952 Jean had a minor injury to her right arm in a gymnasium workout that archery seemed to aggravate. She never competed again. Jean was without question one of the world's greatest women archers of the time. Jean was inducted into the Archery Hall of Fame in 1975.

Ann Marston (born 1938, died 1971); Ann was known as the "Sweetheart of the Bow & Arrow". Ann had won a Cadet, Junior and Intermediate National Championship by 1953. She was NFAA National Champion in 1954, 55, 57 and 1958. Ann was a Miss America contestant in 1958 from Michigan. She won the Talent competition shooting her bow and arrow, this was the first time a sport related talent had won in this category. Ann was on the cover of Sports Illustrated. Ann established herself as an exhibition shooter across the US. Ann promoted archery and shot exhibitions all over the world. Ann died of a stroke 1971 and in 1973 the Ann Marston Memorial Archery Tournament was started. Ann was inducted into the Archery Hall of Fame in 1978.

Holless Wilbur Allen (born 1909, died 1979); Allen had invented one of the most influential changes in Archery, the Compound bow. Allen like many bowhunts was frustrated that a deer could jump before the arrow got to the deer. He experimented with many designs. After reading up on kinetic energy he mounted a small aircraft pulley to the ends of cutoff recurve limbs. He came up with a block & tackle like arrangement. Allen loved to find how things worked. The mechanical knowledge he gained from years of curiosity was a great help to his effort making what he could not afford. Such was the spirit with hours of contemplation in developing a bow to shoot an arrow faster. Studying his pulley bow, what if I positioned the pulley's pivot hole off center? His first compound was crude with wooden eccentrics with a truss handle made of pine boards. But it worked! Let off was 15%, but speed increased 15%. Allen filed for a patent on June 23, 1966. Almost all bow manufactures' got a license from Allen. By 1977 there were a hundred compound models and fifty recurve models to choose from. Allen with his experimentations contrived a complicated device to perform a simple task, shoot an arrow faster. Allen and others fought hard to get approval from state game agencies to allow the compound for hunting. Allen died in a car crash in 1979 coming home from the last court hearing protecting his patent for unpaid royalties. The compound was made legal to hunt with before accepted in NFAA archery competition. The NFAA accepted the compound in 1971 as a regular bow, not a separate division. The PAA accepted the compound for competition in the 1985. The NAA (USAA) accepted the compound in their competitions in 1993. H. W. Allen was inducted into the Archery Hall of Fame in 2010.

Chuck Adams (born1952,-) Chuck is the best known and most widely published bowhunter to date, other then Howard Hill. Chuck started hunting with a rifle at the age of five near Chico, Ca. Converted to bowhunting in his teens. Chuck has more then 111 entries in the Pope & Young Club and 181 Safari Club International records. Every spring he delivers dozens of hunting seminars and keynote speeches around the US. He will not make an appearances during hunting season. Chuck said "I would like to be remembered as someone who helped other people enjoy bowhunting more. If anybody else manages to enjoy bowhunting as much as I enjoy bowhunting and if I have helped in that process-then I am a happy guy." Any money he earns is used to finance hunting trips. He believes hunting on foot is the natural way to bowhunt. Chuck was a Hoyt Pro Staffer. In 1990 he became the first archer in history to harvest all recognized varieties of North American big game, this was repeated four times. Five of Adams's largest animals have been recognized as bowhunting world records. He is a Life member of the Rocky Mt. Elk Foundation. He is a Senior member of the Pope & Young Club and a member of Safari International. He was awarded "The Ishi Award" from Pope & Young. In the 1960's, 70's & 80's he has had 4,700 magazine articles and 10 books published. Chuck was inducted into the Archery Hall of Fame in 2008 and is in the Bowhunters Hall of Fame at the age of 50.

Doug Walker (born 1930, died 2011); Doug was a pioneer of bowhunting for same six decades. He shot archery as a child. At 15 he lied about his age to be trained as a Paratrooper during World War II. After the war he used the GI Bill to become an attorney. After the war he worked to get an Archery only season in his state of Ca. because archers had to hunt during the gun season. Doug was one of first to take a buck and legally tag it during the new archery only season in Ca. in 1947. Doug was the first bowhunter to harvest all 13 big game species of Ca. Doug was introduced to Howard Hill by Doug Easton in 1959. Doug hired on as the Bear Archery Factory Rep. for the West and Southwest area of the US in 1960. He was one of the first regular members of the Pope & Young Club in 1961 was on the Board of Directors and served as their Executive Secretary plus their Records Chairman. Doug had many bowhunter articles published and wrote two books, "Let's Go Bowhunting" 1989 and "Autobiography of a Bowhunter" 2007. Doug ventured into the publishing world by purchasing the Pacific Coast Bowhunter periodical and change the name the Western Bowhunter. The name evolved into the National Bowhunter. Doug being the sole owner. Doug personally know, wrote about and bowhunted with many of the legendary archers of the day. Doug hunted with the bow, promoted bowhunting and wrote many stories about the sport of his passion. He was president of the Ca. Bowmen Hunters and an active supporter of the NFAA. Doug hosted the "Doug Walker Javelina Bowhunter Get-Together" for 13 years and the "Doug Walker's Taxes Safari" for 12 years. Doug founded and incorporated the National Bowhunters Hall of Fame in 1990. He shared his knowledge with anyone willing to listen. Doug promoted all NFAA Bowhunting Programs and was inducted into his Bowhunters Hall of Fame, amazingly he is not in the Archery Hall of Fame.

Freddie Troncoso (born 1933, died 2017); had a toy bow at the age of 4. In 1938 he say a Howard Hill short on Bowhunting. At the age of 12 he harvested his first deer. Freddie became interested in target archery when he taught his wife Eva and her brother to shoot a bow. They both started winning tournaments while he struggled with his shooting in competition. He had a lot of ingrained bad habits which led to experimenting with different setups. Freddie developed and marketed rope release devices. He developed the Pacesetter launcher arrow rest, first called "Lizard-Tongue". Freddie joined the PAA in 1967. He has over 27 archery related patents and started Golden Key Futura Inc. in 1968. Freddie designed the first bolt-on no-drill mounting bracket for arrow rests in 1969. Freddie met Roy Hoff in 1961, Roy encouraged Freddie to writing archery technical articles for Archery magazine. He became a well know coach and lecturer, he was a private top level coach from 1955 to 2010. Freddie &Eva received the Archery Inc. Award of Merit in 1976. Under the courtesy and sponsorship of Easton Seminars in 1991 he traveled Europe for them. The highlight of his bowhunting career was induction into the Bowhunter Hall of Fame in 1992. He was also inducted into the Archery Hall of Fame .

Eva Troncoso (born 1935-?) Got interested in Archery after marrying Freddie in 1956. It wasn't until 1972 that Eva began shooting at a higher level in competition. She won 14 major archery tournaments. Eva first shot Freestyle Limited with a recurve and switch to the compound and release. She joined the NFAA Professional Division in 1973. Between 1972 and 1976 she shoot in 136 tournaments, winning 131 of them. Eva worked with the JOAD Program from 1971 to 1977. Eva wrote the Eva's Kitchen Corner column for Archery magazine from 1990 to 1995. She is in the Ca. Archery Hall of Fame.

Bob Swinehart (born 1928, died 1982); Bob field tested bows for Ben Pearson Archery. Bob designed and built the first NFAA Field range in his area in the early 1950's, he was a promoter of archery. Swinehart was the first bowman to take Africa's "big Five", Cape Buffalo, Lion, Leopard, Rhinoceros and Elephant. He was president of East Penn construction. Bob appeared in Ripley's Believe It or Not after downing a 5000 pound Rino. He hunted with a 100+ longbow and a recurve bow later. Bob was at the front of modern bowhunting. Bob stated "You can't consciously feel fear while hunting big game animals". Bob wrote "Sagittarius" in 1970 and "In Africa" later. Howard Hill said "He not only is an extremely good shot with the bow, but in addition has a great deal of patience, is a fine tracker and possesses great courage". Swinehart was inducted into the Archery Hall of Fame in 2000.

Rube Powell (born 1911, died 1991) Rube took up archery while serving in the US Navy in 1947. He shot an unorthodox high anchor with a high wrist grip. Rube from 1951 thru 1956 was a NFAA National champ. He was very active in Ca. promoting archery, creating archery ranges and assisting new archery clubs. Rube was AAU "Athlete of the Year" in 1955. Rube spent countless hours with city officials, the average citizen and archers in the San Diego area. He retired from the US Navy as Chief Master at Arms. Rube held national records for the Field, Hunter and Animal rounds, plus aggregate tournament scores. There is a Rube Powell archery range at Balboa Park on the South side of Cabrillo Bridge supported by the San Diego Archers active today. Rube was inducted into the Archery Hall of Fame in 1973.

Charles "Charlie" Pearson (born1928?, died 2010); Charlie learned to be a master craftsman bowyer from his father E. Bud Pierson. He built the first indoor archery ranges in the Cincinnati, Ohio area. Charlie loved flight shooting and shot Archery Golf when he could. He was expert at building flight bow. He competed with the longbow, recurve and foot bow winning many titles. Charlie named one of his favorite flight bow "The Sultan Bow!". He collected antique bows going back to Turkish archery. Charlie collected ancient release aids going back to the Mongol Horse Bows thumb ring. Pierson Archery was the place to be for archery. A shop display was always seen at local sport shows and outdoor events. George Helwig and Charlie started the NAA (USAA) JOAD Program in the Cincinnati area. Charlie and his wife Mildred coached and lectured at TWAC for over 50 years. Mildred and Ed Miller of TWAC aired on local TV called the Robin Hood Tournament, using the JOAD format. Being a Quaker and Conscientious Objector Charlie served in a Army Hospital in England during World War II. Charlie was a quiet and gentle man, he always took time to help and answer questions to anyone interested. Charlie ran the NAA Practice Field at any NAA Nationals Target held at Miami University, Oxford range. Charlie and Mildred receive the NAA JOAD Award in 1986.

George Helwig (born 1917, died 2001); George helped found the Junior Olympic Archery program with Charlie Pearson in 1960. He was a professor at Miami University at Oxford for 23 years and NAA Tournament Director for the NAA National Championships held at Miami University many times. Helwig was an avid bowhunter. George was a plant manager for Procter & Gamble. He learned archery as a Bow Scout. George became known world wide as a coach and lecturer for contributing to archery. He was president of the NAA 1973 thru 1976. George was a coach for the US Team in the 1972 Munich Olympic Games, the reintroduction of Archery to the games. He was again with the US Olympic Team in Montreal in 1976. George was a judge at the 1984 Olympic Games for archery in Los Angles. George was a founding Board Member for the Archery Hall of Fame and their Vice resident for over 30 years. George was awarded from World Archery their Silver Plaquette in 1979. He received the NAA Thompson Medal of Honor in 1980. George was a shooter and as a senior won a Gold Medal in the Senior Olympics at the Baton Rouge games. He received the NAA JOAD Award in 1986. George was inducted into the Archery Hall of Fame in 1980.

Bob Lee (born 1928,-); Can't seem to find when Bob started in archery but Bob Lee seems to have been an active lover of archery his entire life. Bob formed Wing Archery Co. in Houston producing handcrafted traditional bows. Bob helped Glenn St. Charles in forming the Pope & Young Club in 1959 and was a charter member. An avid bowhunter Bob's efforts in 1959 successfully got a per-rifle season for archery only hunting season in Texas. Wing Archery produced the first three piece bow (not a medal riser) in 1963. Bob works with the new Archery Manufacturers Organization, AMO in 1968. Bob sold Wing Archery in 1968 and later formed Bob Lee Archery with his son in 1989. Bob was inducted into the Bowhunter Hall of Fame in 2007 and the Archery Hall of Fame in 2012.

Ann Clark (born 1925, died 2018); Ann started shooting archery to bowhunt with her husband in 1952. The two of them opened and ran Clark's Archery & Sports Center from 1952 to 1963. They found E. Bud Pearson & Son an outstanding bowyer and got outfitted properly. In 1953 Ann began exhibition shooting locally. After besting Ann Weber for the NAA National Championship in 1955 she moved on to larger sports shows. The two Ann's became fast friends. Also 1955 she met Earl Hoyt, he was a great help to her. She was shooting at the Cincinnati Sports Show in 1955. She said "I was a pioneer and spokesperson in the industry to bring attention to the women". Ann has won over 300 archery tournaments and was an entertainer at many sports shows. Ann was on the US Archery Women Team sent to Prague for the FITA World Championship in 1957. Ann placed 2nd in the world. She won the NAA Nationals again in 1960, also that year she won the Ben Pearson Open Indoor. In 1962 Ann won the NFAA National Field Championship. Ann has spent her life promoting archery thru bowhunting, competition and exhibitions. She was on "What's My Line" and appeared on Romper Room. The two Ann's helped the first JOAD efforts. She was a recipient of the NAA JOAD Award in 1987. Ann has been a judge at many archery tournaments. Ann has a display as part of the Smithsonian's "Professional Women in Sports". She has stated "Mental attitude will win or loss a tournament", plus "Every place I hunt is my favorite". Ann was part of a group of lady bowhunters called the "Diana's" that hunted all over the US as a group. Ann was a representative and exhibition personality for Ben Pearson Archery. She was awarded the NAA Dallon medal. Ann encouraged an archers choice of shooting style, not to change them but to help guided them. Ann was a Board Member of the Archery Hall of Fame. Ann was inducted into the Archery Hall of Fame in 1984.

Edward "Ed" Rohde (born1926, died 2010); Ed started shooting competition in 1959. In 1962 Ed shot the 1st perfect NFAA Animal Round in competition. Ed won the NAA National in 1963. Ed started bowhunting in 1965. Ed was the 1st PAA member to win all Major Sanctioned tournaments in 1982, which included the Atlantic City Classic, the Las Vegas Shoot and the PAA Indoor and Outdoor Nationals. Ed was a Charter Member of the PAA and Ranked #1 for 5 years in a row. Ed was known as "Mr. Consistency". He was inducted into the Archery Hall of Fame in 2006.

Robert "Bob" Rhode (born1929, died 2000); Bob loved every aspect of archery, the sport, the industry, the history and the people shooting and promoted archery relentlessly. Bob first stood out as NAA National Champion in 1954, don't know when he started shooting. In 1955 he won a silver at the World Archery Championship in Helsinki. Bob went on to win the NAA and NFAA National Championships in the same year. Bob began shooting for Pearson Archery and he enjoyed flight shooting, winning several NAA National Fight Championships . Bob won the NFAA Freestyle Division in 1957 and went on to win the International Field Championship in 1959. In between, in 1958 Bob won the International Canadian Championship. Bob's involvement lead him to help the Professional Archers Assoc., PAA and was their first president in 1962. Bob was a great organizer and helped many archery tournaments and worked as a judge in many. Bob conceived of the visual timing clock for indoor tournaments. Bob got permission from the NAA 1976 to compile their history for their 100th anniversary. He began publishing a series of books on all of Archer History in 1977. Bob received the World Archery Gold Plaquette in 1981. Bob was a life time member of the NAA and NFAA. Bob received the NAA Thompson Medal of Honor in 1989 and the NFAA Compton Medal of Honor. He retired from Hoyt USA as senior Vice President. Bob was inducted into the Archery Hall of Fame in 1985.

Arlyne Rhode (?); Arlyne and Bob founded the US & International Archer magazine in 1981. Arlyne was editor for a lot of Bob's books. Arlyne won nine consecutive Field championships in Minnesota between 1960 & 1970. Shooting Flight archery with a foot bow she entered the Guinness Book of World Records for shooting an arrow 1,113yds, 2ft, 6 ins. She explains archery as a team effort plus individual drive. Arlyne's archery has been a lifetime pursuit that keeps her fit and focused. Arlyne travels the globe to report on archery activities for her archery magazine. She took a job with Bear Archery and there met Bob Rhode. Arlyne earned an accounting degree from Parkland College. Arlyne was inducted into the Minnesota Archery Hall of Fame in 2003. Arlyne won Gold at the Arizona Senior Olympics in 2008. Arlyne's endeavors and work in archery will continue to transcend the sport of archery.

Frank Gandy (born 1936, -); Frank got his first bow at the age of 9 and fell in love with shooting. Frank made a bow in high school shop class, then he bought a recurve later to shoot with. After marrying his high school sweetheart Frank joined a local archery club in the 1950's. In 1967 Frank went to the NFAA National Field Championship, the experience must of did something. He not only won shooting barebow but shot the only perfect 560 Animal Round in that style. He has the only perfect animal round shooting barebow on record with the NFAA at a national tournament. He won again in 1980 and 1981. Frank put on a sight to shoot with the PAA in the 1970's. He won the PAA National Indoor in 1979 and the PAA National Indoor & Outdoor in 1985. Frank won Atlantic City Classic in 1982 and 1985. He won the Las Vegas Indoor in 1984 and 1985. Frank won the NAA National Outdoor in the Masters (over 50) in 1996. The gentleman from Fl. is cordial and helpful to anyone interested in archery. Frank has won archery tournaments shooting in four different styles over five decades. Frank has won two IFAA North American Field Championships and an IFAA World Field Championship. Frank was inducted into the Archery Hall of Fame in 2010.

Ann Butz (born 1935,-); Ann and her husband took up archery in 1955 as a hobby. Ann's skills became apparent in 1966. She came on like a storm winning 18 National Titles. Ann joined the PAA in 1968 winning 72 Professional Tour Events. Ann received the Sports Illustrated Award of Merit. She was the first women to win the "Triple Crown" of Archery topping all three major national events in one year. Ann is considered to be one of the greatest women archer's of all time. Ann won four NFAA National titles, four American Indoor titles, four Las Vegas titles plus four PAA Indoor titles and six PAA Outdoor titles. Ann was inducted into the Archery Hall of Fame in 2011.

Doreen Viola Hansen Wilber (born 1930, died 2008); Doreen got into archery after a customer paid their bill to her husbands auto shop with a bow and set of arrows in 1957. Without coaching or a sponsor she improved over time to be a top amateur competitor. From 1963 to 1973 she never lost an archery tournament in Iowa. Doreen won seven NFAA Sectional Championships from 1962 to 1969. Won the NFAA National Field Championship in 1967. In 1968 she won the Ambassador Cup. Doreen was NAA National Champ in 1969,'71,'73 & '74. She was on US International Archery Team's in 1968,'69,'71 & '73. Doreen was the first US Women to won an Olympic Gold at Munich in 1972 since 1904. Doreen was the first women to shoot over 1200 on the Outdoor FITA Round. Doreen was the first Women to win an Olympic Gold in Iowa's history. There is a life size statue of Wilber with her bow in a plaza near Greene County Community Center with a medal target butt 70M away showing the distance she competed at. Doreen always said "Focus, believe in yourself and shoot only one arrow at a time". She also taunted "As soon as you get the training wheels off that compound bow, you can shot a real bow". She won a Gold at the Championship of the Americas in 1973. Doreen won the NAA National Indoor in 1975. She set 18 national and world records during her archery carrier. The analogies she drew between archery and life with the gracious manner of her humble delivery became a lasting legacy for her competitors and students. Doreen spent many years working with the NAA JOAD program. Doreen was inducted into the Archery Hall of Fame in 1986.

William J. "Bill" Bednar (born 1925, died 2009); In 1958 Bill's wife got him a bow for Christmas. Bill attended the Cleveland Sportsman's Show and shot some arrows at the archery venue set up there. Bill was having some problems, went to an archery shop for help. Bill is right handed but he found out he was lift eye dominant and he was off and running, he switched to left handed shooting. Entered his first archery competition in 1961. Bill was part of the US World Archery Team that won gold in Norway in 1961. Bill joined the Professional Archery Assoc. in 1962. In 1963 Bednar won the first PAA Championship held in Daytona Beach. He with his family started Portage Archery Center. Still a family affair today called Hunter's Outlet Archery Center. Bill won the PAA Championship in 1963, '65 & '66. Also in 1966 he won the Ben Pearson Open at Cobo Hall. Bill was the top money winner in the 1960's and was President of the PAA for a time. Bill became the archery coach at the University of Akron in 1976 thru 1979. Active with the NAA JOAD program and started with the NASP program in 2004. His son Rick became an outstanding amateur archer, qualifying as first alternate on the US 1976 Olympic Team and traveled on several US international teams. Bill won six gold medals form 1987 to 1997 in the Senior Olympic Sports events. Started shooting a crossbow and was on the US World Crossbow Senior Team going to New Zealand in 1992. Founded Ten Point Crossbow Technologies in 2000. Bill has several archery related patents for the crossbow. Bill was inducted into the Archery Hall of Fame in 2007.

Jim Dougherty (born 1936, died 2015); Jim got his first deer with a gun at the age of 10. Got his first bow shortly after that and harvested his first mule deer with the bow at the age of 14 in 1950. Jim was asked why he hunted with a bow "Why do I bowhunt? Because I love it!", boy did he. Jim was a bowhunter, communicator and educator of untold influence for 3 generations of bowhunters. Jim wrote "Trails End" on the back page of Petersen's Bowhunting magazine for 25 years. He had bowhunted in 33 US states, 4 Canadian provinces, Mexico and Africa as he described it "with some success". Jim shot for Ben Pearson Archery. He was a member of Pope & Young since 1973 and was given a Honorary Lifetime Senior Membership to Pope & Young in 2005. Jim was past President of Pope & Young and the American Archery Council. Two of his books "Guide to Bowhunting Deer" and "Trail's End" are still out there. Jim was one of the National Bowhunter Education Foundation Board Members and Chairman of Bear Archery Bowhunting Council. Founder of Jim Dougherty Archery, his shop in Tulsa. Numerous Pope & Young Record Book Entries, Lifelong archer and World Champion Varmint Caller. Jim received the Professional Outdoor Media Association's 1st Fred Bear Award in 2008. He is in the Bowhunters Hall of Fame and inducted into the Archery Hall of Fame in 1997.

Pete Shepley (born 1953?,-); in the 1960's Pete worked on his grandfather's farm in the summer. Grandpa Gale showed Pete how to make bows out of Osage Orange. Pete got an engineering degree at Southern Illinois University. He worked for Magnavox as a product engineer while shooting competition as a hobby. Pete started making plastic vanes, cushion plungers, release aids and bow slings on the side. Pete was shooting a Jennings compound and he had some ideas on how to improve the design but to no avail, Jennings wasn't interested. Pete made his own compound and shot it at local archery tournaments. Within a short time he had orders for 500 of his newly designed compound bows. In 1971 Pete started Precision Shooting Equipment, PSE, in 1982 PSE moved to Tucson. Pete has over 20 patents on archery items. Pete has bowhunted all over the US including Alaska, Canada and Africa making films to promote PSE. Pete is in the Bowhunter Hall of Fame. His company is one of the major archery manufactures today.

Clarence "Bud" Fowkes (born 1920, died 2006); In 1949 Bud picked up a bow and fell in love with archery. Bud started coaching his son and helping other archers. Bud shot competition, coached and promoted archery. He worked with the Miller's at TWAC and was active with the NAA JOAD program. Bud was an active NAA National Judge at many archery tournaments over the years. Bud made and sold crossbows from his home. He worked at Gulf Research, has a seismograph he worked on in the Smithsonian Institution. Bud was a coach for the US Olympic Team in 1972. Archery was reinstated as an Olympic Sport that year after a 52 year absence. He was the coach for the US Archery Team in the 1976 World Field Championship. Bud was a coach in 1979 and 1983 for the US Archery Team at the Pan American Games. He was a co-author for the first NAA Instructor's Manual. Bud traveled to Bhutan in 1983 to coach their national archery team for the Olympics' and many other countries. He was coach for the US Archery Team for the 1987 World Archery Championships. Bud was inducted in the NY Archery Hall of Fame in 1996. He was inducted into the Archery Hall of Fame in 2014.

Dave Staples (born 1939, died 2008); Dave first shot a bow in 1951 and he remembers the thrill of hitting the target that 1st time. Dave worked in his uncle's small archery shop in NJ. Dave was not a great bowhunter or an outstanding shooter at tournaments but he got involved and improved the image of all archery. Dave owned and operated Dave Staples Archery Lanes from 1960 to 1982. He sold and installed Spectre Archery Enterprise automatic archery lanes. Dave promoted the JOAD program and the Bowhunter Education program. Dave was a founding member of the Archery Lane Operators Assoc. Joined the PAA in 1964 served as president in 1969 for five years and then served as PAA tournament director. Dave also served as PAAs Advanced International Coaching Program. Founder & President of Images Group Inc. in 1982. Dave started writing about archery at the age of 20, he was a prolific writter for magazine articles on archery. Dave was an avid bowhunter since the age of 13, joined the Pope & Young club in 1979. Co-founder of the Archery Hall of Fame in 1971 and president from 1996 to 2008. Was involved with the American Archery Council and was president from 1973 to 1976. Dave was on the Senior Coaching Staff an TWAC from 1976 to 1985. Dave was a co-author of "Peak Performance Archery". Dave was a sales rep for Darton Archery. In 1974 he received the Karl E. Palmatier Award of Merit. A tireless promoter Dave was on over 300 TV & Radio sports talk shows. In 1986 Dave was the first recipient of the Pete Shepley Archery Career of Excellence Award. Dave was the first person to be recognized with the Archery Hall of Fame Lifetime Achievement Award. Dave said "I would have to say the main reason I was drawn to archery and have stayed involved is the people I have met. Nothing in this world can take the place of persistence." Dave was inducted into the Archery Hall of Fame in 2008.

William "Bill" Wadsworth (born 1917, died 1991); Bill was known as "The Father of Bowhunter Education". Bill grow up in NY graduated Fulton High School in 1933 and Syracuse University in 1938. Bill graduated from the National Training Academy of the Boy Scout's in 1944. Bill was in the Boy Scout camp Onondaga Council from 1949 to 1962. He developed the Boy Scout's High Adventure programs' in 1985. Bill founded and was president and is a life member of the Central New York Bowmen. Bill was a member of the National Council of Boy Scouts of America. Bill launched an In-State Training program to teach bowhunting basics in 1969. He was Vice President of the New York State Field Archers and Bowhunters for some 25 years. Bill retired in 1978 after 36 years with the Scouts. He brought his bowhunter education to the National Field Archery Assoc., NFAA and it became the National Bowhunter Education program, it grow very fast. In 1979 with the blessing of the NFAA his program became an independent 501c3 foundation called the National Bowhunter Education Foundation, NBEF, known today as the International Bowhunter Education Foundation. Bill's enthusiasm led national and international bowhunter education efforts. Bill was elected to the North American Association Hunter Education Hall Assoc. Hall of Fame in 1989. Bill was inducted into the Archery Hall of Fame in 1998.

Victor "Vic" Berger (born 1936, died 2013); Vic Berger was born in Germany, Vic moved to the US in 1956. Vic shot for Bear Archery and was known as the White Knight, wearing traditional archery dress. Vic used a mirror under his arrow rest as a draw check and helped develop the cushion plunger which was called "The Berger Button" in the late 1960's. His first major win was the PAA Outdoor Nationals in 1967, he won again in 1969 and '70. Vic won the US Open Indoor Limited Championship in 1970 and '72. Vic Berger won the 1984 PAA National Indoor. Vic opened an archery shop in Springfield, Ohio in 1975 called World of Archery. He promoted indoor shooting leagues, archery classes and coaching, used the JOAD program and shot 3-D indoors. Vic was a volunteer instructor at TWAC. Vic was inducted into the Archery Hall of Fame in 2013.

Dick Lattimer (born 1935, died 2011); Dick got into archery when he hired on at Bear Archery for advertising and promotional work in 1966. Dick took to bowhunting and public relations. Dick was founder and executive director of the Fred Bear Sports Club starting in 1972. Dick was president/CEO of the Archery Manufacturers Organization, AMO. Dick was Vice President of the Archery Hall of Fame from 2001 to '07. He was President in 2008 & '09. Lattimer served as Television Chairman of the International Association of Fish & Wildlife Agencies. He was Co-Chairman of their full Communications Committee in Washington, D.C. Dick was a member of the NRA Hunting and Conservation Committee. He was on the NRA Bowhunting Sub-committee plus on the NRA's Public Affairs Committee. Dick was on the Board of Directors of the United Conservation Alliance. Dick moved to Gainesville in 1979 with Bear Archery. Dick wrote several book about Papa Bear. Dick had many interest, he wrote "Space Station Friendship", "All we did was Fly to the Moon" and "The Jesus Digest". Dick was a Fellow of the British Interplanetary Society. Dick also wrote poetry under the name Joshua Carpenter. Dick was inducted into the Archery Hall of Fame in 1999.

John Williams (born 1953,-); John started shooting as a youth with his parents. John had the distinction of being the first archer to hold all 3 World Titles in the same year. At 16 he placed 2nd at the World Championships. At 17 he won the IFAA World Championships in York, England. In 1971 he won the NAA National Championship and the Ambassador's Cup in Vancouver. He won the IFAA World Field Championship and went on to capture the 1st Gold Medal at the 1972 Olympics for the US. John joined the PAA in 1973. John's first outing as a Pro he placed 6th at Las Vegas. In 1978 he was the Grand American Pro Champion. John was a coach for the US Olympic Team in 1984. He was in several books on Archery. John was inducted into the Archery Hall of Fame in 2015.

Leonard "Len" or "Lenny" Cardinale (born 1939,-); Len had a strong but positive influence on archery in the New York metropolitan area. He opened his archery business "Butts and Bows" in 1964. Len was a former Olympic Rifle competitor. His shop was pure City people who would had never experienced competitive archery or bowhunting. Lenny was proactive and loved bowhunting. Len organized bus trips for his customers to bowhunt state land in rural NJ. He held woodchuck and carp contest plus leagues' and archery classes. Lenny got involved nationally through the Archery Lanes Operators Assoc., ALOA, he was a founding member. Len became a sought after Judge and Coach. He got involved with the PAA and became their advanced coaching instructor, he was an NFAA Master Coach. Len was a lecturer for four NAA US Olympic Teams and was active at TWAC. Lenny was a senior member & official measurer for Pope & Young for some 30 years. Lenny was on the Board of Directors with IBEF, AAC and Bowhunter Who Care. Len became a technical editor and advisor for Bowhunter magazine, Archery World and had articles in Outdoor Life in the 1980's. He made four videos on basic shooting through advanced shooting distributed world wide. Lenny believed if your actions inspire others to dream more, learn more, do more and become more, you are a leader. Len is in the Bowhunters Hall of Fame and was inducted into the Archery Hall of Fame in 2005.

Darrell Pace (born 1956,-); Darrell started shooting in Cincinnati at Charlie Pearson's indoor range with a coupon found on his dad's car. Darrell placed 5th at the age of 15 participating in the US Olympic Trials in 1972. At the age of 16 Darrell became the youngest member of the US World archery team. Pace won the NAA National Championship in 1973 thru 1976, '78 & '79. Darrell set a World record at the World Championships in 1975 shooting a 1316 on the FITA Outdoor using an all aluminum arrow shaft. Pace won the World Field in 1978 and the World Outdoor again in 1979. Darrell is the only archer to win two Olympic Gold Medals 1976 and 1984. The US didn't send athletes to the 1980 Games. He won the 1979 World and was expected to win the Gold in 1980. Darrell won the Pan Am Games Gold Medal in 1983 & 1991. Pace was the NAA's Athlete of the Year in 1984. He won 1st place at the Championship of the Americans in 1986. Darrell was on four time US Olympic Team member, his efforts help win a Team Silver in 1988. In 2011 Darrell Pace was declared the greatest male archer of the 20th century by FITA. Darrell is active today promoting Olympic Archery. Darrell was inducted into the Archery Hall f Fame in 2015 and still helps archery locally.

Mathew "Matt" McPherson (born 1958,-); Matt's father was an Assemblies of God minister. His father became an archer because his mother was not comfortable with guns. He and his brother Randy made bows at shop in high school. Matt married Sherry in 1980, she was a pianist and he played guitar in a Christian music group. Matt opened an auto body shop and studied metallurgy and engineering for fun. Matt as a bowhunter felt his direction was going towards the archery business. In 1983 he thought of a new technologically advanced compound bow. In 1985 he started McPherson Archery with some investors and made the bow to sell. Matt and the investors did see eye to eye on the direction of the company. He sold out his interest by 1989. In 1991 Matt visualized the single cam compound bow and started Mathew's Archery that same year. Matt and Sherry pursued there love of music by starting Autumn Records. Matt created McPherson Guitars. Matt has some 20 patents some in archery, he expressed the journey itself is as important as the destination and "I'm not really interested in being important; I just want to do what's important". Mathews is a major manufacture of archery equipment today. Matt was inducted into the Bowhunters Hall of Fame in 1998. I'm sure he will be inducted into the Archery Hall of Fame.

CHAPTER 5

Individuals Patent of Archery over time

Patent search results for Archery Improvements from 1872 to 2000? There are many patents not listed I couldn't find

I have used the US Patent web site and Google to search with many results, plus the Archery Hall of Fame and the Bowhunters Hall of Fame. I have patent #'s and names of people I found. I have talked to people at the US Patent office and they said they can't run a search for me but tried to explain to me how, it was as clear as mud. Some of the information I have below is first showing individuals names then patents pending numbers and then granted patent #. If your interested in more information you can easily search by patent #.

These are archers I can't find all of their Patents

Doug Easton started his company in 1922. He made Custom Yew Wood Bows and hardwood arrows in Watsonville, Ca. His process to dovetail wood shaft to make a Footed Arrow was an advance in wood arrows. He also made the first aluminum arrow, When? He made aluminum arrow in 1939. The NAA National Meet was won in 1941 shooting his aluminum arrows. He introduced his 24RT-X shaft in 1946 and his XX75 in 1958. The earliest patent I could find was arrow components was 1983.

Dr. C. H. Hickman was an archer and worked for Bell Laboratories after 1929. I know he patented the Bazooka but I'm not interested in that. I know he had a lot of patents. He made the first shooting machine in 1927 and the first portable coronagraph called a "Spark Coronagraph" about the same time. He designed sights for the longbow and designed a radical new type bow that was never produced. I found a patent #2285031 for silk fiber backing dated 1938 for improving longbow cast.

Howard Hill was a showman and promoted archery by doing. He shot for Ben Pearson Archery, was the star in "Tembo" a move of him bowhunting in Africa. He taught the archers and Earl Flynn to shot archery in the move "Robin Hood". He did more demonstrations and movie shorts for the public then anyone of the day. He was the "Worlds Greatest Archer" for promotion of archery. Howard Hill and his brother produced Longbow to give speed, stability and cast about 180fps. The only patent I found was #2256946 dated 1939 for bow staves laminating bamboo to wood bow limbs.

Ben Pearson was the first to mass produce archery equipment starting in 1927 and is in business today, by 1970 I read Ben Pearson Inc. produced 50% of all bow sold in the US. The earliest patent I could find #2426283 was for a takedown bow dated 1943. I know he had many patents, was considered the "Father of Modern Archery". In 1927 he moved to Pine Bluff an worked in a workshop in the backyard. He dreamed of mass-producing archery equipment to make them more affordable. In 1938 an oilman named Carl Haun stopped by his shop to buy some arrows for his grandson. He was so impressed that he financed Ben Pearson Inc. that same year.

Fred Bear got into archery in 1927 after watching "Alaskan Adventure" in a theatre staring Art Young, he actually met Art Young later. Born in Pa. he moved to Detroit and began advertisements for the car industry. He started Bear Archery in 1933 and was the first to advertise bowhunting and making bowhunting movies without showing the kill. He was concerned about archery's public image. He had numerous patents I have found patented #2665678 the process to laminate wood and fiberglass front and back to make bow limbs dated 1950. He may of patented other archery equipment? . In 1941 he flow to Alaska to bowhunt with friends and had to check in his bow. When they got off the plane his bow couldn't be found. He was left handed and all his friends were right handed. He started developing a takedown bow so he could carry it on the plane with him. The earliest patent I found was for a takedown bow #2464068 dated 1946. He bowhunted world wide and made many film with his takedown recurve. Considered the Father of Modern Bowhunting he made films, published books, appeared on several TV shows and contributed to outdoor magazines.

Tom P. Jennings was a master bowyer in 1936 and later known as "Mr. Compound Bow". He was a partner in S & J Archery. He was an archery technical writer for Archery World magazine. Tom purchased the first license from Allen to manufacture and sell his Jennings Compound Bow. He patented both two and four wheel compound bows but he wasn't the first. The earliest patent under Jennings name was #05961760 dated 1978. I know he had many other patents.

Holless Wilbur Allen patent US3486495 was the first compound bow dated 1966. He gave his first bow design to Archery World magazine for evaluation. It was sent to Tom Jennings for testing. The bow was faster then a recurve with a 15% let off in draw weight. Allen wanted a faster bow to deer hunt with, he had a deer jump the string and he missed. I wanted to see his first design, I know it was not the hang bracket design that he produced to sell? Allen's patented design was a split limb, cam design but it was to expensive to produce for the time.

Gail Martin shot his first bow in 1937 and started his archery company in 1951. He had several bow designs trying to get around Allen's Patent. He made a bowstring jig, did he patent it? or any of his bow designs? He patented a lot of archery bows and accessories, I can't find them? The only patent I found was and improvement to the compound #08336276 dated 1994.

C. H. "Chuck" Sanders he made the Sanders archery matt, a standard for archery competition at the time. He was an archery equipment distributor and had a lot of accessories his company patented. But did he patent any of them?

Henry A. Bitzenburger I know he had a patent on his flitching jig. I have the #US3333842 in1967. I ran a search with out the number and could not find anything? did he patent anything else?

Earl Hoyt Jr. He and his father started making archery equipment in the 1930's. He has designed some of the best performing tournament bows to date. I know he patent base limb stabilizers for his bows. His first product for a bow was a base limb stabilizer, set at the top and bottom if the bow riser. What else has he patented?

There are many people promoting a positive image of archery around the country that you never hear of that do a great job in less public ways, some of the archers I have worked with, judged with and heard good things about but I don't have a bio on them, they are listed here, maybe you know one.

Tim Austin, Barnsdale, Jay Barrs, Rick Bednar, Deborah Blum, Phillip Bowdowski, Randy Brabec, Bob Brenneman, Allen Campbell, Jerry Carter, Jackie Caudle, Dennis Cline, Liz Colombo, Dave Cook, Paul Davison, Ed Eliason, Rodney Estrada, Kirk Ethridge, Lee Ford, Tom Green, David Hughes, Jane Johnson, Richard Johnson, Jean Lee Lombardo, Rick McKinney, Jesse Morehead, Nancy Myrick, Denise Parker, Frank & Becky Pearson, Bernie Pellerite, Dean Pridgen, Dan Rabska, Robert Ragsdale, Terry & Michelle Ragsdale, Sheri Rhodes, Steve Robinson, Ken Rogers, M.J. Rogers, George D. Ryals IV, Mary Anne Schumm, Frank H. Scott, Brian Sheffler, Jim Shubert, Bud Simon, Randi Smith, Rick Stonebreaker, Tim Strickland, George Teckmitchov, Frank Thomas, Diane Watson, Dee Wilde, Larry Wise, Jim White, Rod White, Terry Wunderly, Vic Wunderly.

A must apologize for not knowing or listing the numerous lovers of our sport that promote archery every day to help our local archers and the general public understand us better.

Archery Patents I Found

There are many types of searches for patents, I have found more then one that worked for me, some by accident. Mostly I only have a name? patents # and dates, few pictures or marketed product names. I'm trying the compile information on the progress of archery history as to when and were things improved to help archery grow to what it is today. Each patent has the date and number at the top with the inventors name at the bottom. A patent does not give the product name as sold to the public, in fact many never go into production.

Longbow and Recurve Bows

The oldest patent US126734A granted 1872-05-14 for a takedown bow with medal limbs, inventors name E. S. Morton.

Patent US218199A granted 1879-08-05 for a lamination of the bow limbs, no material names given, inventors name Charles A. Howe

Patent US261610A granted 1882-07-25 for a bow with pulleys at it's limb tips with an adjustable handle, inventors name John W. Sutton.

Patent pending US 1709630A 1928-05-07 granted US1709630A 1929-04-16 for takedown longbow, inventors name Phillip Rounsevelle.

Patent pending US1810335A 1927-10-15 granted US 1810335A 1931-0-16 a longbow with tubular bow limbs, inventors name George E. Barnhart.

Patent pending US1960477A 1929-03-05 granted US1960477A 1934-05-29 a tubular laminated longbow limb, inventors name Robert H. Cowdery.

Patent pending US2000832A 1932-04-02 granted US2000832A 1935-05-07 a rawhide laminated longbow, inventors name Charles B. Fisher.

Patent pending US 1926845 1932-01-06 granted US1926845 1933-09-12
a center shot longbow, inventors name William M. Folberth.

Patent pending US2186386A 1937-06-10 granted US2186386A 1940-01-09
A center shot arrow rest for a longbow, inventors name John O. Lowell.

Patent pending US2307021A 1940-08-05 granted US2307021A 1943-01-05
a deflex limb design for a longbow, inventors names Cordrey Hancil & Walter J. Duvall.

Patent pending US 2228823 1939-10-18 granted US2228823 1941-01-14
A two piece takedown longbow, inventor name T. E. Helm.

Patent pending US2256946 1939-05-27 granted US2256946 1941-09-23
a laminated bamboo bowstave for a longbow, inventors name Howard Hill.
Patent pending US2285031A 1939-02-21 granted US2285031A 1942-06-02

a single stave longbow with a material fiber reinforced limb, inventors name Clarence N. Hickman.

Patent pending US 2316880A 1941-10-28 granted US2316880A 1943-04-20
A laminating process for deflex longbow limbs, inventor name Walter L. Miller.

Patent pending US2344799 1941-05-12, granted US2344799 1944-03-21
an offset handle for a center shot with a teardrop at the tip of the longbow limbs for the bowstring, inventors names Thomas B. Brown & Marion L. Stansell.

Patent pending US2423765A 1945-03-10, granted US2423765A 1947-07-08
enlarged bow handle with laminated semi-recurve limb tips on deflex bow limbs, inventors names William M. Folberth & Paul Permelee.

Patent pending US2426283A 1947-08-26, granted US2426283A 1947-08-26
a hinged fold down bow, inventors name Ben Pearson.

Patent Pending US2457793 1945-04-18, granted US2457793 1948-12-28
a hinged fold down bow, inventors name Fred B. Bear.

Patent Pending US2613660A 1946-02-15, granted US2613660A 1952-10-14, single stave non-recurve bow with fiber reinforced limbs, inventors name Fred B. Bear.

Patent pending US2665678A 1950-04-21, granted US2665678A 1954-01-12
an enlarged handle section with fiber reinforced semi-recurve limbs, inventors name Fred B. Bear.

Patent pending US2689559 1952-05-15, granted US 2689559 1954-09-21
a recurve bow that can be shot right or left handed, inventors name Leonard S. Meyer.

Patent pending US2894503 1955-08-04, granted US 2894503 1959-07-14
Laminated recurve bow limbs with reinforced limb tips, inventors name Ennis B. Pierson.

Patent pending US2900973 1956-07-25, granted US2900973 1959-08-25
bolt on semi-recurve limbs with medal riser and built in sight. inventors name Charles A. Diehr.

Patent pending US2957469 1956-09-05, granted US2957469 1960-10-25
medal riser center shot with parallel straight limbs, inventors name E. D. Wilkerson.

Patent pending US2995130 1956-09-04, granted US 2995130 1961-08-08
reinforced full working recurve fiber limbs with enlarged semi-pistol grip handle, inventors name Earl H. Hoyt, Jr.

Patent pending US3015327 1959-09-04, granted US3015327 1962-01-02
honeycombed core for reinforced fiber semi-recurve limbs, Joseph F. Lightcap.

Patent pending US3038830 1959-11-16, granted US 3038830 1962-06-12
laminated process for pre-stressed archery bow, inventors name Harold W. Groves.

Patent pending US3040728 1958-07-21, granted US3040728 1962-06-26
medal riser with bolt on limbs with an adjustable arrow plate, inventors name Naseeb Nieman.

Patent pending US3055353 1959-07-31, granted US3055353 1962-09-25
bolt on limbs to medal riser with adjustable handle grip, inventors name Joseph S. Perrucci.

Patent pending US3207146 1962-12-13, granted US 3207146 1965-09-21
medal riser with bolt on adjustable angle limbs, invertors name Phillip B. Grable.

Patent pending US3326200 1965-09-20, granted US3326200 1967-06-20
vertical laminated bolt on limbs to magnesium riser, inventors name Phillip B. Grable, sold as Golden Eagle.

Patent pending US3397685 1965-10-09, granted US3397685 1968-10-20
laminated limbs bolted to solid riser with a torque free handle, inventors name Beeby G. Walker.

Patent pending US3407799 1965-10-26, granted US3407799 1968-10-29
one piece laminated bow with handgrip alignment apparatus in riser, inventors name Robert J. Reynolds.

Patent pending US3412725 1965-03-29, granted US3412725 1968-11-26
one piece bow with base limb resiliently mounted stabilizers, inventors name Earl H. Hoyt Jr.

Patent pending US3415240A 1965-10-14, granted US3415240A 1968-12-10
laminated bow having a handle section and a pair of separate limbs including tapered socket members in the ends of the handle section which receive tapered butt portions of the limbs which lock and unlock, inventors name Fred B. Bear.

Patent Pending US3517658 1968-01-18, granted US 3517658 1970-06-30
Sq. riser section with laminated limbs attached with torque free grip mounted, inventor name Donald E. Shurts.

Patent pending US3537440 1968-11-04, granted US3537440 1970-11-03
a one piece bow with riser section with different specific gravities material that has high static and dynamic stabilities, inventors name Tadao Izuta.

Patent pending US3537439 1968-11-22, granted US3537439 1970-11-03
a bow mounted at the upper and lower ends of parallel riser elements the risers are connected to each other by means of a shelf element adapted to provide support for an adjustable handle and adjustable arrow rest. portions of the riser extend to form mounts for extending torque rods, inventors name William H. Joslin and Muncle Indiana.

Patent pending US3552373 1969-01-06, granted US3552373 1971-01-05
a bow with a 1st and 2nd limb pivotally attached to the ends of the bow riser section, inventors name Jerome M. Van Hecke.

Patent pending US3804072 1970-02-21, granted US3894972 1971-02-17
a bows handle section with one stabilizer attached on the belly side which extends obliquely downward, may have a 2nd stabilizer attached to the handle extending out of the back of the handle, inventors name Tadao Izuta.

Patent pending US3814075 1972-07-21, granted US3814075 1974-06-04
bow limbs detachably connected to the riser section in a close fitting relationship into portions of sockets formed in the riser section. A fixed pin extending forward at the bottom of the socket with a 2nd pin entering a hole from the rear to hold the limbs in lateral alignment, invertors name Earl H. Hoyt Jr.

Patent pending US3901210 1973-12-14, granted US3901210 1975-08-26
bow limbs having multiple reversal curves built in at substantially equidistant from the riser, inventors name William R. Stewart.

Patent pending US3921598 1973-10-15, granted US3921598 1975-11-25
a take down bow having a socket and a rib to receive a notched limb end with a restraining band, inventors name James C. Helmick.

Patent pending US3957027 1975-01-08, granted US3957027 1976-05-18
a bow which permits the limbs to be either detached or folded with respect to the handle, the draw weight may be adjusted through the connectors without modifying the limbs, inventors name Harry E. Drake.

Patent pending US4819608A 1987-08-24, granted US4819608A 1989-04-11
a laminated bow limb consisting of plurality of hollow micro spheres in a matrix of hard synthetic resin "syntactic Foam" in thin facing and backing strips of high tensile and compressive strengths for a higher recovery rate, inventors name Earl H. Hoyt Jr. and Gary W. Filice.

Compound Bows

Patent pending US3486495A 1966-06-23, granted US3486495A 1969-12-30
bow with draw force multiplying attachments cams or pullies for a compound bow, inventors name Holless W. Allen.

Patent pending US3841295 1973-10-20, granted US3841295 1974-10-15
a bowstring is secured intermediate its ends to eccentrically pivoted cams mounted at the outer ends of the limbs of the bow. Adjustable control cable operatively interconnects each limb. The terminal end of each end segment of the bowstring is secured to the lever associated with the opposite limb, the control cable connection is to balance a maximum pull weight. Adjustment of the length of the control cables effects adjustment of the tension of the limbs, inventors name Lafayette D. Hunter, assignee Donald S. Kudlacek.

Patent pending US3923036 1973-11-12, granted US3923036 1975-12-02
a compound bow riser structure including upper and lower limbs joined to a lightweight metal handle section. The handle section also includes side ribs positioned adjacent the front and rear surfaces, inventors names Thomas Paul Jennings, John Monroe Williamson & Carl Sumida.

Patent pending US3854467 1974-03-14, granted US3854467 1974-12-17
bow includes a pair of eccentric sheaves are revolvably mounted on he handle and a pair of pulleys are revolvably mounted on the ends of the limbs. a bowstring has its ends anchored to the handle and the eccentric sheaves and pulleys. a pair of concentric sheaves are each connected to one of the eccentric sheaves and an endless crossed cable that rotate in unison during movement between drawn and rest positions, inventors name Russell Hofmeister, assignee Herter's Inc.

Patent pending SU3987777 1975-02-10, granted US 3987777 1976-10-26
bow with an improved construction for reducing the holding force at the end of the draw. With a bowstring passing over each said eccentric pulley and said concentric pulleys to assure equality of motion as the arrow is drawn to a release position, inventors name Rex F. Darlington.

Patent pending US3990425 1977-09-26, granted US3990425 1979-06-12
compound bow with bowstring cable spacer, invertors name Paul D. MacWilliams.

Patent pending US4005696 1975-03-28, granted US4005696 1977-02-01
a bow having a lower and upper limb connected to the center portion and eccentrically mounted bowstring pulleys mounted at the outer ends of each bow limb. Each of the support members includes an upwardly extending outer end which is shaped and positioned to maintain a bowstring. Thru the end of a bowstring may be readily connected to the inner bowstring holder by passing a closed loop at the end, inventors name Thomas Paul Jennings.

Patent pending US4060066 1975-12-11, granted US 4060066 1977-11-29
An eccentrically mounting pivotal cam members at its outer extremity. A bowstring for projecting an arrow comprises a working stretch and a pear of separate end segments, then passes through a diametric bore in the cam member to the opposite side (two wheel hang bracket closed system), inventors name Donald S. Kudlacek.

Patent pending US4061124 1975-11-10, granted US4061124 1977-12-06
a compound bow having limb members adjustably pivotally mounted on opposite ends of a handle member by a limb adjustment assembly including as arcuate rib and groove connection an adjustable bolt fixedly holding the limb members. Having a rotatable shaft member upon which the cable may be adjustably wound and unwound to change the effective length of the cable. Having an eccentric wheel assembly mounted on the tips of each limb with the limb adjustment wheel assembly to enable tuning and timing relationships to be established, inventors name Norman Arlo Groner.

Patent pending US4078538A 1976-11-17,granted US 4078538A 1978-03-14
compound bow is disclosed which is formed by a air of opposed limbs joined to a centrally positioned handle section, a pair of pulleys are mounted by brackets extending inwardly fro the ends of the limbs, a cable system for holding the bowstring in a tensioned condition is passed through the two opposed pulleys a two wheel compound bow, inventors name Paul E Shepley.

Patent pending US4201177 1977-12-07, granted US4201177 1980-05-06
compound bow with one of the wheels or cams may be quickly manually adjusted with respect to the other without disassembling the strung bow, a ball and socket type quick connect and disconnect device is provided for dead ending the bow cables, inventors names Rudolph G. Holman and Frank W. Ketchum.

Patent pending US424171 1978-11-17, granted US4241715 1980-12-30
a compound bow a coupling the bowstring between the draw cables to provide a continuity between the bowstring and the draw cables each operatively coupled to a limb at a position near the end of the associated limb. Each of the draw pulleys permitting variations of the point of intersection between the path and at least one of the first and second grooves providing an adjustment in the draw length and the draw weight of the bow, inventors name Thomas P. Jennings.

Patent pending US4333443 1980-10-14, granted US4333443 1982-06-08
a compound bow with cable end terminals are adapted to be removable coupled together whereby to facilitate field disassembly over which a preferably segmented cable system is wound having an end revolvably associated with a pulley and an opposite end axially secured to the bow. A bowstring extending between opposite bow limbs coupled to the teardrop fitting for propelling an arrow, inventors name David Roelle, assignee Ben Pearson Archery Inc.

Patent pending US4241715A 1978-11-17,granted US4241715A 1980-12-30
a compound bow with each of the cables having a peripheral portion and a central portion, 1st and 2nd grooves in the peripheral portion and a path leading through the central portion and connecting the 1st and 2nd grooves, each of the draw pulleys permitting variations providing an adjustment in the draw length and the draw weight of the bow, inventors name Thomas P. Jennings.

Patent pending US5368006A 1992-04-28,granted US5368006A 1994-11-29
a dual-feed single-cam compound bow, a cable passes around the pulley to form a bowstring section and a 2nd cable section, both sections forming a dual feed single cam compound bow, an anchor cable is provided t tie the two limbs on the bow together during the flexing of the bow, inventors name Mathew A. McPherson, assignee Bear Archery Inc.

Patent pending US5515836 1994-11-08, granted US5515836 1996-05014
a tiller adjustment system for an archery bow includes a tiller adjustment knob for precisely adjusting the tiller of a bow limb, a biasing mechanism in the form of two spring pocket to urge the bow limb into engagement with the tiller adjustment knob, inventors names Gail H. Martin, George T. Newbold, Fredrick L. Hatfield & James A. Lloyd, assignee Martin Archery.

Patent pending US6257219B1 2000-02-11, granted US6257219B1
2001-07-10; bow stabilizers or vibration dampers, a rotating member for use with a compound bow including a body having a rotation point for journaling the body to a bow limb, the body including a damping device for absorbing vibrational energy, inventors name Mathew A. McPherson.

Patent pending US6446619B1 2000-01-23, granted US6446619B1
2002-09-10; an archery bow having a substantially constant draw weight, the bow also having an upper rotational assembly rotatably mounted upon the upper limb for rotation about a 1st axle, the lower rotational assembly having at least a 1st lower cable track and a 2nd lower cable track, inventors name Mathew A. McPherson, sold as Genesis.

Patent pending US9581406B1 2016-10-21, granted US 9581406B1
2017-02-28; compound bow wedge lock limb pocket, a limb mounting pocket receives butt ends of split limbs of a bow, the pocket includes a top wall extending above the butt ends. An actuating member which may be a tapered wedge is disposed between the free ends of the 1st and 2nd tabs fro pushing the 1st and 2nd tabs generally away from each other, inventors names Samuel S. Nevels and Allen C. Rasor Jr. assignee Precision Shooting Equipment.

Arrows

Patent pending US1648376A 1927-04-04, granted US1648376A 1927-11-08
clamps for feathering arrows, a hollow housing with three ribs that clamps can be attached holding fletching against an arrow shaft, inventors name George W. Blodgett.

Patent pending US1789575A 1927-07-02, granted US1789575A 1931-01-20
tubular metal arrow with inserts for point and nock, inventors name Samuel C. Allen, assignee Dayton Steel Racquet Co.

Patent pending US1794051A 1928-05-03, granted US1794051A 1931-02-24
fletching a medal arrow shaft, an open housing to held a shaft level with a clamp hinged to hold a feather against the shaft, inventors name Samuel C> Allen, assignee Dayton Steel Racquet Co.

Patent pending US194051A 1928-05-03 granted US1794051A 1931-02-24
arrow fletching jig, a method of making a medal arrow, inventors name Samuel C. Allen.

Patent pending US1842540 1927-07-05, granted US1842540 1932-01-26
method of making a medal arrow in composing point and nock with groves for fletching, inventors name Robert H. Cowdery.

Patent pending US1896536A 1931-11-20, granted US1896536A 1933-02-07
arrow fletching jigs, inventors name Belshaw Thomas

Patent pending US1999601A 1932-03-11, granted US1999601A 1935-04-30
tubular material to make arrows, inventors name Louis Tengel, assignee American Fork & Hoe Co.

Patent pending SU2137014A 1938-01-04, granted US2137014A 1938-11-15
an arrow head comprises an impact or cutting plate and a specially designed slotted tip of bullet shape for receiving the plate, arrow head construction for hunting wild game, inventors name Arthur J. Brochu.

Patent pending US2265564A 1939-09-29, granted US2265564A 1941-12-09
a single bladed head for hunting wild game, inventors name Paul E. Klopsteg.

Patent pending US2337080A 1940-05-14, granted US2337080A 1943-12-21
a fletching jig for securing feathers or vanes to an arrow shaft, which is particularly simple and economical to make and operate for various kinds, sizes and lengths may be easily placed and secured to an arrow shaft of different diameters. For holding the feather or vane clamp at the desired angle with respect to the shaft for arranging the feathers or vanes at the desired spiral on a shaft. I have devised an arrow jig having certain novel feathers of

construction, combination and arrangement of parts and portions, inventors name Henry A. Bitzenburger.

Patent pending US2836208A 1955-04-15, granted US2836208A 1958-05-27
to provide a generally new and improved arrow fletching jig of simple and inexpensive construction and dependable operation for semi-skilled operator may accurately position and glue feathers or vanes to an arrow shaft at one time. The device comprises a rigid frame having triangular end plates which are spaced and rigidly fixed in parallel relationship by three parallel shoulder rods, inventors name Earl H. Hoyt Jr.

Patent pending US3572716 1968-11-25, granted US3572716 1971-03-30
a hunting arrow head including a pod readily attached to the broadhead for the automatic dispensing of a tranquilizing composition upon entry of the head into the flesh of game, inventors name Fred B. Bear.

Patent pending US3595579 1968-04-26, granted US3595579 1971-07-27
vanes made from a sheet of adhesive backed plastic material, each vane being formed from a section of a sheet of adhesive backed plastic material which is folded, so that both sides of the fold are bonded together by the adhesive, except for strips at the ends thereof, by which the section is bonded to the arrow shaft, inventors name Alfred E. Benolt.

Patent pending US3741542 1971-02-11, granted US3741542 1973-06-26
a readily disassemblable hunting arrowhead including a first blade engaged in a slot communicating with the front end of the collet and a 2nd blade, orthogonal to the 1st, inventors name Richard S. Karbo, assignee Brunswick Corp.

Patent pending US3756602 1972-11-24, granted US3756602 1973-09-04
archery arrow vane, is provided with a vane means including two flight vanes carried by a mounting vane, it is mounted with a slight helical spiral to cause rotation of the arrow during flight, inventors name Richard F. Carella.

Patent pending Des, 243527 1975-08-20, Des, 243527 1977-03-01
an artificial arrow fletch, polyvane fletch item. inventors name Leonard Henery Schnipke.

Patent Pending US4050696A 1976-08-17,granted US4050696A 1977-09-27
a pile (point) has removable ball bearings, or a threaded weight plug and/or a scored attaching portion which is readily breakable for shortening and lightening the pile in order to regulate the spine and balance of the arrow for improved performance, inventors name Fernando Troncoso Jr.

Patent pending US4141554 1977-02-03, granted US4141554 1979-02-27
an arrow shaft socket is disclosed which solves the problem on inserting a hollow threaded socket into a cavity in an arrow shaft to flow onto the threaded portion, an alternate

embodiment can include the provision of one or more axial grooves along the outside of the insert, inventors name Donald D. Sherwin.

Patent pending US4234190 1978-02-06, granted US4234190 1980-11-18
a carbon fiber-reinforced plastic arrow is disclosed having a tubular shaft, the tubular shaft is constructed of carbon fiber-reinforced plastic to include an interior section in which the carbon fibers run in two direction, an outer section in which substantially all of the fibers are parallel, Tom P. Airhart.

Patent pending US5971875A 1998-03-31, granted US5971875A 1999-10-26
vaneless arrow shaft, with the use of a smaller tube which fits inside the nock end of an arrow shaft and the smaller tube having molded in it a spiraled grooves which acts upon dimples that are molded in the arrow shaft body and when the bowstring drives the smaller tube into the arrow shaft causing the whole arrow shaft to spin, the results of which allows the arrow shaft to oscillate less, fly straight without vanes and faster with more penetration and will enter a close range target straight, inventors name Christopher Columbus Hill.

Target Butts

Patent pending US1602441 1925-01-08, granted US1602441 1926-10-12
an archery target made of two fabrics held apart by spacing bars supported by two post tied into the ground, inventors name Ellis Mallery.

Patent pending US1818939 1929-03-18, granted US1818939 1931-08-11
archery target, a fiber material bound into strips and wound in a round matt with a fiber covering to holds its shape, inventors name Harry M. Brading.

Patent pending US1961511A 1933-02-24, granted US1961511A 1934-06-05
archery target, a container with special means for dispensing contents for dispensing thin flat articles in succession contained between two walls with means to stop an arrow, inventors name Homer M. Sinclair, assignee American Tissue Mills.

Patent pending US2423347A 1944-04-27, granted US2423347A 1947-07-01
archery butt, a machine to process a swamp grass into a tightly bound round matt with a dense core to stop arrows, inventors name Charles A. Saunders.

Patent pending US3367660 1964-07-21, granted US3367660 1968-02-06
archery butt, using a fibrous material with laminated layers into a round matt by reinforced means, invertors name Dominic P. DiMaggio.

Patent pending US4093227 1976-06-28, granted US4093227 1978-06-06
a marksmanship target supported by a moveable support arm with a shock absorber interposed
between the targets and support arm. The shock absorber includes eight thin resilient ribs extending
from a circular hub mounted on the support arm to a marginal edge of the targets and integrally
formed with the target which moves back if hit by an arrow, inventors name Charles A. Saunders.

Archery Accessories

Patent pending US1885962 1932-02-09, granted US1885962 1932-11-01
anchor strings for an archery bow, a string system anchored to the bow handle, below the
nocking point on the bowstring and lower limb tip, a maximum draw check, inventors name
Alvin L. Swenson.

Patent pending US1926845A 1932-01-06, granted US1926845A 1933-09-12
a cutout at the handle to make a center shot arrow rest, inventors names, William M. Folberth
& Frederick G. Folberth.

Patent pending US1961517A 1931-12-03,Granted US1961517A 1934-06-05
longbow sighting device, a bar with a slide block, holding a sighting device that can be adjusted
up and down and right and left to hold a sight pin on the bullseye from varying distances. the
block also holds a pendulum pin for long distances, inventors name Paul E. Klopsteg.

Patent pending US2271173 1940-05-20, granted US2271173 1942-01-27
method of making a bowstring with loops at both ends and a center serving, inventors name
Nathaniel B. Lay.

Patent pending US2275870 1940-06-19, granted US2275870 1942-03-10
a medal post that sticks into the ground with a loop at the top two feet off the ground, a ground
quiver to hold arrows, inventors name Horace D. Sheldon.

Patent Pending US2464068A 1946-01-16,granted US2464068A 1049-03-08
a quiver is a device used in archery for containing arrows, a bowquiver mounted on the bow,
disclosed a quiver formed to be detachably but secured to the bow whereby it forms a part of
the bow enabling arrows to be carried by the quiver to the bow, inventors name Fred B. Bear.

Patent pending US2483928A 1947-08-18,granted US2483928A 1949-10-04
arrow clamp at the arrow rest, an arrow holder, inventors name George S. Ott.

Patent pending US2542501A 1949-02-23,granted US2542501A 1951-02-20
a sighting device mounded to the belly of the bow with a medal slide strip with a sliding block
holding an adjustable pin to sight on a target at varying distances, inventors name Bert E.
Fredrickson.

Patent pending US2593789 1946-03-25, granted US2593789 1952-04-22
a medal post that sticks into the ground with a loop and a double hook at the top to hold arrows and the bow, inventors name Ben Pearson.
Patent pending US2768669 1954-09-27, granted US2768669 1956-10-30
a side quiver designed to hold broadhead arrows secure and is adjustable to
arrow length, inventors name James L. Kinnee.
Patent pending US2769179 1953-11-02, granted US2769179 1956-11-06
an archery shooting glove, a three fingered glove of leather that goes over the finger tips with the leather extending back to a strip that stamps around the wrist, inventors name Alfert J. Love.

Patent pending US2788701 1955-06-28, granted US2788701 1957-04-16
a range finding device for a bow, using multiple mirrors mounted of the bow that parallax intersect on the target, inventors name George G. Browning.

Patent pending US2964166 1960-05-05, granted US2964166 1960-12-13
a hard bow case with devices inside to hold arrows and bow for travel, inventors names William L. Lehner & Milan L. Lincoln.

Patent pending US2974319 1957-09-27, granted US2974319 1961-03-14
a double layer of leather with strips extending for three fingers to hold a bowstring with a leather loop to place the center finger through to hold the tab in place, there is a space between the first and second finger strips for the arrow to fit, this will protect the drawing fingers and give a smooth release of the bowstring, inventors names Jack K. Wilson, Norman E. Wilson & Robert S. Wilson.

Patent pending US2980097 1959-01-28, granted US2980097 1961-04-18
an arrow rest device that screws into the handle at the shelf with a arrow support wire to rest the arrow on while shooting, inventors name Harold F. Rothgery.

Patent pending US3163697 1961-07-13, granted US3163697 1964-12-29
a sight bar mounded with two extending rods holding a sight utilizing optical rangefinder and coupled sighting element, inventors name David S. White.

Patent pending US3196860A 1061-07-03,granted US3196860A 1965-07-27
bow stabilizers or vibration dampers mounted at the base of bow limbs and edge of riser on a one piece bow, inventors name Earl H. Hoyt Jr.

Patent pending US3244161 1964-05-07, granted US3244161 1966-04-05
an arrow rubber holder at the arrow rest that detaches as the bow is drawn, inventors name Stanley N. Jenson.

Patent pending US3253587 1964-05-08, granted US3253587 1966-05-31
archery bow stringer, a cord with leather cups to fit over the bow tips, standing on the cord to pull the bow up and relax bowstring tension to slid the bowstring loop on to brace or take the bowstring loop for unbracing, inventors name James A. Pearson.

Patent Pending US3292607 1963-05-06, granted US3292607 1966-12-20
a device mounted through the bows riser with an adjustable plate that you can mount an arrow rest to, inventors name Earl H. Hoyt Jr.

Patent pending US3318298 1965-02-02, granted US3318298 1967-05-09
an adjustable inlayed sight assembly in the sight window with a brush arrow rest at the bottom of the mount, inventors name Fred B. Bear.

Patent pending US3342172A 1965-02-25,granted US3342172A 1967-09-19
archery bow limb shock cushioning means having a bracket with pivotally mounted weighted extended arms, inventors name John DeWitt Sanders.

Patent pending US3365800 1967-08-07, granted US3365800 1968-01-30
a bowhunting sight what is mounded holding a plate wit two slits holding pins with different size circles to fit the shoulder area of a full grown deed at different distances, inventors name Richard F. Carella.

Patent pending US3372686 1965-09-30, granted US3372686 1968-03-12
archery bow handle with resiliently biased arrow rest that screws into the riser at the window, leveraged upright arrow rest to set an arrow on but collapses forward as the arrow is shot with a spring push helping forward movement, inventors name Earl J. Losh.

Patent pending US3410644 1967-11-21, granted US3410644 1968-11-12
a telescopic bow sight wherein the ocular lens is mounded in the bowstring to magnify with a lens in the bow sight, inventors name Alvin E. Lendon.

Patent pending US3443558 1967-02-15, granted US3443558 1969-05-13
arrow actuated clicker for shooting a broadhead arrow, inventors name Maynard W. Peck.
Patent pending US3446200 1966-08-11, granted US3446200 1969-05-27
a tubular device with air plunger that attaches to the bow handle and bowstring, so the bow may be drawn and fired without an arrow, the plunger absorbs pressure for the release of the bowstring, inventors name Norton M. Gross.

Patent pending US3482563 1967-07-13, granted US3482563 1969-12-09
an archery bow spring-biased plunger, mounted in riser above the arrow rest so the arrow rest against the plunger as the arrow is being shot, inventors name Norman L. Pint.

Patent pending US3524440 1968-01-17, granted US3524440 1970-08-18
a bow sight comprises of an upper mirror and a lower mirror are mounted on the riser, the two mirrors are aligned substantially vertically with each other. A cross hairs or other target alignment to place on the target, the lower mirror is focused on the target while the upper mirror is focused on the lower mirror and reflects the target image to the archer's eye. The mirror mounting the cross hairs may be adjusted vertically to compensate for distance, inventors name Walter D. Hill.

Patent pending US3524441 1968-03-25, granted US3524441 1970-10-18
an archery bow stabilizer having an isolated shock cushion mounted base, a resilient, compressible elastomeric bushing in the base provides a captive support for attaching the rod and head to the bow, inventors name Owen E. Jeffery.

Patent pending US3574944 1968-09-10, granted US3574944 1971-04-13
a sighting device in which a sight member is carried by a range member and the range member is supported in spaced relationship from the bow, a range member support device is adjustable in length, inventors name David William Reynolds.

Patent pending US361578 1970-02-02, granted US3651578 1972-03-28
a bow square for checking and recording the bracing height, nocking point and locations for a kisser and peep sight of an archery bow, an elongated plate provided with a graduated scale for measuring the bracing height and a cross bar extending transversely of the elongated plate and having a scale extended parallel to the bowstring, inventors name Thomas Allen Sanders.

Patent pending US3669059 1971-01-02, granted US3669059 1972-06-13
a clacker adapted for attachment to an archery bow window, a spring element that is sandwiched between metal strips. The spring element is biased outwardly from the bow by the arrow during the drawing of a bowstring, when the spring element moves out of engagement with the arrow, the element will slap the bow and a noise is produced indicating to the archer that the arrow has been drawn the proper distance, inventors name Frank T. Stuart.

Patent pending US3612029 1970-01-08, granted US3612029 1971-10-12
a bowstring silencing device constructed of a tough, flexible synthetic thermoplastic material having a central core inserted between the strands of the bowstring, having a plurality of flexible integrally formed vibration damping arms radiating from the core of the bowstring, inventors name Cornelius F. Carroll.

Patent pending US3672347 1970-12-03, granted US3672347 1972-06-27
the shaft of an arrow is supported in the sight window of an bow by an arrow rest comprising a flexible finger which laterally as it is engaged by the feathers of the arrow after release, the tab is formed of sufficiently heavy plate stock to be rigid and remain in the desired position under lateral force, inventors name Holless W. Allen.

Patented pending US3703728 1971-08-27, granted US3703728 1972-11-28
a light weight lattice like shield including integrally formed loops for receiving adjustable, flexible and elastically extensible bands for securement of the shield to the forearm of an archer, inventors names Thomas Allen Saunders & Eugene F. Saunders.

Patent pending US3769956 1972-01-13, granted US3769956 1973-11-06
a retractable arrow rest to support an arrow in proper position for shooting. The arrow rest includes an L-shaped member having an upright arm rotatable mounted in a sleeve that is connected to a bow mounting member with an arrow supporting leg. The supporting arm is spring biased outwardly from the bow it retracts out of the way upon forward movement of the arrow, inventors name Miroslav Andrew Simo.

Patent pending US3787984 1972-09-22, granted US3787984 1974-01-29
a bow sight is provided with a sight mount which is both vertically and transversely adjustable wit respect to a supporting bar. An anvil and base assembly serve to attach the support bar to a bow and include fastening means permitting of both forward and lateral tilting of the support bar and its sight mount, inventors names Fred B. Bear & Owen E. Jefferey.

Patent pending US3845504 1973-03-01, granted US3845504 1974-11-05
a finger tab to draw a bowstring includes a flexible leather tab projuscting forwardly from an elongated base, the width of the tab is dimensioned to be interposed between the bowstring and the two middle fingers only, the end projections of the base are arranged for engagement by the index and little fingers, an elastic retaining strip is secured at opposite ends of the base for receiving the two middle fingers to draw and release, inventors name Gerald I. Killian.

Patent pending US3846998 1973-08-09, granted US3846998 1974-11-12
a machine is provided for testing the straightness of arrows, for localizing and measuring any want of straightness and for mechanically correcting any defect of this nature that may be discovered. The machine desirably includes a central stand on which a deflection meter is mounted, together with a straightening lever. Arrow supporting and rotating carriages are mounted on the trackway with freedom for independent adjustment, inventors name William E. Lock.

Patent pending US3854217 1974-03-18, granted US3854217 1974-12-17
an arm adapted for attachment to the side of a bow, supports an elongated base which mounts an elongated micrometer screw extending parallel to the plane of the bow. A sight-supporting block is mounted on the base for slidable movement parallel to the screw and a latch is pivoted to the block for releasable engagement with the screw. The assembly is reversible for mounting on either side of a bow, a sighting pin mounted on a rod below a leveling bubble, inventors name Gerald I. Killian.

Patent pending US3865096 1973-12-28, granted US3865096 1975-02-11
arrow rest with an upwardly and forwardly projecting free standing resilient arm connected at its lowest rear end to a horizontally extending base support, the arrow rest provides improved arrow flight, inventors name Fernando Troncoso Jr.

Patent pending US3880136 1973-11-07, granted US3880136 1975-04-29
an accessory for an archer to be worn on the drawing hand to anchor with the bowstring under the chin, device includes an arcuate shaped member adapted to fit a portion at the chin of a user when the bowstring and arrow are drawn to fully extended position so as to aim and shoot an arrow with greater accuracy at a consistent draw, inventors name Ivan P. Leidy.

Patent pending US3945127 1974-03-27, granted US3945127 1976-03-23
a sighting device wherein one to ten sighting pins containing light conducting fibers are used to align the arrow. The sighting pins are adjustable both vertically and horizontally and are battery operated, inventors name Phillip G. Spencer.

Patent pending US4011853 1975-07-31, granted US4011853 1977-03-15
an archery peep sight adapted to be mounted in the bowstring of a bow for aligning the path of an arrow, a disc having a centrally located sight opening is attached to the bowstring in fixed space relation with the nocking point. A semi-conical recess is formed in the second end of the disc, Bowstring receiving channels are formed on opposite sides of the disc, inventors name James D. Fletcher.

Patent pending US4133334 1977-02-01, granted US4133334 1979-01-09
an arrow supporting device with a mounting plate adapted to be affixed to the bow window, with a closed loop spring member having two ends pivotally attached at the ends to the mounting plate, the closed loop spring member is movable towards the mounting plate to permit the stabilizing structure of the arrow to clear the arrow supporting device, inventors name Richard D. Tone.

Patent pending US4170980 1978-03-24, granted US4170980 1979-10-16
an archery bow arrow rest includes a hollow cylinder threaded externally for removable attachment in a threaded opening through the riser of an archery bow and threaded internally for removable attachment of a hollow, externally threaded guide sleeve which anchors a support plate and slidably guides a spring loaded plunger for axial movement on the longitudinal axis of the cylinder, with an arrow rest arm mounted pivotally at one end on the support plate, inventors name Gerald I. Killian.

Patent pending US4177572 1978-06-28, granted US4177572 1979-12-11
an individual lighted sight pin for an archery bow which provides a small point of light for aiming an arrow. A fiber-optic rod transmits light from a light-emitting diode (LED) activated by a voltage source to the sighting end, inventors name Ted E. Hindes.

Patent pending US4535747A 1983-03-17, granted US4535747A 1985-08-20
an archery bowsight arranged for removable attachment to the handle portion of a bow, is supporting a longitudinally extendable mounting aim with horizontally adjustable bowsight windage carriage which mounts an elevation carriage provided for micrometrically graduated vertical movement. An elongated sight pin mounting block mounts a plurality of sighting pins individual adjustment, in order to provide yardage and elevation adjustment, inventors name Donald S. Kudlacek.

Patent pending US5896849 1998-03-30, granted US5896849 1999-04-27
arrow rest provides complete radial support to an arrow disposed in a ready-to-draw position even if the bow is tilted, such radial support is provided by an inverted coil brush comprising a disc-shaped structure, no angular orientation of the arrow vanes to the arrow neck is required, the arrow rest can be used with any diameter arrow, inventors name Wilfred Isaac Branthwaite.

Release Aids

Patent pending US2000015 1933-10-03, granted US2000015 1935-05-07
a safety arrow release device for bows in archery, a handle grip that fits into the palm of the hand with a device extended forward to hook onto the bowstring to draw, extended device has a triggering device to release the bowstring, inventors name Godfrey Flury.

Patent pending US2637311A 1950-08-03, granted US2637311A 1953-05-05
a pistol grip to pull with that has a pin in the front of the grip that can lock into the bowstring securely and be released by a triggering device at full draw, inventors name Harry J. Rose.

Patent pending US2965093A 1959-10-23, granted US2965093A 1960-12-20
a squire medal device with finger slots to held with a mechanical device at the front what has a pivoting ledge that locks onto the bowstring and can be triggered at full draw, inventors name Jean J. Arsenault.

Patent pending US3072115 1959-06-15, granted US3072115 1963-01-08
an adjustable leather wrist strip with an adjustable forward strip that wraps around the bowstring and is held by pinching the leather strip wrapped around the bowstring, pull to full draw and relax the pinch to release the bowstring, inventors name Jesse E. Johnson.

Patent pending US3604407 1969-03-28, granted US3604407 1971-09-14
a plastic handle with a double leather strip to wrap around the bowstring and pinch with your thumb the leather strip against the plastic handle to hold the bowstring, to release the bowstring relax the thumb, inventors names Jack K. Wilson, Norman E. Wilson & Robert S. Wilson.

Patent pending US3656467 1971-01-15, granted US3656467 1972-04-18
a hand held bowstring drawing and release member having a notch formed for engagement with for drawing the bowstring, a finger engaging portion formed for the drawing the bowstring to a stable bow tensioned position with a single finger and another finger engaging portion positioned to provide a trigger release of the bowstring upon squeezing down on the several finger portions. The finger engaging portion used in drawing the bowstring is aligned with the notch in such a way that the mid-point of this portion will be directly behind the notch while the bowstring is being drawn by a single finger, inventors name Dale F. Halter.

Patent pending US3757763A 1971-07-15, granted US3757763A 1973-09-11
a trigger operated bowstring mechanism for receiving a bowstring and shooting the arrow incident to a triggered release of the bowstring. A hand-supported stock carries the releasing mechanism which includes a bowstring engaging hook pivoted to the stock on a vertical axis. The hook is held in its string engaging position through engagement in a notch provided in the lower edge of a trigger which itself is pivoted to the stock on a horizontal axis. The notch is disengaged from the hook to release the bowstring when the trigger is pivoted upward by rearward pressure of the archer's forefinger on the top end of the trigger, inventors name Patrick R. Pinti.

Patent pending US3749076 1971-06-18, granted US3749076 1973-07-31
arrow nock and trigger actuated release, an archer's handgrip including support structure for supporting the nock on the rear end of an arrow against lateral deflection. The support structure includes a finger releasable latch mechanism releasably engageable with notches in the nock portion of the supported arrow and retains the supported arrow nock against forward movement relative to the support structure, the latch mechanism and support structure being engageable with the rear end portion of the associated arrow nock rearward of the forward end of the bowstring accommodating slot of the arrow nock, inventors name Michael D. Suski.

Patent pending US3757763 1971-07-15, granted US3757763 1973-09-11
a hand-supported stock carries the releasing mechanism which includes a bowstring engaging hook pivoted to the stock on a vertical axis. The hook is held in its engaging position through engagement in a notch provided in the lower edge of a trigger which itself is pivoted to the stock on a horizontal axis. The notch is disengaged from the hook to release the bowstring when the trigger is pivoted upward by rearward pressure of the archer's forefinger on the top of the trigger, inventors name Ross A.

Plnti.

Patent pending US3853111 1974-02-25, granted US3853111 1974-12-10
an adjustable rope release for an archery bowstring, triggered by squeeze action of the fingers, which permits the archer to set the point in the squeeze motion at which the arrow id released. The rope release comprise a hand grip, for grasping by the index and middle fingers of the drawing hand, from which a rope cord is looped around the bowstring and held by a hooked

pin whose angle of projection relative to the grip member is adjustable by set screws. Squeezing of the middle finger of the hand causes the hand grip to pivot laterally relative to the drawn bow to a point which permits the rope loop to suddenly slip off the hooked pin, thereby releasing the bowstring and projecting the arrow toward its intended target, inventors names Melvern B. Stanislawski & Daniel F. McKinney.

Patent pending US3952720 1975-04-11, granted US3952720 1976-04-27
a bowstring release mechanism, the mechanism is released by the use of a trigger, which is adjustable and features a sear that aids in reducing applied force, resulting in an easier trigger pull. It includes the use of a flexible rope loop that is looped around the bowstring and held by a rotary holding member, which is locked by a sear. The sear is locked by a sliding trigger, which, when actuated, will free the sear and the holding member, allowing the loop to escape, inventors name Hugh R. Wilson.

Patent pending US3998202 1975-08-04, granted US3998202 1976-12-21
a bowstring release device comprises a one-piece, T-shaped body including a handle portion forming the crossbar of the T-shaped body and a leg portion extending outwardly from the handle portion and terminating in an outer free end portion. A bowstring receiving notch is formed in the free end portion and a transverse slot is formed in the free end portion normal to the bowstring receiving notch. A lock is pivotally mounted in the transverse slot for releasably locking the bowstring in the notch. A latch pin is slidably mounted in the enlarged bore and is spring biased outwardly into the transverse slot. A release lever is pivotally mounted along side of the handle portion while retaining the bowstring until the latch pin is retracted by operation of the release lever, inventors name Frank E. Boyko.

Patent pending US4041926 1976-02-18, granted US4041926 1977-08-16
a bowstring release device includes a frame, a pair of opposable jaws pivotally connected to the front of the frame with the pivotally connected to the front of the frame with the bowstring-retaining ends of the jaws at the front thereof and with the opposite or rear ends thereof defining a space when the front ends abut. A plunger with a specially configured head having a wider diameter at its front end is slideably disposed in the frame, the plunger head being urged forward into the space by a spring so as to keep the front ends of the jaws closed, trapping the bowstring. A trigger is secured to the plunger and enables the archer to urge the plunger rearward in the frame and out of the space so as to permit the front ends of the jaws to open and release the bowstring. An adjustable stop may be provided to finely control the extent to which the head can be urged into the space and thus the extent of rearward movement. An adjustable collar, usable on the archer's wrist or elbow, is attached to the frame by a cord to enable the archer to draw the bowstring by the release device, inventors name Fernando Troncoso Jr.

Patent pending US4105011 1977-09-23, granted US4105011 1978-08-08
bowstring release, a hand-held operated archery bowstring release has a generally lazy-T-shaped member contoured as a handhold. A pair of forwardly projecting jaw members retain

a tensioned bowstring until released by a single slight downward movement of an associated plunger. Following such release an open helical compression spring acting on the plunger resets the jaw member to the bowstring holding position. The plunger has a circular cross section and has a plurality of longitudinally spaced coaxially aligned and small diameter segment and an upstanding conical frustum segment, inventors name Van B. Chism.

Patent pending US4173210 1977-12-29, granted US4173210 1979-11-06
a bowstring release device, a trigger device for facilitating pulling of a bowstring and for quick release of the taut bowstring for propelling an arrow from the bow, said trigger device comprising a main body portion provided with suitable substantially perpendicular to the main body portion having a bowstring hold and releasing latch mechanism carried thereby. The latching mechanism comprises a flexible loop member adapted for encircling the bowstring and engaging a loop receiving recess provided in the secondary body portion. A latch member extends across the open end of the loop receiving recess and is openably connected with a release trigger by way of a pivotal bell crank and a lever member whereby a light touch of the trigger member by the finger of the archer quickly causes the bell crank and lever member to operate to release the latch for release of the taut bowstring, inventors name Loyd S. Napier.

Patent pending US4249507 1979-03-14, granted US4249507 1981-02-10
a bowstring draw and release device has a frame in which a hammer is mounted in such a way as to cooperate with a trigger and latch to effect release of the bowstring with a relatively low trigger pressure. The device includes a frame having a recess in its front end and a pivotal latch member adapted to extend across the recess for engaging a loop which is formed into a bight around the bowstring. A latch sear is releasably engaged with the latch and has a portion disposed in the path of movement of a spring biased hammer normally held in a cocked position by a hammer sear connected to the trigger. A suitable handgrip extends rearwardly from the frame and is designed to enable the user to actuate the trigger with his index finger. Rearward pull on the trigger causes the hammer sear to disengage the hammer and release it from the locked position, whereby the hammer advances forwardly to engage and pivot the latch sear for causing it to disengage the latch, inventors name Paul Marra.

CHAPTER 6

After World War II

Paralympic Archery started in 1946 as a form of rehabilitation for war veterans with spinal cord injuries. The first Para Archery competition for those with physical impairments was held on the lawn at the Stoke Mandeville at a Hospitals in 1948 in Great Britain. During those days, the rounds shot were the St. Nicholas Round for novices (48 arrows shot from 36.6 meters and 36 arrows from 27.4 meters). There was the Albion Round for established archers (36 arrows each shot from 73.2 meters, 54.9 meters and 45.7 meters away). Para archery was one of the eight sports at the Rome 1960 Paralympic Games. Athletes were assessed by doctors and given classifications for competition, which they then participated in. In the Paralympics in Barcelona 1992, held two weeks after the Olympic Games other athletes with impairments beyond spinal cord injuries were included. In 1998 FITA piloted the sport with a specific classification system, which is used today. The Paralympic competition has individual and team events in both standing and wheelchair competition.

1946 Archery was ready

Archery exploded, equipment was available do to the promotion of the people listed above. All those solders coming home, many wanted to hunt and learn to bowhunt. Many NFAA members around the US fought to get archery only hunting seasons and they worked at organizing their clubs to show interest in bowhunting by the numbers of their membership, voting people interested in bowhunting. Today I believe almost every US state has a bowhunting season separate from gun hunting. Now we have a market for Archery to grow. The NFAA members just before the Second World War were ready, they now hosted their First National Outdoor Field Championship in 1946 at one location as a national archery organization. By the end of the 1950's the NFAA had almost 30,000 members across the US. The NAA continued it's traditional long distance shooting until the late 1960's using FITA Rounds. Archery was reintroduced into the Olympic Games in 1972. The NAA membership was growing slowly by staidly to about 2000 members. Now for the NAA the old debate came back, what is a professional archer and how to define an amateur for Olympic competition? The Olympics' required amateur competitors only. In the 1960's the NAA classified all Manufacturers and makers of archery tackle as Pro's because they made a living by selling and making archery equipment for money. Of course if you shot archery for money prizes? no question. You didn't even have to win money but just compete for money and you were no longer eligible for amateur competition.

CHAPTER 7

Shooting Archery for Money

The NAA rejected money prizes in the 1880's, years ago. Lets start with Howard Hill, he was the greatest Professional Archer of the 20th century. He shot archery in films and exhibitions and got paid. In 1940 the Archery Manufacturers Assoc. sponsored the **Great American Open Tournament, GAO** to be held in Milwaukee 1940 with $5000 in cash for Men, Ladies and Junior shooters. This archery tournament had options to shoot over 3 days. They had 5 archery events; you could shoot 5 Target events, 3 Target events and 2 Field events or just compete in one event. One of the Field events was moving targets, bowhunters loved that. There was an immediate request for entry forms from archers in 10 states. This upset archery traditions of the NAA, they couldn't get away with. There were 216 archers entered in the events to be shot over the 3 days. There were many archery manufacturers tents open for business. The manufacturers were amazed at the sales and interest in archery products. Russ B. Hoogerhyde won the Target event and Howard Hill won the Field competitions. It just didn't create that much interest and the war was coming.

It wasn't until 1958 that the next big money tournament was held. The **Fred Bear Money Shoot** with a $5000 purse, no pretense. This tournament followed the NFAA National Field Championship. The top eight shooters from the NFAA Championship were invited to shoot for the money. They shot 56 Field and 56 Hunter targets. The ranges were set up for spectators with a mobile scoreboard. Bear sponsored the money tournament to answer some of his questions about archery. Can archery be made interesting to a gallery of spectators? Will newspapers and magazines give archery the attention it deserves? Fred Bear wanted only one Men's and one Women's Champion. Joe Fries won the NFAA Field Championship and the $2000 for the Bear Money Shoot. Ann Corby shot barebow in the NFAA Nationals and won $1000 shooting with a sight for the Bear Money Shoot. Fred felt the many divisions in archery competition led to confusion and discouragement in the press for coverage. There had to be a thousand spectators following archers around the courses at this tournament. The courses were laid out so everyone was perfectly safe for spectators to watch and enjoy.

1959 **Ben Pearson Open Indoor Championship,** this was the first money shot indoors. It was shot in Detroit at the Coliseum, this was not an all cash shoot. There were no divisions of styles of shooting, just highest score. Money divisions were Men, Women and a Team competition. There were 52 target butts with 2-16" target faces on each butt. Above each target was the archers name and a number flip tablet to keep a running score for the spectators to see. By the half way point spectators were speculating on the high scores so far as to the outcome. They shot two lines, one at 1pm & one at 4pm, both lines were full. James Caspers won the men's earning $1000 and a Diamond Ring. Key Clay won the Ladies earning $1000 and a Silver Blue Mink Stole. The Team, L.C. Whiffen won $1000 and a Ben Pearson Trophy.

1960 **Ben Pearson Open Indoor Championship** was the second indoor money shot in Akron, Ohio held in the Akron Goodyear gym. The Cleveland and Akron newspapers covered the tournament with some TV coverage with 379 shooters and around 400 spectators. (I kind of feel most of the spectators were family and other archers). The shooting was top quality shooting the Chicago Round at 20 yds. at a 16" target face, shooting 96 arrows for each of the two rounds for completion. James Caspers won the men's winning $1000, Ann Clark won the women's winning $800.

1960 the **Bear-Easton $10,000 International Invitational** shooting 42 Field targets held near the Bear Factory for a $20 fee. They had Men's Freestyle & Barebow plus Women's Freestyle & Barebow with some 500 spectators. It was agreed that ties would be broken with the highest 14 target total of the three rounds shot. Except the judges decided on breaking toes with the most hits, no disagreement. Sometimes you have to go with the flow. Bob Kadlec and James Mackel tied anyway and won $1000 each. Women's freestyle Lou Shine won $1000, Barebow Men James Palmer won $1000 and women's Barebow Faye Sconyers won $1000.

1961 the **Ben Pearson Open Indoor Championship** at Fort Wayne, Indiana in the Memorial Coliseum with 460 shooters. The 3rd Ben Pearson Open was the 1st big archery tournament after new rules were set forth by the NAA concerning amateurism, few knew what the rules meant. Many delayed their decision as to shooting Open or Amateur Divisions, a new attendance record was set. This was the 1st time for the Ben Pearson to establish an Open and Barebow Division. Those competing in the amateur divisions could shoot without jeopardizing their amateur standing. They gave out merchandise for amateur prizes, but if the prize was worth $70 and accepted by the shooter they lost their amateur standing. Three of the prizes were worth more and were refused by the winners. Ben Pearson Company gave them a new bow, it must of been worth less? All the targets had the archers name on their target with a flip number cards to keep a running score. There were 3 shooting times, Sports Illustrated covered the tournament. Men's Freestyle Bill Partin winning $600, Ladies Freestyle Margaret Tillberry won $500. Men's Barebow Allen Froats won $600, Ladies Barebow Gertrude Hitt won $500. The Team was won by the Ohio Archers winning $500.

The Professional Archers Association, PAA

In 1961 the Professional Archers Association was formed to define a Pro archer. They established a minimum score requirement for members or they had to have won a state championship to join. Your first year was an apprenticeship and then you were accepted as a full member. The

PAA had a dress code and a code of conduct. Most PAA members never accepted a trophy at any tournament, only money as a prize. Some would compete in a local tournament but refuse a trophy or donated it back. The PAA started scheduling their Tournament Money circuit in 1963. The PAA had their own Archery Instructors School for new members. They were the most clean cut and dedicated archers I have ever associated with. There were many very good shooters that had the scores but never joined the PAA. I knew of their tournament circuit or schedule and on an open date I hosted what they called a "Pot" shoot. I couldn't have a guaranteed purse so each archer paid a fee to shoot and 90% of that fee was returned as prize money. A lot of non-PAA Pro's shot but still never joined the PAA.

The **Colt-Sahara & NFAA Indoor Championship** held in Las Vegas, Nevada in 1962. This information is from "Archery Magazine" reported by Roy Hoff. Many an archer had never seen legal gambling and the best entertainment in the US. There was no reason to even leave the Sahara Hotel. A TV show called "Panorama Pacific" covered an hour of the shooting with Life Magazine and Sports Illustrated there as well. There were 5 ranges with 20 targets per range with 8 archers per target. Neither Life Magazine or Sports Illustrated printed anything about the largest archery money tournament ever held, just weren't impressed. Some shooters objected to their names and scores being announced over the PA system as the tournament was active, so it stopped. So overall no announcer or scoreboard was there to keep the spectator advised on who was doing what to try in hold the spectators interest. This was new and we are learning. They used a new target face for scoring that was impossible to see arrows in the targets. There were a great many archers who were displeased. The tournament had Men's and Ladies Freestyle and Barebow divisions, no mention of amateurs. Men's Freestyle Matt Yurick won $700, Ladies Freestyle Lou Shine won $500. Men's Barebow Lon Stanton won $700, Ladies Barebow Teressa Carter won $500.

The **Ben Pearson Open Indoor Championship** was held in Fort Wayne, Indiana 1962. They shot Open & Amateur divisions shooting a double Chicago Round. There were 4 shooting times each day. There were 40 target butts with 4 targets on each butt with name cards and flip numbers to keep a running score. They used the new PAA indoor target face with 585 shooters attending. Archers coming always check the registration list posted to see who was shooting and on what target butt and when. The first shooting line started at 9am and the last shooting line was at 7:30pm. The money winners Men's Open Bill Partin won $1000, Ladies Open Jane Waite won $1000, the Team winner was the Ohio Archers winning $500.

The **Ben Pearson Open Indoor Championship** in Detroit, Michigan in 1963 with 701 archers. There were archers from 28 states and Canada. They hosted an Open, Amateur and Team competition. There were 6 Open Teams making the shoot off out of 46 teams entered. The shoot was held in the Coliseum Building using 50 target butts. All ties were broken by the most 9's shot. Men's Open Jim Pickering won $1000, Ladies Open Margaret Tillberry won $1000. No mention of the Team and any amateur shooters.

Point of interest Jim Pickering went to the Ben Pearson Open with the understanding that his Indoor range and Pro shop was to pay his iterance fee. When he got there he had not been pre-registered. He had a hard time coming up with the fee but did and won. Let me mention here that the Ben Pearson Open was the only money tournament that paid the men and ladies the same amount of money. Even today the ladies receive less of a money prize. But over all, archers are the greatest competitors, not just in winning but in the joy of participation in just shooting itself, there are no real losers.

The **National Outdoor PAA Championship** of 1963 held at Daytona Beach, Fl. This 1st PAA national tournament was held on the country club of a resort city. Shooting the new PAA outdoor round forming a large "V" helping spectators with a better view of the action. There was some disappointment at the turnout and some dispute with sponsors over prizes and prize money, growing pains. They shoot four rounds on the new course shooting two each day. There was some 700 spectators present with an announcer helping all to under stand what was happening. Non-archers watching were amazed at the excellent shooting and the archery equipment. They had a scoreboard which kept a running score for all to see. Many PAA shooters stepped back into the spectators after shooting and answered questions. The new target faces allowed spectators to see every hit clearly. The judges used a golf cart to run around to call arrows and replace target faces. Both CBS & ABC made movies for their winter programs, local TV was their also. One local newspaper had daily stories. PAA Men's Champ William "Bill" Bednar won $1000, PAA Ladies Margaret Tillberry won $1000, no team or amateurs shooting.

The 1963 **Enchanted Forest Shoot** was held in Las Angeles, Ca. Publicity stated $10,000 in money and $10,000 in prizes. This tournament may have been the biggest flop in the archery world. None of the vouchers given to the winners instead of cast were honored, this was very unfortunate. At the last moment the PAA found out there were problems about payments and there were sponsors of the shoot for the PAA members. The Enchanted Forest sponsoring the shoot and promises made by them that the money would be there, so the shoot continued. The PAA hired Doug Easton's lawyer to see that the archers didn't come out on the short end. The Enchanted Forest said they would have the money available next week. Why standard procedure wasn't pursued further will never be known. The PAA learned that firmer rules to make sure all prize money was their and not let just anyone sponsor their money tournaments. Freestyle Men Jim Pickering won $1000, Ladies Freestyle Marcie Bangert won $500, don't know if they ever received their money.

The **Ben Pearson Open Indoor Championship** was held in Detroit, Michigan at Cobo Hall in 1964. The hall had 80 target butts with names of archers above and below the four target faces per butt with a flip card for keeping a running score. There were 959 shooters participating with 320 archers shooting on each of three shooting times. It was said some 6000 spectators were watching over the two days. This tournament received the best press & TV coverage so far. The amateur winners shot exceptional scores. Wayne Blowers set a new record with his Barebow scores. Men's Freestyle Bill Bednar won $1000, Ladies Freestyle Margaret Tellberry won $800. The Team competition was won by the New York State who won $500.

The **Ben Pearson Open Indoor Championship** held at Detroit, Michigan in 1965 at Cobo Hall using the PAA target face. Considered the largest one of the largest indoor archery tournaments in the World with 1174 shooters. For the first time money awards went to the 25th place in the Men's Open Division. The tournament was PAA sanctioned shooting 12 ends of five arrows twice using 94 target butts with four target faces per butt. Half of the target butts were on one wall and half were on the opposite wall with a large grandstand for spectators in the middle. It was estimated some 6000 watched the shooting both days. The bow racks would accommodate archers having a backup bow. There were large tables behind the bow racks to place your bow case and tackle close by. The lighting was perfect, you didn't even need a flash to take pictures. They shoot three lines; one at 9am, 11:30am and the 3rd at 3pm. Team members not in the individual contest could shoot their team scores at 6pm. On the 2nd day all shooters were placed with their competition by score. Ties were broken by the highest individual round. They hosted an Open, Amateur, Youth and Team competition. There were 72 Pro's registered. The PAA made a colored movie film at this tournament to show prospective sponsors, don't know what happened to it. The Men's Open Jim Ploen won $1000, Ladies Open Gwen Learn won $800 with the Team, American Team winning $500.

The **National Outdoor PAA Championship** 1965 held at Detroit, Michigan in Rouge Park with a $4000 purse. They had a PA system set up for the "V" shaped range of the 20 target course, announcing past champions and a running score as the action progressed. They shot two rounds each day with a total of 240 arrows to complete. The event was covered by 3TV stations with interviews on local radio. Local newspapers gave extensive coverage with pictures. The Men's William "Bill" Bednar won $550, Ladies Margaret Tellberry won $300. The PAA was presenting a positive image of archery to the public.

The **Ben Pearson Open Indoor Championship** of 1966 was held at Detroit, Michigan at Cobo Hall. This tournament was renamed the International Indoor Championship. It was still referred to as the Ben Pearson Open. The PAA indoor target faces seem to be standard for indoor shooting now. Ben Pearson Archery offered $1000 cash prize for a perfect round of 300. Ed Rohde of Iowa shot a 299. The Ben Pearson Open hosts Open, Amateur and Team competition, adding this year a men's and ladies Team competition. The men's Open Lester Gervais won $1000, Ladies Open Gwen Learn won $800. The men's Team Indiana #1 won $500, Ladies Team Michigan won $359.80.

The **Colt-Sahara Indoor Championship** was held in Las Vegas, Nevada at the Convention Center. This tournament was advertised as the 1966 Sahara-Colt US Open Indoor Archery Championship. Competitors came from 27 states shooting for $12,000 in cash and merchandise. This was a PAA sanctioned shoot. 348 registered, both Pro's and amateurs, there were 38 four man teams entered. The Teams were competing for the new "Colt Cup" a Sterling Silver Bowl, given a value of $1,250. Each archer dropped a penny into the cup as they picked up their score card for luck. Jim Pickering and Bill Bednar were tied at the finial arrow. Bill won in a sudden death shoot off over Jim. Dead silence is a big distraction. In the shoot off Jim shot an arrow that hit an arrow in the 5 ring and deflected into the 4 ring. The rule was an arrow scores as it sets in the target, not fare but that was the rule at that time. They also had a handicap competition with merchandise prizes. The Men's Open Chuck Wertz won 1st, Ladies Open Roma Squibb won 1st, I couldn't seem to find the money amounts for Pro winners.

The 1966 **PAA Outdoor National Championship** I couldn't find any information other then it was held at Point Pleasant, West Virginia. The Men's William "Bill" Bednar won $2000, Ladies Marie M. Stotts won $1000.

CHAPTER 8

The Compound Bow When?

Up until World War II all archers shot longbows and wood arrows. By the end of the 1950's almost everyone was shooting recurve bows and aluminum arrows. In 1933 the first one piece release aid was patented. I couldn't determine when in the 1950's archers started using a release aid in competition with the recurve bow. But Wilbur Hollis Allen patented a design for an archery bow with draw force multiplying attachments, a compound bow in 1966. Allen sent every archery company he could find his new design wanting financial help, no takers. Allen went to Dearborn Michigan in 1966 to see if Fred Bear would be interested in his new bow design, again no interest. Allen when living in Ca. bought a Bear Grizzly recurve for parts to made his first compound bow with wood eccentrics. Allen sent a right and left handed compound bow to Archery World magazine for testing and evaluation. They sent the bows to Tom Jennings their archery technical writter. Tom Jennings tested and bought the first license from Allen and helped made Allen's first bows for sale. The hearsay is Archery World received these first Allen & Jennings bows to advertise for sale with a full page add in 1967. Both Allen and Jennings made improvements on their version of the compound and sold them. Jennings was already a known bowyer which helped. Allen was a bowhunter looking for a faster bow, Jennings said at one time Allen didn't invent the compound bow, don't know were that can from Allen did patent the design for the first compound bow.

Jennings had the first license under the Allen patent and improved and sold his compounds. Jennings had better distribution because he already produced recurve bows and accessories. Allen was manufacturing and selling his own compound bow. Jennings was the driving force to get the compound bow accepted for bowhunting and competition. The compound bow was made for bowhunting and archers found it quickly. Other Archery manufactures began producing the compound bow for their market with a license from Allen. In the early 70's Allen sued all the bow companies for patent rights plus royalties for every compound sold and won the suite. Several bow companies had to stop production of the compound bow because they couldn't come up with the money for the bows they had already produced and sold. Anticipating this Earl Hoyt Jr. put money aside from every compound he produced and sold. Unfortunately Allen died in a car accident on his way home from the last court appearance on the patent royalty rights. Mrs. Allen blamed Jennings and refused him the right to produce a compound bow. Tom Jennings did not stop producing the compound until 1982, he owed a lot of royalties' to the Allen patent rights. He never filed bankruptcy because Bear Archery bought all of Jennings assets from the bank. All of this was after Allen's patent had run out. I find it amazing that W. H. Allen was not inducted into the Archery Hall of Fame until 2010 and I didn't find him in the Bowhunters Hall of Fame, the bow changed archery.

The compound bow didn't look like a bow of the time, it was outlawed for use by the NAA and PAA immediately as it hit the archery market in 1967. Remembering that the NFAA is a bowhunting organization, their members starting using the compound bow to hunt with and shot it in NFAA tournaments. In 1971 the NFAA accepted the compound bow as a legal bow for their competitions, at that time it was not a separate style of shooting just a bow. The NFAA started their own Professional division in 1973 with the compound bow for money. Top archers wanted to shoot their best scores possible. The compound bow and a release aid did that. The PAA didn't accept the compound bow in their competitions until 1985. Today the PAA isn't active and the USAA (NAA) didn't accept the compound bow until 1993.When World Archery (FITA) had accepted the compound bow as legal but in a separate division in their world competitions, but not for the Olympic Games.

CHAPTER 9

NFAA (continued)

In 1977 there were two agenda items as mentioned, one to change Field to metric distances and the other to change scoring to 5, 4, 3 on the new metric target faces, there would be metric target faces for the Field, Hunter and the International Rounds. As stated earlier it was assumed the agenda item to change to metric distances was the way to go to make Field archery an International game. A national championship was coming up and the NFAA office needed target faces for the event, they had to be ordered, no time. The NFAA Executive Committee made the decision to order the new targets in centimeters. Now the agenda item was defeated to change to metric distances and the NFAA was to remain with yard distances, what now? The new scoring passed so they just used the new cm target faces with little objections. They also established a new Indoor Championship target face in centimeters at 20 yards which was used. Again the NFAA lost a lot of their membership due to the scoring change. Myself, I had just obtained my 500 patch on Field, now it was harder to obtain with the smaller five for score. The following year they established the Bowhunter Freestyle Limited class for their competitions. In 1979 the NFAA suffered a financial crises and suspended the publication of Archery magazine for a time. Bow & Arrow magazine became the official NFAA publication the next year. 1980 was the year the NFAA hosted their first Indoor National Championship in Omaha, NE with 524 shooters. The NFAA has had an indoor league program since 1943 but never an National Indoor Championship at just one location. At most NFAA National Championships there is a Pro/Am team competition held before the NFAA Championship starts. It is good publicity for the Pros and great practice for the rest of us. The NFAA Instructor School was inactive but was reestablished in 1982. The old program discontinued to one location the year after Mr. Cushman's death. The **new NFAA Instructors School** restarted with all new updated material basically because there was no record of the old program. Written in 1981 by the new NFAA Instructor Chairmen Mr. Veit who rewrote the material and traveled to give the new program. Their were three NFAA Schools that first year with NY being the first.

In 1982 the NFAA published and sent a newsletter to their membership as a supplement to the Bow & Arrow magazine with current information. In 1983 the first **North American Field Archery Championship**, NAFAC was held in London Ontario, Canada sponsored by the International Field Archery Association, IFAA. This tournament was determine by hosting archers living in Canada, the US and Mexico as a North American Field Championship, this was to be an annual event. The next year it was held in the US 1984 at Colorado Springs at the Air Force Academy and the next year it was held in Mexico 1985. Today it is mostly held in the US as a annual North American Championship by the NFAA.

At the annual 1983 NFAA Directors meeting there was a new proposal to accept the 3-D round as an official NFAA round. Point if interest: 3-D started in the 1970's as a novelty round by NFAA clubs for their bowhunters. In 1973 our archery club in Ohio hand made life size Styrofoam animal targets and shot them in a more realistic hunting condition with our bowhunting equipment from unknown distances. At first we used the Field Range but everyone could figure out the distances from the Field markers. So we had to have a completely isolated course to get true bowhunting conditions. By 1980 their was a **3-D Triple Crown** tournament being held in the Mid-West drawing a lot of shooters. Mostly because there were commercial 3D targets being sold and being used. Now in 1983 the NFAA was considering making 3D a new part of its program. There was much discussion, there was one problem, being the NFAA they tried to come up with standardized distances for the 3D round targets. All the other NFAA rounds were standardized, the NFAA rounds where the same wherever they are shot. Because this couldn't be achieved the proposal was voted down. The next year 1984 the International Bowhunters Organization, IBO was formed, mostly in the Mid-West and northern states. In 1986 the Archers Shooters Association, ASA was formed in Georgia through a Sports TV program and some other Southern states. 3D archery today still has no standard configuration for their course. They are set out before a tournament and taken down after the competition. Of course the IBO & ASA have different rules for equipment classes and maximum distances shot. But there 3D tournaments draw a lot of bowhunters. Unfortunately it is considered a competitive round and most shooters do not use their bowhunting equipment to shot 3D.

In 1984 the NFAA began publishing Archery magazine again and offering it as part of the NFAA membership. In 1986 the NFAA offered a state membership fee to be billed along with the annual NFAA membership dues. That is you only received one invoice for both your home state and NFAA membership, that is the way it is today. The NFAA National Indoor Championship was moved to Kansas City, Mo. In 1988 the IFAA World Field Championship and NFAA National Field Championship was to be held in conjunction for the five days of shooting at Darrington, Wa. The NFAA Pro Style Divisions for their competition was reduced to just Freestyle and Freestyle Limited in 1990. The Traditional style of shooting was added for adult shooters that year in the regular NFAA competitions. The NFAA Foundation was established the same year to help promote archery with some scholarships offered to youth shooters. In 1991 the first NFAA Unmarked 3D National Championship was held in Hickory, NC. This same year the NFAA established a requirement for behind the shooting line clearance and minimum lighting for any NFAA certified Indoor ranges. 1992 was a big year, the NFAA challenged the NAA to the USOC (NAA) as National Governing Body for control of Olympic Archery in the US. Up to how you had to be an NAA member to try out for any World Archery Team, that team was to represent the whole of the US.

The NFAA started recognizing all FITA styles of shooting for their major tournaments in 1992. In 1994 the challenge was withdrawn with the signing of a **reciprocal participation agreement** with the NAA & NFAA. That is if you are an NAA or NFAA member in good standing you could participate in the others regional, sectional and national tournaments. This did not go down too state archery organizations competitions but some states agreed to accept it.

It was in 1994 that the scoring for the Field and Hunter rounds were changed back to 5/3. The old center spot became just an aiming spot again, this was optional to states and clubs until 1996 so clubs could use up their old stock of targets. The NFAA lost a lot of members when they started marking the target distances and now changing the Field scoring? not good. They still maintained around 20,000 members. Arlyne Rhode had started publishing the Archery magazine for the NFAA in 1996. Today Archery magazine is published by the NFAA itself. Arlyne has moved on to US, International Archer magazine, check it out. In 1995 a **Senior Division** for age 55 and over was established in all NFAA styles of shooting. Previously the seniors shot in their regular style of shooting and received a complementary award for their age group. The NFAA Senior is over 55 years of age, a senior (adult) shooter in the NAA is a regular adult, 20 to 49 at that time. If a senior shot well in the NFAA they could win the championship and the complementary senior award with the NFAA. This was the year the Redding's Western Classic Trail Shoot was sanctioned as the NFAA Marked 3D National Championship.

It was 1996 that the NFAA website was implemented. Also the IFAA World and NFAA National Indoor was held in conjunction again at one location. In 1997 the NFAA went back to their new/old scoring of 5, 4, 3 for their Field, International and Hunter Rounds, you confused? In 1998 Maple Leaf printing became the official supplier of all NFAA target faces. The IFAA & NFAA Indoor Championships were held together again in 1998. In 1999 the NFAA purchases the World Archery Festival, the Vegas Shoot. The World Archery Festival became a separate corporation from the NFAA. This was also the year the NFAA started a pilot program called the Development in Archery Youth Shooters, DAYS to help youth into archery around the US. Never really got off the ground but is still on the books. Also in 1999 the FITA styles were dropped or no longer recognized in NFAA competitions. Finger shooters went back to one division. When the NFAA dropped the FITA style classes, after adding them for 7 years. Archers using these recurve finger classes felt left out, they couldn't compete against compound finger shooter or that is what they thought at the time. From 1971 to 1994 they had been competing against each other in Freestyle Limited, no one said anything then. There was enough pressure from the membership to create a new style of shooting. Now the NFAA was afraid of leaving some one out, the new class was named Recurve/Longbow Freestyle Limited style to pacify the complaining archers. They didn't retain any other FITA classes, they were to small a group to bother about, I guess. They worried about Recurves competing against Compound, what about Longbows competing against Recurves in this new class? The IFAA has separated Compound and Recurve shooters for years in all divisions. In 2000 the NFAA Outdoor Field Nationals went to a three day tournament instead of five day competition. They still shoot for five days but only three scores would count for the championship, 1 Field,

1 Hunter & 1 Animal round, confused again? The NFAA museum at headquarters was open to the public in 2000 in Redlands.

In 2001 the NFAA's World Archery Festival purchases the Atlantic City Archery Classic. Also in **2001 the NFAA included a Seniors Division** for 50 and over, the Masters Division for 60 and over plus the Master Senior Division for 70 and over. In 2002 the NFAA's World Archery Festival implements the three Star Archery Tour; Vegas, Atlantic City and the NFAA National Indoor. 2001 the year the NFAA added a bonus spot for one point extra if hit for their Animal Round targets, mandatory at Sectional and National Championships. NFAA Sectional Southwest, states Nevada, New Mexico, Utah, Hawaii, Colorado, California and Arizona. NFAA Sectional Midwest, states South Dakota, Nebraska, North Dakota, Missouri, Minnesota, Kansas and Iowa. NFAA Sectional Southeast, states South Carolina, Tennessee, North Carolina, Kentucky, Georgia, Florida and Alabama. NFAA Southern Sectional, states Oklahoma, Texas, Mississippi and Louisiana. NFAA Sectional Great Lakes, states Ohio, Michigan, Wisconsin, Indiana and Illinois. NFAA Northwest Sectional, states Oregon, Montana, Washington, Idaho, Wyoming and Alaska. NFAA New England Sectional, states Rhode Island, New Hampshire, Vermont, Maine, Massachusetts and Connecticut. NFAA Sectional Mid-Atlantic, states Delaware, Pennsylvania, New York, New Jersey, Virginia, Maryland and West Virginia.

Finding information on any phase of Archery is hard, persevere it is really worth it. Most adults look for archery for their kids. If the kids get involved the parents will follow. I known it is hard but you could start your own archery activity but it must be safe. To find more information just Google your "State Name" & Archery. You can't say the NFAA was not trying, their rules are submitted from the membership and voted on by their Board of Directors. There are changes almost every year. One director from each US state. The USAA (NAA) rules are from World Archery. Olympic Archery rules are governed by World Archery with many member countries, each country has one vote on any change. The compound bow is more popular even thru it is not used in Olympic Archery competition.

CHAPTER 10

NAA Continued
1946 to 1978

After four years of NAA Mail-In tournaments during the Second World War the NAA held it's **1946 Annual Meet** in Cincinnati, Ohio on August 5-10 with the largest participation to date; 137 Ladies, 176 Men and 12 Junior shooters. There where participates from 30 US states and Canada with 100 targets on the field. There where some 250 archers shooting their first NAA National in years. They held a Team Round competition but I couldn't find the results. There was a picture of a Crossbow shooter but I couldn't find their results. This year the NAA added a Veteran's Trophy with six shooters over 70 years of age. There were several perfect ends shot earning a membership in the Six Gold Club.

At the Business meeting with over 100 attending. Amherst, Mass. was selected for 1947 National Meet. There also was a vote to increase dues from $2 to $4. The official magazine was the American Bowman-Review with over 5000 printed each month. They approved the 20 yd. Chicago Round as the official NAA Indoor Round. The NAA finances are in excellent condition. The NAA was look progressively forward, attempting only what seems reasonable, sound and sensible moving into the future. The NAA's job is to undertake procedures that will strengthen their usefulness to the recreational phases of archery. Maintain a close relationship with existing national archery organizations serving all of archery.

There where 10 displays by known manufactures encompassing bows, arrows, testing devices, gadgets, targets, etc. for all to examine with much interest. Several flight shooters shot qualifying distances for the "Wing Club" membership, Flight Shooters only. They shot the York Round under English rules with targets at both ends of the field. They held an unofficial Field Round, little interest.

Results: Women's Champ Ann Weber - 2185, Men's Champ G. Wayne Thompson - 2975, Jr. Girls Champ Alice Ann Bredshaft - 2084 and Jr. Boys Champ Jay F. Reeg - 2664. Flight contest (Class 1 only): Women's Champ Mrs. Jack Stewart - 383 yds., Men's Champ Mike Humbert - 468 yds., Jr. Girls Peggy Dunoway - 418 yds. and Jr. Boys Jay F. Reeg - 298 yds.

1947 NAA National Meet at Amherst, Mass had 378 archers from 25 states, Canada and Sweden. There was an interest shown in the changing trend from wood to metal arrows with the inclusion of scopes and binoculars on the shooting line. With Crossbow competition included but I could not find any scores posted for crossbow. A new rule kept the scopes behind the shooting line and no coaching was allowed on the shooting line until all arrows were shot. There were 26 Men's Teams and 10 Ladies Teams mentioned but with no posted scores as results. They established a Classification Committee with a flexible method to correct any imperfections or errors, to establish proper brackets with comparatively equal skills. The NAA sponsors Mail-In Matches for Clout, Flight, Team Jumbo, Target and Indoor shooting around the year. The NAA helped establish the Olympic Bowmen League some 20 years ago. Now shooting the Indoor Chicago Round at 20 yards and the Olympic Round based on 90 arrows at 30 yards outdoors. Plus the Inter-Collegiate Target Mail Match, all not requiring NAA membership. The NAA membership was approaching 1000. In the NAA Junior Divisions they can earn a felt emblem, classification certificates and medals in any sponsored NAA tournament at local, state, regional and national competitions.

Results: Women's Champ Ann M. Weber - 3383, Men's Champ Jack K. Wilson - 3084, Jr. Girls Champ Lorraine Avery - 1956 and Jr. Boys Champ Jerome Moga - 2868. Flight contest (Unlimited Class only): Ladies Champ Millie Hill - 401 yds., Men's Champ Don Gourley - 553 yds., Jr. Girls Champ Virginia Hersh - 308 yds. and Jr. Boys Champ Dick Finke - 314.

1948 NAA National Meet at Reno, Ne. At the Board of Governors meeting there was discussion on the Rule for Scopes and coaching during shooting for score. The Classification System Committee was trying to establish groupings from the "Leading 100 Archers" list. Next years location for the NAA National Meet was to be Fond du Luc, Wisconsin. There was discussion of a guarantee of no loss for the host club. The Board felt it was an honor to host their National Meet and a maximum fee of $5 for shooting was established. There was a proposal to hire a AP Reporter to promote the NAA. It was felt a newsman's angle would help the NAA's image to the public but no action was taken. The Hook & Flipper was made legal in flight shooting as long as there was no mechanical parts.

At the NAA Annual Business meeting Fond du Luc, Wisconsin was announced as next years National Meet location. The following committees gave their reports Crossbow, Junior, Flight, Membership, Research, Legal and Nominating reports were read. It was suggested that a Crossbow Representative be included on the Tournament Committee. It was thought the weight limitations for the crossbows was unnecessary. The hand loading rule was sufficient and urged that material used in lock & trigger mechanism need not be made of wood. The Junior Committee suggested three age groups for Youth: a Midget Class for under 12, another group between 13 thru 15 and a third group 16 thru 18, No action taken. The Flight Committee suggested a change in their rules, the shooting platform area should be roped off, the flight field should be marked for a 200 yard width and a 100 yds distance marker longer then the Associations record distance, plus add a 10 yard foul line as a clear indicator of limits. New rules should be submitted by M. B. Davis to be discussed and submitted to the Board of

Governors at a later date. It was Moved, seconded and passed that Rebounds shall count 5 points. There was much discussion on a uniform color of the target faces. It was suggested that a 2 or 3 inch black spot be added to the center of the Gold. It was urged to leave the colors alone.

It was passed that all scores be kept on a cumulative bases daily with archers reassigned after each round shot. It was decided that Local, Regional meets be allowed to determine weather or not they wish to use mixed rounds for their championships. The subject of shooting for money consumed over an hour and proved heated. A local Reno group was willing to host a money tournament with a $10,000 purse indicating this would propagate interest in Archery. There would be a sanction of a money tournament to be referred to for a Mail Vote. The mail vote would only ask about a money tournament and avoid the word professional (I couldn't find the results of the vote).

Results: Women's Champ Jean Lee 3622, Men's Champ Larry Hughes 3152, Girls Champ Betty Bowersack and Boys Champ Rowland Richards Jr.

1949 NAA National Meet the 65th was at Fond du Lac, Wis, labeled the "Tournament of the Century" with 26 national records broken with one world record broken. There were 51 perfect of ends shot with new members added to the "Gold Club". Archers from 24 states, Alaska, Canada, England and Sweden attending. Television & Newsreel cameras were literally all over the place for the week of shooting with 100 targets on the field plus many manufacturers displays. They stated the youngest archer was four years old and the oldest was 82. Sights mounted on the bow were now dominating NAA competitions. The NAA Intermediate, Junior and Cadet divisions were established.

Results: with 76 Women, Champ Jean Lee 3680; with 124 Men, Champ Russ Reynolds 3217; with 9 Intermediate Girls, Champ Grace Frye 2228; with 16 Intermediate Boys, Champ Edward Berg Jr. 2880; with 2 Junior Girls, Champ Ann Marston 1886; with 6 Junior Boys, Daniel Stahl 2144 and 3 Cadet shooters (Girls & Boys) Charles Lee Carroll Jr. 935. Flight (Unlimited only) Women Eunice Modlin 575 yds., Men Clarence Haugan 617 yds., Jr. Girls Grace Frye 260 yds., Jr. Boys Edward Berg Jr. 447 yds, plus in the Free Style Paul Berg shot 719 yds.

1950 NAA National Tournament at Lancaster, Pa. with a new Secretary stating that there are many unwritten rules & regulations which we must now put on paper and in our records so that everyone will know about them. The Golden Gate Archers became 100% NAA membership (the first). I think they have initiated a very progressive step which if followed could make the NAA the kind of organization we would like to have.

The FITA Fund to send our Man & Woman NAA champions to the 1950 FITA World Meet in Copenhagen had raised $750 which is inadequate. The archers made up the balance to attend. NAA decals put out by John Siegle were sold for 25 cents each. The Wings Club group is showing some dissatisfaction and wish to be brought up to date. We need files on the records of all our member clubs; state and regional associations. Letters have gone out but the response has been slow. We must remember the NAA is a volunteer organization. The state organizations object to paying the $7.50 club annual fee. Because of a lack of state and regional records there is a question about Six Gold pin applications membership. A monthly bulletin to clubs and individuals giving current information is needed.

The Board of Governors meeting was a general session and as everyone was not there many items were left to the next session. At the Annual Meeting 1950 discussion as to what has been going on with the matter of incorporation. It was discussed, the difficulties the committee was running into on incorporation. After the Professionalism Money Shoot Committees report it was decided that the **NAA make no distinction** between amateurs and professionals. The Women's Committee suggested that a group of 100 shooters be divided into groups of 25 or divided into class A, B, C & D. That Ladies shoot the Double American the 1st day so these scores could be used for the above classifications. Such classifications be placed on the back of their membership cards, no action. There was a report on the FITA meeting at Copenhagen by Dr. Rowland Richards.

Results: Women's Champ Jean Lee 3812 with 81 shooters, Men's Champ Stan Overby 3249 with 131 shooters, Intermediate Girls Champ Betty Wager 3311 with 11 shooters, Intermediate Boys Champ Michael Moga 3060 with 9 shooters, Jr. Girls Champ Janet Lehmer 2150 with 5 shooters, Jr. Boys Champ Harry Edwarss 2786 with 11 shooters, Cadet Girls Champ Catherine Richards 1150 with 3 shooters and Cadet Boys Champ Bob Taylor 1927 with 8 shooters. Flight (unlimited only), Women Evelyn Haines 433 yds., Men Irving Baker 602 yds., Jr. Girls Barbara Van Papering 335 yds. and Jr. Boys Harold Duppre 329 yds.

1951 NAA National Tournament at Les Angeles, Ca. Board of Governors meeting, there was a schedule misunderstanding about the Juniors shooting their official Wand Round. Jr. shooters showed up at the original time were allowed to shoot with supervision. Jr. shooters showing up at the corrected time on the new schedule shot unsupervised and turned in their Wand Round scores. After much discussion the scores as official were the ones shot at the corrected schedule. It was suggested that a special award by given for the scores shot at the original scheduled times, but it didn't happen.

There was a question about Jr. shooters whose age changed during the week of shooting? Which would result in their changing classification. It was agreed that the age of the shooter at the opening was their age for classification at that tournament. It was suggested that fundamental bulletins be made for NAA Official files on: Now to organize & run an archery Club. Tips on how to conduct an archery tournament. A Junior bulletin explaining Junior competition. Answers to technical questions on tackle making, est. and a special sheet of approved rules.

It was proposed that a volunteer be established for their NAA area, and should be known as a Field Representative of the NAA. To police the rules of the NAA and be able to award Six Gold Pins on the spot after an official NAA tournament. These Representatives would not be able in any way to make decisions in the name of the NAA but would serve in an advisory capacity only, no action at this time. The Chairman then told about the contract the NAA had with the American School Supply Co., who would make up material to sell to archers. For every sale, the NAA would get a certain percentage of the profit.

Annual Business Meeting, 1952 NAA National Championship was to be in Jackson, Mich. with Earl Avery the new NAA President. Awards were given to the men on the basis of Total score and Women based on the afternoon American Round. For next years Nationals it was suggested a letter of invitation be sent to the President of the United States and his immediate family to attend Opening Ceremonies. And send a letter of invitation to the Governor of the state if the US President was unable to attend. That the NAA President in a brief note introduce the defending Champions. It was asked that thought be directed toward the creation of an NAA flag. It was suggested that the By-Laws be changed to start the NAA Nationals on Fri. instead of Mon. The feeling was there would be more participates, no action.

Results: Women's Champ Jean Lee 3700 with 36 shooters, Men's Champ Russ Reynolds 3177 with 68 shooters, Intermediate Girls Laurette Young 3376 with 4 shooters, Intermediate Boys Jerry Hash 3206, No Jr. Girls, Jr. Boys David Peterson2497, Cadet Girls Catherine Richards 1533, Cadet Boys Robert Easton 2060. Flight (unlimited only), Women Babe Bitzenberger 395 yds., Men Harry Drake 623 yds. and Jr. Boys Jim Easton 432 yds.

1952 NAA National Championship at Jackson, Mich. The Park Department of Jackson County cooperated in allowing the use of the Ella W. Sharp Park. This year the Tournament Committee tried a sextuple American Round for archers who do not like to shoot the York Round or those whose equipment might not be adequate. These archers did not compete for the Championship but shot for the pure fun of the sport. In addition there were 8 men and 4 women who shot instinctive Target archery (becoming rare). A more detailed analysis of these events may indicate the desirability of continuing them in future tournaments. There were 151 archers participating.

Results: Women's Champ Ann Weber 3679, Men's Champ Robert Larson 3113, Intermediate Girls Lorna Price 3424, Intermediate Boys Bob Schafer 3048, Jr. Girls Ann Marston 2293, Jr. Boys Ronald Ockerman 2631, No Cadets. Flight (Free Style only) Women Mildred Miller 395 yds., Men Charles Pierson 624 yds., Intermediate Girls Dorothy Breneman 167 yds., Intermediate Boys Ronnie Ockerman 291 yds.

1953 NAA Annual Tournament at Amherst, Mass. Annual Business Meeting at the Recreation Room, Baker Dormitory, University of Massachusetts. Treasurer's Report June 1953 showed $149.06 profit for the year with a bank balance of $754.03. It was voted to give the West the first refusal of invitation for the 1954 NAA Nationals. The Board approved a Six-Golds range bar to be attached to the Six-Golds pin for the National Company of Crossbowmen, they will furnish these bars. The NAA is to provide buttons of distinctive colors for varying distances to be awarded to members of the NAA after they have received their Six-Golds pin. The engraving on the button will indicate the distance shot. Mr. Hoyt & Mildred Miller have worked on the problem of classification. It was stated there will not be a report on the Classification Committee. There was an alternate plan. 1. Memberships coming directly through NAA as they now stand, 2. Memberships through the club secretaries. Through this plan all NAA memberships would be handled by the individual club secretaries. Each affiliated NAA club must have ten NAA members. Dues would be based as follows; $3 for individual, $4 for family and $4 for club affiliation. The classification for proposed mail matches could run through the summer as Six-Golds shoots. Clayton Shank discussed their classification in Pa. This proposed club plan does not include associations. New rules were discussed and it was stated that a copy of these rules would be sent out to each member club. Wednesday's meeting recessed.

Second part of the meeting on Thursday. Requesting usage seed-letter received from England. A letter from a German women asking for old arrows & bows to be used as models. The first Six-Golds button is to be awarded with the Six-Golds pin. Buttons may be purchased at $1.25 by those already possessing Six-Golds pin. No Old Business - New Business - The new revised flight rules has been drawn up and handed out. Suggested that Wing pins be revised with additional numbers indicating distance, send to Flight Committee. Subject of International Rounds discussed, suggestion that NAA foster **FITA rounds**. It was suggested "Weeping Sheets" be mailed out to archers that attended the National Tournament but who did not attend the banquet, to be sent out upon request.

At the tournament site there was a panorama of 100 colorful targets identically marked with red, white & blue divisional markers. With the majority of the archers dressed in the traditional "white" made a sight which may be unequaled. At Regional, State and National Shoots white costumes give a touch with which no other form of dress can compare. Back of the shooting lines convenient benches and tables were positioned for each group at each target with colorful beach umbrellas. Food and comfort facilities were located near the shooting lines. There were 87 Women, 100 Men, 26 Intermediate, 10 Juniors and 14 Cadets shooting.

Results: Women's Champ Ann Weber 3579, Men's Champ Bill Glackin 3178, Intermediate Girls Ann Marston 3196, Intermediate Boys Albert Ankrom 2697, No Jr. Girls, Jr. Boys Wayne Glazier 2644, Cadet Girls Jackie Couse 1491 and Cadet Boys Albert Boehm 1846. Flight (longest distance shot), Women Lucille Gourley 420 yds., Men Charles A. Pierson 675 yds., Jr. Girld Nancy Breneman 317 yds., Jr. Boys Ronald Ockermen 425 yds. and Cadet Boys Gary Couse 205 yds.

1954 NAA Annual Tournament at Sacramento, Ca. Prexy, have every reason to be proud, McClachy High School offered a perfect site. There were 165 archers participating. New Champ Robert Rhode of Minneapolis with a new Double York record of 280-1834 replacing the 218-1775 established last year (that is hits & total score). You were starting to see semi-recurves laminated bows with sights all along the shooting line.

Results: Women's Champ Laurette Young 3520, Men's Champ Robert Rhode 3282, Intermediate Girls Peggy Bosonetto 2930, Intermediate Boys Richard Carlson 3455, Jr. Girls Barbara Glaser 1912, Jr. Boys Grant Calkins 2710, Cadet Girls Kay Volkman 2131 and Cadet Boys Joey Moeller 2342. Flight (Longest Distance only), Women Margaret Breneman 336 yds., Men Peter P. Martinek 529 yds., Jr. Girls Nancy Breneman 365 yds., Jr. Boys Gary Couse 217 and Cadet Girls Gretchen Flo 118 yds.

1955 NAA Annual Tournament at Oxford, Ohio, Miami University. At least 39 records fell during the tournament. There were 89 Six-Golds shot by contestants at this meet. The first Six-Golds was shot by Dr. Roberts in 1929. There was a Six-Golds shot at 80 yds., only the 4th time in NAA history. In a business session George Helwig was elected to the National Board of Governors. Through the years the Intermediate, Junior and Cadet Divisions have been under different age groups and called by many different names. The first National that had a Junior Division was in 1914, that year the girls and boys competed together. It was to be 14 years until there were divisions for the young shooters. It was in 1949 that the three youth divisions were added.

Results: Women's Champ Ann Clark 3606, Men's Champ Joe Fries 3252, Intermediate Girls Nancy Breneman 3411, Intermediate Boys Richard Carlson 3476, Jr. Girls Kay Volkmen 2292, Jr. Boys Gerald Kapela 2792, Cadet Girls Jackie Couse 2175 and Cadet Boys Peter Wagner 1599.

Flight (Longest Distance only): Women Dorothy Humbert 536 yds., Men Charles Pierson 774 yds (World Record), Intermediate Girls Bertha Modlin 267 yds., Intermediate Boys Jim Dillon 357 yds., Jr. Girls Nancy Breneman 383 yds. and Jr. Boys Larry Medlin 553 yds.

1956 NAA Annual Tournament at Lakewood, NJ. Board Meeting #1 Aug. 11 at 2pm in the Hotel Manhattan. A report on the FITA Fund Raising Committee. There was a $620.97 in the pass book account needing joint signatories. Board members agreed to a five session schedule. The question was raised as to how much money the NAA should receive out of fees collected from special shoot competitors who shoot only one day. It was suggested the NJAA pay one-sixth of the total fees collected to the NAA. It was also suggested one-half, the matter has nor been resolved to act on this matter, be it resolved when a full quorum is present. There was a report from a questionnaire on inclusion of the Hereford Round in the Women's Championship events was discussed. The reaction against the Hereford was not entirely reliable. There was an agreement that the inclusion of the Hereford in the Championship events made sense. It was decided to include the Hereford as part of the Ladies Championship events for subsequent years. The question was to be brought up at the annual business meeting. It was decided to hold all discussion or classification until a full quorum had arrived.

It was suggested the Six-Golds to be awarded on the basis of having been shot on the official NAA Target face during an official NAA round. The Board noted that a special award for Six-Golds at 80 and 100 yds be of a different color from any now in use. It was suggested that the FITA effort can and should be supported without the necessity for shooting the FITA rounds. The entire Board present felt that the two FITA faces should be made up and controlled as the new official face that has been copyrighted and produced. There was a concern with variation in most paper that allows the official face to shrink or expand any appreciable amount. A short review of the FITA competition and rules was passed out on prepared sheets of the FITA Amateur status. It was stated that money shoots will cast doubt on the amateur status of any US archer. The Amateur Athletic Union has no influence over the NAA. We are not an amateur sport. We will not attempt to make a distinction between amateur and professional participants. We cannot maintain **FITA Olympic competitive rules** in their present unrealistic form.

Board Meeting #2 later the same day, same location. Board voted to allow secretary to use any amount up to $50 for purchase of necessary equipment and repair of same at the NAA office. The contract for all subsequent tournaments shall request a minimum of $300 towards the expenses of the Secretary-Treasurer. A special new account called a Reserve Account to be built by a $2 deposit per registrant fee collected at this tournament. Every effort shall be made to build this fund over time. It was felt that the membership should be told the Constitution & By-Laws had been clarified, not changed. The Secretary reported that a real need existed for copies of the Constitution & By-Laws before a Handbook could be published. There will be no advertising included in the Handbook. The Board stated we simply wish Board approval before making any move. Since other Board members were missing it was difficult to act on matters.

Board Meeting #3 Aug 12 same location 9am. Board feels inclusion of the Hereford should be a mandate from the women in the NAA. It should be a women's vote only. While men could vote at the business meeting, they should be asked not to vote on this matter. Any classification system which meets the needs of a local area will be encouraged by the Board. The NAA will not adopt any classification system other than the official one now in operation. The idea for a special "100 Leading Archers of the NAA" patch which can be offered to qualified archers at a nominal fee. A request of a clear definition be set up as to what qualification should exist for the following NAA Honors: Thompson Medal of Honor, Honorary Membership and Life Member. Placement on the "100 Leading Archers List" shall be determined by age according to NAA rules. Box Scores shall be reported separately for Juniors and Intermediates. It was suggested that one-day shooters at all National Tournaments be allowed to register for the Team events.

Board Meeting #4 Aug 12 later in the day. NAA members are to vote for people in their region only for representation. The Constitution makes mandatory mail voting for nominations each year. The Board was unanimous in recommending that more than one candidate shall be offered for each region. Any dealer will be allowed to purchase the stamp at cost if their 48" plates for target faces adhere to our rigid standards. A royalty of .05 cents per face is mandatory. The question of incorporation arose which cannot yet be solved because of factors of cost. It was implied that Bear and others may in all probability buy from Sanders who could supply all faces to all archery dealers. It was preferred that a official meet run exactly as the FITA competitions. It was felt two FITA Rounds be shot under FITA procedures. Tournament to be non-profit with no awards to be given just certifications only to raise moneys. Contestants must be NAA members during all phases leading to eligibility. Contestants must be amateurs under FITA rules. Any NAA member may participate in the European Shoot if they pay their own way. The Board reserved the authority to use any trophy donated by anyone to the NAA in any manner the Board deemed best.

Board Meeting #5 Aug. 13 at same location. There was an explanation of the Northwestern National's archery insurance Plan. Forms of this plan were passed around to every member present. It was suggested that suitable cases for perpetual NAA trophies be built for transport of same. The question of permanent versus perpetual trophies was discussed. We cannot please everybody we should have to plan on the continuation of perpetual trophies. It was requested to contact Minero-Newcome on the possibility for producing an NAA membership pin. It was suggested that such a pin not feature the target face of the NAA but be a distinctive pin.

Board Meeting #6 Aug 14, 1956 at Mansion House, Lakewood, NJ. Discussed reluctance of Sylvan Archers of Oregon to accept a bid for the 1957 NAA Annual Tournament. There were two other possibilities but no particulars at this time. The Board voted to hold this matter until a report could be made on all possible bids.

Board Meeting #7 Aug. 17 at Seagirt Inn. The Secretary/Treasurer was reappointed for the year 1956-57. It was stated the NAA should be looking forward to the possibility of a full-time secretary, a paid secretary. The Chairman asked about committee work, no committees appointed except for the Finance Committee.

NAA Annual Meeting 1956 at Clefton School, NJ. The Chairman of the Board announced that at this time there was no bid for next years Nationals. When a formal bid has been accepted the membership will be notified. It was announced that the Constitution & By-Laws had been clarified and printed. The membership may write to the NAA office for copies. It was stated a special committee was formed in the question of how best to insure NAA trophies is under advisement. The FITA Fund Chairman called attention the offer made by Minero-Newcome in donating free plaques to those NAA clubs who donated the proceeds of an entire tournament to the FITA Fund. A review for a special FITA Qualifying Shoot was discussed stating the European Championships are to be held every other year. The total FITA funds to date were $610.39. There was a sincere plea for NAA affiliated clubs to host two FITA shoots per year. Much discussion on adding the Hereford Round to the women's championship rounds. The Hereford Round for the ladies was tabled for at least three years until a complete report from sections be studied. A lengthy discussion followed on the International Round and on the proposed Qualifying shoots. The Chairman explained that arrangements and details were still in the process of being worked out, meeting adjourned. There were 242 shooters.

Results: Women's Champ Carole Meinhart 3682, Men's Champ
Joe Fries 3311, Intermediate Girls Lynne Smathers 3112, Intermediate Boys David Peterson 3432, Jr. Girls key Volkman 2565, Jr. Boys Kenny Smathers 2816, Cadet Girls Loy Volkman 2220 and Cadet Boys David Oelerking 1929. Flight (longest only), Women Barbara Van Popering 449 yds., Men Charles A. Pierson 686 yds., Intermediate Boys Roy Van Tassel 391 yds. and Jr. Boys James Dillon 405 yds.

1957 NAA Annual Tournament at Sacramento, Ca. Board Meeting #1 Aug 3 at Hotel Senator. The problem of retiring some NAA trophies was reviewed. Conceder retiring NAA Trophies to the city of San Diego's Roger Jessup Museum which houses an excellent archery collection. They may be reclaimed by the NAA at any time. No trophy may be retired at any time without full Board authorization. The Board agreed that Junior Awards ought to be simple and permanent. No new awards could be approved until designs were submitted as outlined in standards for perpetual trophies. It was requested that a list of missing trophies be printed. The Constitution of the National Company of Crossbowmen was not to be included in the NAA Handbook. Much discussion with respect to the FITA Qualifying Meet ensued. Concern was voiced at the cost of the meet, particularly to contestants travel and a loss financially. Since the world Meet was to be held in Brussels in 1958 it was suggested the FITA Shoot be held with the 1958 NAA Nationals, no action taken. The report on the FITA Meet was read as information. The question of obtaining visas in time for the FITA World Meet was brought up. The Board felt this would offer no real problem except for "Iron Curtain" countries. The Board felt it was not possible to name a long list of alternates to any official US Team sent to represent America in Europe. NAA members not members of the official team would be welcome to shoot as individuals at their own expense. The Eisenhower "People to People" program which involves an exchanging of information between nations. It was felt Archery should be involved, meeting recessed.

NAA Board Meeting #2 Aug 4 at same location. It was suggested a reduction in dues for children over 18 living at home with only one copy of TAM was desired for that membership. It was so ordered by the Board. This matter is not to be publicized. The matter of individual NAA memberships without TAM was discussed. The problem was not resolved. It took 60 to 90 days for NAA material to reach NAA members through TAM but the Board felt that TAM must do for the present. Doug Easton offered to write John Yount on the policy of the NFAA in offering membership without their field magazine. Current communication is an old problem to which at present there seems to be no solution. It was suggested that individual latter be feed to local papers and magazines for news of top archery activities. It was suggested the NAA pattern their news releases after the NRA. But in establishing such a magazine it is clear the NAA would face at least a five year financial loss, no action. Archery particularly needs increased recognition on the world, national and regional level. Much discussion, no solutions.

Board Meeting #3 Aug 4 later that day at the same location. The Board discussed Al Volkman's proposal for making Junior, Intermediate and Beginner awards at his cost. Even thou the proposal was sincere, after study it was not accepted. The Secretary was instructed to send a brief letter to each Board member asking for a clear expression of feelings on the matter of retirement of perpetual trophies. There was a misunderstanding regarding FITA rules, FITA does **not allow sights** on bows for shooting. There was a protest because after traveling to the FITA Qualifying Shoot a shooter was not allowed to shoot and wanted a refund. The Board felt under no circumstances could money be refunded. Latter Saunders Archery Target Company, they were reluctant to print an appreciable number of the new official NAA target faces because of slow sells. Saunders would be contacted on this matter. The Secretary was instructed to inform all clubs and associations that official faces must be used for Six-Golds tournaments, meeting adjourned.

Board Meeting #3 Aug 6 same location. Bid for the 1958 NAA Annual Nationals was granted to the Minnesota State Archery Assoc. It would be formally announced and approved at the Business meeting. It was suggested and approved that photos of the top shooters be taken for the NAA Handbook. The NAA Handbook was to have 30 title listings on current Rounds & Material. It was discussed that additional funds were necessary to send a team and official delegate to the FITA World Championship. The matter of pageantry at the National tournament was discussed and felt it desirable.

Board Meeting #4 Aug 9 at the same location. Secretary was reelected to another year. Ballots for Chairman and Vice-Chairman were to be sent to absent members as soon as possible and the results announced.

NAA General Business Meeting-a report was read on the FITA Qualifying tournament and Fund Raising Committee. There was a report on the World Tournament in Prague and the teams activities in Prague. It was asked why there was so little publicity on FITA World tournament here in the US. The NAA was aware of the publicity problem at all archery levels of activity. It was stated that it is up to the archers to cooperate with the newspapers locally. Than there was a strong appeal for everyone to help raise the money to send the US team to Brussels in 1958. The secretary reported the NAA Handbook was about 70% complete and should be available next summer. A Financial report showed a balance of $1,053.60 available. It was moved that the 100 Leading Archers list be changed. A very animated discussion followed. Suggestion that the list to be only 50 in each category.=, only list the top 25, not list the York Round, a substantial majority insisted it remain the same. The bid from Minnesota was accepted but the date was left open in an attempt to coordinate with the NFAA. So the two tournaments did not conflict. Also so the meet might tie in with the 1958 FITA World. It was stated that professional archery is coming and they need to be thinking about it. It was pointed out that a professional archer cannot compete in FITA. It was felt that our best shooters would be unable to represent the US because they are not amateurs. A good deal of heated discussion followed on the amateur-professional status.

Results: Women's Champ Carole Meinhart 3784, Men's Champ Joseph Fries 3333, Intermediate Girls Kay Volkman 3509, Intermediate Boys Jim Yoakum 3410, Jr. Girls Loy Volkman 2402, Jr. Boys Robert Oxnam 2974, Cadet Boys Alan Stafford 2240. Flight (Longest only) Women Mararet Breneeman 305 yds., Men M.B. Davis 489 yds., Jr. Boys Jim Yoakum 393 yds. and Cadet Boys Dick Bloedon 217 yds.

1958 NAA Annual Tournament at St. Paul, Minn.

Board Meeting #1 at St. Paul, Minn. After a brief highlight of the recent FITA Meet it was agreed that a team captain must accompany contestants to FITA Meets. The question arose as to how funds should be raised to support US Teams to FITA meets. Some feeling was expressed that it might be difficult to continue to raise funds at present levels without new sources of support. Considerable discussion took place on the possibility of including the FITA Round as part of our National Tournament program. It was agreed that adopting the round for NAA purposes at National Tournaments might take a reasonable amount of time to work out. All Board members are to encourage all NAA clubs to shoot a FITA Round for its members to familiarize them. The Board agreed to discuss the matter of cost of official NAA faces at a subsequent meeting, recessed.

Board Meeting #2 later that day at the same location. The first matter on the agenda was the cost of official NAA faces. Saunders claimed the NAA royalty of 5 cents per face had increased his list price by 30 cents. Some New England clubs were holding non official Six-Golds Shoots to protest. It was decided to write to Saunders asking if it was possibility for

THE SECRETS OF MODERN ARCHERY ▼ 105

clubs ordering targets directly or the possibility of target orders be routed through the NAA, no action. It was maintained that Ben Pearson is now negotiating to produce target faces. It was reported that FITA is most impressed with what the NAA have done about official faces. There was a concern about the manner in which the NAA should continue to honor shooters from Canada or foreign countries at their nationals. Should the NAA require archers from out side the US join the NAA or should a "courtesy" membership be issued or ought we award special medals gratis. Decision was all contestants are to pay registration fees & join the NAA. Individuals from foreign countries may not be awarded any NAA Perpetual Trophies. There was a request to change the name of the NAA Olympic Bowmen League to avoid trouble with present day Olympic archery activity. The present Olympic Committee is desirous of our title change. It were changes to the NAA Indoor Winter League. There was a problem of scheduling the next NAA National and coordinating this activity with the FITA Meet and our Qualifying Tournament. This is particularly frustrating since it will be impossible to avoid conflict with the NFAA meet. It was suggested the Qualifying Meet be held separate from the NAA Nationals in spite of financial and scheduling difficulties, no vote. There was questions as to how long can the NAA keep raising the money needed for the FITA Qualifier Meet and sending a US Team to the World Championship. The Board felt that interest in World archery activity would possibly keep the financial ball rolling. The Board was in firm agreement that the World FITA Meet takes precedence over all other archery activities. After the FITA Meet the Board should consider our own Nationals, the Qualifying Tournament, then regional, state and local meets in that order for master scheduling purposes. It was discussed on how to pick shooters for the US Team sent to the FITA World. A committee ought to be appointed to select a point system for shooting a national, regional and state meets. These and other factors, including personality qualification should be considered. Do we want this person to represent us at a World Meet. The Board appointed Clayton Shank to be the new FITA Chairman, meeting recessed.

Board Meeting #3 Aug 4 at same location. Board members were needed to help with registration on the field. Because of the Aug. date for the World Meet July was considered, no vote. A further review of selection of a US Team was entered into. We are sending Americans who are reflecting the attitudes and convictions of this nation. The Board also agreed that no one not a senior (that is their adult) be allowed to compete in the Qualifying Meet. A suggestion with respect to FITA participation no individuals at a World Meet may sell bows or accessories, no individual is to capitalize on his having won a place in international competition, any and all fees derived from Radio, TV appearances, lecture tours and any income realized from FITA Tournament experience should be revert to the NAA FITA Fund. A FITA Selections Committee was formed. Some sort of a point system which shall be used for inviting NAA members to the Qualifying Meet. The Board agreed that a special "10 pin" for FITA Rounds be made and not use the NAA Six-Golds pin. The Olympics as it affects archery was taken up to explore all possibilities for affiliating the NAA. The NAA will be ready to assume the leadership in the establishment of an Amateur and Open class for our association, recessed.

Board Meeting #4 Aug 4 later in the day. The entire meeting was devoted to reviewing every decision the Board had made to date for the benefit of the members. EVERY motion made and every suggestion recorded in the minutes of the first three meetings were voted upon. The question of classification was raised. The basic system was discussed and found to be fair. It was recommended the classification be used at all meets in the future, recessed.

Board Meeting #5 Aug. 5 at the same location. It was requested that more shoulder patches be ordered, approved. It was passed that new larger patch be ordered. The Board agreed that the same uniform design should be retained for an eventual membership pin, patch & decal. A committee was formed to help in the choice of a new decal emblem. After the committee agreed on a new design it would be forwarded to the Board members for reaction. The Financial Report was reviewed in detail. In spite of the recommendation to increase club dues the Board decided it would be unwise at this time. The matter is to be held over until the next year. The Board approved the resumption of the three year membership plan but no changes under the Club Plan. There was a question about the Classification system and questioned why they did not enjoy greater success with it. The Board agreed that every effort should be made to encourage its use at all NAA clubs tournaments. The title of the "100 Leading Archers" is to be changed to "Highest Scores Shot by NAA Members in (year)" passed unanimously. Discussion about pay for the Secretary-Treasurer of an annual salary of $1000. It was unanimously rejected and the Secretary-Treasurer resigned, meeting recessed.

Board Meeting #6 Aug. 8 at Parade Ground Field, Fort Snelling. The matter of the "100 Leading Archers" list was reviewed an a fold insert card printed in TAM would be in the Nov. or Dec. issue to submit scores. The NAA Handbook was discussed at some length. The matter of commercial editorship was thrashed out. It was the opinion that such editorship is disastrous to archery. The NAA Handbook is a modest start. The same Secretary-Treasurer stated he would serve another two years, possibly three, but no more. The Secretary will send out a complete voting total when the other ballots are received. The last matter on the agenda involved the question of drinking on the shooting line. There would be instruction to all shooters that drinking while on the line would not be permitted. The Board voted unanimously to add this to the 1959 program the following: 1. All archers shooting are to act as ladies & gentlemen, 2. All archers are **requested** to dress in white and 3. Drinking on the line is not permitted and may be cause for removal from the field. This rule has always existed but it will be enforced.

NAA General Business Meeting Aug. 7 at Hotel St. Paul. It was announced that the bid to hold the 1959 Nationals at Pennsylvania State College in July or Aug. had been accepted. The Chairman explained briefly the highlights of the recent FITA Meet in Brussels. It was stated some of the information from the FITA Congress: Olympic archery competition is for **men only**, Archery may be included in an Olympic Meet only at the request of a host nation and FITA had 27 member nations working on a uniform code for shooters. Any code adopted will affect the FITA organizational members world wide. The official change of three arrows shot per end was changed to six arrows per end as we have in America. For the two short distances, 50 & 30 meters, the ends shall remain three arrows per end. Flexing of the bow before shooting in now permitted. It was announced that the new FITA "10 pin" was for perfect ends made in the FITA Round. The new title of "The 100 Leading Archers" of the NAA will be called "Highest Scores Shot by NAA Members in (year)" was stated to all. The Team Event will be listed as procedure of aggregate scores as being totaled to show the achievement of **states** even though a team may be shooting as a registered **club team**. The FITA report stated after an expenditure of $6,703.21 with all bills not yet received, the fund had $2,511.19.

It was moved that nominations be closed for Regional Representatives, ballots were passed out. The candidates for election were asked to stand, they did so. It was asked from the floor for more time at official practice, it was stated anyone could come as early as they wished to for practice. It was moved that a specific time be announced as official practice in all future meets, it was passed. It was stated that there was three official ends of practice at the longest distance to be shot. It was asked that all archers be required to pre-register noting in every case over planning has caused of financial loss. It was stated they agreed with this idea in principle but in order to have it work pre-registration blanks must be available well ahead of meet. It was moved that pre-registration blanks be printed in TAM in the months of April, May, June and July, passed. Considerable discussion took place on the date at which the coming National is to be held, it was left up to the host club. Results of the elections were announced, Motion for recess until Friday evening at the Banquet.

Results: Women's Champ C. Meinhart 3637, Men's Champ Robert Bitner 3419, Intermediate Girls Key Volkman 3236, Intermediate Boys Dennis O'Neill 3600, Jr Girls Loy Volkmaan 2466, Jr. Boys Blake Renslow 2939, Cadet Girls J. Sudberry 1755 and Cadet Boys S. Paulson 2132. Flight (Longest only), Women E. Estervog 318 yds., Men H. Allen 790 yds., Intermediate Boys R. Deller 609 yds., Jr. Boys R. Victor 234 yds. and Cadet Boys G. Smith 260 yds.

1959 NAA Annual Tournament at Lancaster, Pa. the **Diamond Jubilee.** Board Meeting #1 Aug 15, New Secretary-Treasurer transfer of business office to begin at once. Six-Golds pins and range buttons have to be sent by Air Express that are needed for this tournament. Discussion of Classification system the need of presenting cards to secretaries of clubs at Six-Golds tournament so that classification would be possible. How to prevent unscrupulous archers from "sand bagging", no action. The board had question to be sent to TAM; can the tear-out in TAM be made into an NAA Membership application, add the NAA dues schedule and if the time lag between submission of material and publication could be eliminated. That the editor of TAM be invited to meet with the Board to discuss mutually pertinent problems.

Board Meeting #2 Aug. 15 later the same day. Editor of TAM present, he was asked to include a tear-out coupon in the magazine. The coupon type invitation to join NAA will be in the present front insert. He was asked about lag time. After considerable explanation about printing procedures he stated the lag will be shortened by about a week. A long discussion took place on the NAA Handbook. It was requested of the Board to consider the presentation at the business meeting the idea that one FITA round be substituted in the NAA Championship program, Board agreed. The matter of the 5 cent royalty on each Official Target face was discussed. It was suggested to reduce the royalty to 2 cents per face so the manufacturer could absorb this cost, voted in favor and passed. The matter of standardizing the official target face so that only one type of target face be printed for all Championship rounds. The standard face could also be used for the FITA rounds long distance if the faces were printed with a ten ring, matter tabled.

Board Meeting #3 Aug 16 same location. The first item on the agenda concerned a communication from the US Naval authorities inquiring whether the NAA would cooperate with their Recreation Division in establishing standard rounds in archery that they could use in building up their program. It was agreed the NAA should by all means take advantage of this opportunity. Information sent, possible score for any given round, existing National records for all rounds and suggested "top" category for Naval awards. It was discussed they may be limited to indoor ranges. It was suggested to the Naval authorities they participate in our National Indoor League. The matter of possible participation in the Olympic Games. The 1964 Games were to be held in Japan and that archery (men only) will be included in these games. The final conclusion was that we would keep an open mind on the subject., meeting adjourned.

Board Meeting #4 Aug 16 same location. The matter of the contract between NAA and sponsoring organization was discussed and it was agreed that the present form be retained with such necessary modifications to conform with local conditions. FITA activities and fund raising was discussed. In the matter of using these funds to send teams abroad, it was agreed that we abide by the rules as written to send six archers and a Team Captain. In case of a tie for the team membership, special funds must be raised for such people through means other than the general fund for FITA Team members. The Board feels that it is most desirable for a time limit to be set for clubs to bid for the privilege of conducting the Qualifying Tournament. The deadline provision to entries must be published. A discussion ensued in regard to the "100 Leading Archers" list, a new method of handling this seems desirable. The NAA Nationals were to be held on the West coast in 1960, no bids. It was suggested the facilities at Miami University be used but information was needed before the business meeting. It was voted to accept Oxford but to make no announcement of a specific place. The financial report came up for discussion but evoked no comments that needed action of the Board. The Board authorized $500 for office equipment needed. The chairman spoke of the report on the special Youth Committee. The Board agreed to look into this standardized Youth program and its possibilities at some future time. The matter of a design for an NAA emblem, several designs were displayed, none were exactly what was being sought, meeting adjourned.

General Business Meeting at Franklin & Marchall College, Lancaster, Pa. Aug. 19. There was a report of the FITA Fund and of the Team's trip to Sweden. It was felt that fine progress had been made in establishing a good relationship with archers of other nations. Response from all over the country was most gratifying and provided the means to give archers the opportunity to compete in the World Matches. The date of the 1961 FITA Tournament are set in Aug. at Oslo, Norway. There was a brief report on preregistration. It was emphasized that it was much better to know how many archers to plan for. The financial report was read and accepted as read. The Chairman presented the slate of candidates for membership as Board of Governors and Regional representatives. Nominations were opened for nominations from the floor. Any nomine must be willing to serve and would assume responsibility of the office, nominations were closed. It was discussed the State Teams should be incorporated into the National Tournament program. It was felt it should be studied from the state level first, the motion defeated. The motion was changed to "that we have state team competition in the national program; that team members may shoot with either a club or a state team.", motion passed. It was explained this would not change the NAA Constitution. The results of the election was announced. It was announced that the 1960 NAA National Tournament would be at Miami University in Oxford. It was explained that the Western states could not provide a location. The matter of including a FITA round in the National program was explained, that the Board felt it wise that this be discussed in home groups to be thoroughly studied. This would entail a change of the NAA Constitution. It was agreed that this should be tried out at home clubs, and have them report back. The NAA should poll member on the general use of the 10 ring target face. There was a request not to hold the Flight Competition on a busy airport in the future as it was last year, motion to recess until the banquet.

Business Meeting at the Banquet, Franklin & Marchall College Aug 20. The new Chairman of the Board was announced, this closed the 75th Jubilee Tournament.

Results: Women's Champ Carol Meinhart 3732, Men's Champ Wilbert Vetrovsky 3473, Intermediate Girls Loy Volkman 3312, Intermediate Boys Kenneth Samathers 3281, Jr. Girls Carol Strrausburg 2534, Jr. Boys Jim Leder 2921, Cadet Girls Deborah Clark 2209 and Cadet Boys David Paulson 2284. Flight (Longest only), Women Mildred Miller 681 yds. and Men Danny Lamore 937 yds.

Jan. 1960 NAA Board Meeting at the Union League Club, Chicago, Ill. To open the meeting there was an express purpose of discussing problems confronting the Board of Governors and to reach solutions if possible or appoint committees to study special problems. The following are given in the FITA order of the agenda for the sake of clarity and continuity. An agreement with the publishers of TAM will be negotiated in regard to the memberships that had expired and have not been deleted from TAM files. It was felt that some would appear on the Life Membership list but should rightfully be on the Honorary list. A revised list was made. There was a request of the Company of Crossbowmen to be considered a NAA membership on the Club Plan Membership. It was felt they are an association and not a club. With the Editor of TAM in agreement, it was decided to offer NAA memberships without a subscription to TAM at a reduced fee. There was great confusion about the NAA Club Plan Membership. It was decided to establish a consistent membership fee schedule. It was stated that the Classification was intended as an incentive to improve shooting skill not a means to secure awards only. There was a committee to look into improving the classification system. A Finance Committee was formed. A fee schedule was set for the 1960 NAA Nationals as: Senior Fee $16 per person, Crossbow Fee $21 per person, Intermediate Fee $12 per person, Junior Fee $10 per person and Cadet Fee $8 per person. There was discussion on the Crossbows higher rate, there are only two Crossbow entries assigned per target and more targets needed to be used. A Committee was formed to review the Constitution and prepare it for inclusion in the proposed NAA Manual.

Participation for the World Tournament was including in our Qualification Tournament. It was felt that we reeducate ourselves to use the term "World Championship Round" instead of the FITA Round. In regard to participation in the Olympic Games, participation hinges on "Amateur Status". It was suggested in an attempt to reach an agreement with the American Olympic Committee on **amateur status** for archers, no commitment at this time. It was pointed out that the Olympic Games of 1964 held in Japan would include archery for men. Our young male archers should be informed now what they must do to protect their amateur status. The Interscholastic League has been run by Mr. Louis C. Smith for many, many years at a deficit. Mr. Smith asks to be relieved of the responsibility of conducting this tournament at the age of 90. Mrs. Alice Hilton accepted the assignment, there are a number of colleges participating. The list known as "Best Scores of (year)" had entry forms in TAM. This was to be a personal responsibility of sending your best scores for the year. This plan failed to produce sufficient response to produce a reasonably accurate list. The project was now to go through the club, they will receive a new plan for reporting scores. Much discussion on the up coming NAA Manual, no firm date was given.

1960 NAA Annual Nationals at Oxford, Ohio Results: Women's Champ Ann Clark 3945, Men's Champ Robert Kadlec 3486, Intermediate Girls Carol Strousburg 3535, Intermediate Boys Jim Leder 3415, Jr. Girls Debbie Clark 2322, Jr. Boys Larry Mann 2767 and Cadet Boys Ken McMahan 2268. Flight (Longest only), Women Mildred Miller 653 yds., Men Charles Pierson 873, Jr. Girls Nyla Mullins 238 yds, and Jr. Boys Dave Sparks 446 yds.

1961 Joint Meeting at Oak Brook Polo Club House, Oak Brook, Ill. attending NAA, NFAA, AMADA, ABA & PAA. These are the notes of an informal meeting of the above noted archery organizations. It was stated this was not to decide anything definite but to make some effort to coordinate on mutual problems and to get the word Archery before the public. It was stated the meeting was not solely for those shooting but to a greater extent to those who will shoot tomorrow. A report from the NAA Chairman of the Eligibility Committee. Right now the amateur is a problem to some. Most problems are created by the archers themselves. The entire amateur situation revolves around "intent" and to determine intent is sometimes impossible. In archery the amateur rules are quite liberal in comparison to other sports. It was stated the NFAA has resisted interpreting the amateur rules. The NFAA would abide by the NAA decision in each case. There should be an operational letter to be sent to archery clubs & associations. Discussion was on awards at various type at tournaments to obviate the possibility of converting them into cash. It was stated that a more comprehensive interpretation of the rules would be published as soon as possible. This portion of the discussion was concluded by the reiteration that it was agreed an amateur may not compete for cash.

The question of reinstatement to Amateur Status was discussed. It is impossible to forgive reception of money, but any other offender may have his case reviewed. The machinery for that process is not yet completed. It was asked that a Glossary of Terms be developed and sent to all National and State Archery Associations. Report that archery will not be in the 1964 Olympics, contrary to previous expressed. An Archery Hall of Fame was briefly discussed but will need additional study. It was decided it was not vital to work jointly on age definitions for various divisions. All delegate were asking to consider & study all media of archery instruction. Suggestions were forthcoming for setting up joint committees, no action. It was stated all the organizations present were fundamentally interested in one thing, getting more people to shoot archery. Also that no one cared how they shot, aside from safely and good sportsmanship. Let each organization sell itself and its pleasures.

NAA Regulations Governing Amateur Archery Competition Jan. 1961. "An amateur archer is one who engages in archery solely for the pleasure and physical, mental or social benefits he derives there from and to whom archery is nothing more than an avocation." 1. The amateur archer may not compete for cash prizes in any sum. May not compete for trophies or awards of any kind worth more than $70.- 2. The amateur archer may not exhibit his skill as an archer for pay. 3. The amateur archer may not accept pay for instructing or coaching in archery. 4. Endorsement of an archers name or picture is not permitted for advertisement or endorsement of any company or product. 5. Expenses an amateur archer may request, receive or accept only actual expenditures. 6. Employment by an amateur may not accept money from a firm or individual engaged is some phase of archery promotion without regularly being on the payroll and work at a specific job. He may not receive paid time off during normal work week for practice of archery. 7. Self-Employment an amateur if in the manufacture of archery tackle must not use his shooting prowess or his name or photograph as a basis for selling his wares. 8. An amateur archer may participate in competition with a non-amateur only where the tournament entries are confined to the bona fide member of a club. 9. The amateur may not compete with non-amateur at the state, regional or national level. He must compete in a different division.

NAA Board Meeting at Palma House in Chicago Jan. 1961. A discussion of the forthcoming NAA Tournament with the presentation of the plans of the host club of Oak Brook International Polo Club near Chicago. Sunday was a warm up event, most likely a Double American.

Monday included the Flight, Wand and Clout Rounds.
Tuesday the Men's and Women's International Round.
Wednesday the Men's York, Hereford for Inter. Boys, National & Columbia Round for women & Inter. Girls.
Thursday the Double American for all with Friday the Team shoots.

The Annual Meeting on Wednesday evening and the Banquet held Friday evening. Crossbow schedule the same as listed in 1960. In order to shorten the shooting time there will be 3 shooters per target, with one shooter on the line at a time. having 2 1/2 minutes to shoot three arrows, using the ABC system rotation used in International tournaments. The NAA was asked for recognition of a new Crossbow Assoc., the NAA will not recognize another crossbow assoc. but would include the crossbow program in the schedule. The 1961 host would retain the same schedule of fees as in 1960. Pre-registration shall be made no less than 30 days in advance of the tournament. Anyone registering late may do so only with the permission of the Tournament Committee. After discussion it was moved that the NAA file a Tax Exemption Certificate, motion passed. A discussion was held concerning proposals from manufacturers for the price of items bearing the newly designed NAA emblem, no decision. It was moved that the NAA extend an invitation to the International Federation to hold its tournament in the US in 1965. This should be included on the agenda for the meeting at Oslo, motion carried. It was moved that the NAA appropriate the money to copyright the NAA insignia, motion carried. The Trophy Chairman gave a list of missing trophies, in order to check the cost of prizes. It was moved that all retired trophies be packed and placed in dead storage until, motion carried.

NAA Amateur & Professional Qualifying Tournament. First matter was approval of the Proposed Regulations Governing Amateur Division Competition. Change the words "Professional" and "Open" to read "non-amateur" anywhere they appear in these rules. "Those competing in the open division are not amateurs". Sponsors of the Qualifying and NAA Tournaments were advised to designate "Amateur" on registration blanks and score cards. It was moved that the rules be adopted as amended by the Board, motion passed. It was recommended an advisory committee be appointed. Be it known that the burden of proof rests with the archer, not with the NAA. It was moved that any archer who has not received a cash prize in excess of $70 or who has not been paid for putting on an archery exhibitions be accepted as an amateur, motion carried. It was moved that the NAA apply forthwith for a Voting Allied Membership in the Amateur Athletic Union, motion carried. All existing trophies remain in the Amateur Division. A new medallion shall be designed for the Open Division. There was a motion that the majority of the Board be of amateur standing, motion defeated. It was directed that the above changes be included in the invitation to the NAA tournament, meeting adjourned.

NAA Annual Meeting at Elmhurst College in Elmhurst, Ill. Tournament Committee Report-very few archers abided by pre-registration. Facilities will be made available for archers registering late only if possible. For FITA rounds all holes on the target faces will be taped at the end of scoring for that end. Nothing will be scheduled for Friday afternoon but announcement will be made the Chicago Bowhunters Field Course will be open. Announcement of establishment of amateur and non-amateur divisions. The NAA Constitution was so amended by vote. There were those committees renamed to Eligibility Committee, Rules Committee and Amateur Rules Committee. Motion to apply for Allied Membership in the Amateur Athletic Union was tabled. Motion and discussion to agree to make NAA emblems and merchandise available to the membership at a reasonable profit, motion carried. Shall the NAA remove its 18 year age limitation for participants in International archery competition, motion tabled. It was stated that a FITA committee is considering the adoption of a **Field Round for International competition**, a motion that the NAA approve the NFAA Field Round as suitable for International competition, motion carried. There was a report on the initial impetus for a Professional Archers Association, PAA which the NAA will support. The Board decided to accept the offer of the National Sporting Goods Assoc. to use its posted box number in Chicago as a permanent NAA mailing address. It was stated that the Eligibility Committee needs a clear statement on "instruction vs. coaching" "merchandise awards vs. gifts". Winners at the

National Tournament shall be known as National Amateur Champion and National Non-Amateur Champion. The Six-Golds pin name was accepted as Six Gold pin. It was informally decided to urge the use of the 10 ring target face. It was unanimous that the current 16" face for the Chicago Round be made an official NAA target face for the indoor round. The NAA will incorporate within the State of Illinois, papers of incorporation to be drawn up, unanimously carried. Discussion as to the manner of proceeding with all time records of the NAA since the establishment of a non-amateur division, no decision.

1961 NAA Annual Tournament Results: Women's Pro Champ Margaret Tillberry 3695, Women's Amateur Champ Victoria Cook 3548, Men's Pro Champ Gene Ellis 3610, Men's Amateur Champ Clayton Sherman 3642, Intermediate Girls Carol Strausburg 3323, Intermediate Boys Jim Leder 3519, Jr. Girls Debby Clark 2552, Jr. Boys Dave Keaggy Jr. 3044 and Cadet Boys Kevin Park Oderman 2294. Flight (Longest only) Women Mildred Miller 433yds., Men Maj. F. Levings 634 yds., Men Non-amateur Robert Rhode 656 yds., Inter. Boys Trent Niemeyer 448 yds., Jr. Girld Julie Sudberry 310 yds., Jr. Boys John Levings 370 yds. and Cadet Boys Kevn Oderman 197 yds.

1962 Joint Meeting of NAA, AMADA, NFAA, & PAA at Oak Brook, Ill. A Joint Meeting of the above archery associations was called by the NAA. The purpose of the Joint Meeting is to develop a common interest among the associations to get more people to shoot a bow. It was asked about the status of individual club shoots. It was stated that it was not possible for an individual to accept cash prizes. Cash could be given through a club to cover expenses, much discussion followed. To be an amateur prizes it cannot exceed $70. Because this is a new problem precedent has not been established by past rulings and each case must be treated individually. Once declared a professional in archery an individual is ineligible for amateur competition in any and all sports.

A Title is an award and an amateur and a professional cannot compete for the same Title. The NFAA members want a non-amateur status and will not accept a professional status for the average archer in their organization. It was stated now it may jeopardizes the eligibility of the individual. The group was advised the NAA wants to set up a Junior Olympic Archery program but it needs to obtain approval from the USOC. The NFAA stated it may be interested at lest for a start. The 1963 FITA Championship will be in Windsor, England. The 1965 FITA Championship will be held in the US with yet the location not determined. The NFAA recognizes the NAA as the World's Championship archery organization and at present there is no World's Championship Field Archery activity. The NFAA said that there were plans for this to be considered in the future. It was stated that the 1968 Olympic possibilities for archery were very good. It was stated that there should be cooperation between the NAA and the NFAA in regards to the Olympics. FITA has adopted the Field Archery rules as drawn up by the NFAA. It was announced the National Collegiate Archery Field Championship will be held in conjunction with the NFAA Nationals in 1963 at Lake Arrowhead, Ca., the Joint Meeting officially closed.

1962 NAA Annual Tournament at Oak Brook, Ill. Board of Governors Meeting Aug. 5. A report was given on the 1961 tournament that there were 147 participants and the host absorbed a substantial loss on the conduct of the tournament. They had purchased new targets and target butts that they did not resell. They were using them for additional tournaments. If an intermediate declaring himself a senior he must pay full target fee for a senior. Prizes will be withheld until ruling by the Eligibility Committee on any participant whose classification as an amateur is in doubt. A motion that archers be rotated in the American rounds as well as in the FITA round, motion passed. There was requested that the NAA ask an opinion from the Joint Meeting on the individual association's understanding of the word "non-amateur". In addition that the NAA spokesmen inquire as to the interpretation of the professional & amateur status. In that the NAA National Champion will be an amateur event. It was moved that the NAA request the USOC grant the privilege of using the word Olympic in a proposed Junior Archery Olympic program, meeting recessed.

Board Meeting at Elmhurst College Aug. 6. The first item was to review the mail match, it was suggested that the NAA office handle the mail matches. The NAA should try to make a profit and the cost of trophies and postage be covered. The tournaments will be comprised of 30 arrows at 20 yds. and a ten-ring face should be used. It was stated that FITA had a mail match which should be considered at a later date. A statement if income and expense was read and approved. It was stated to the Board concerning the handicapped archers and the need of special rules for these people. There was an outline given of the activities that had been engaged in on behalf of handicapped persons and the terrific enthusiasm they had for archery. There was a review of the current dues rate and membership requirements in the association. It was the decision of the Board that a Junior who applies independently must pay full membership dues. However, the Board decided that there should be consideration of a special dues structure for a proposed junior program. It was considered the establishment of a amateur card to be offered for 25 cents to non-members of the NAA and free to NAA members upon signing of an affidavit that they were bona fide amateurs. The Board was presented with the question of the aiming spot from the Eastern Archery Assoc. after considerable discussion it was decided that this should be presented at the annual meeting to be considered for a vote. It was proposed the word "professional" be used in place of "non-amateur" this was passed, meeting recessed.

Board Meeting as Elmhurst College, Aug. 8. It was asked that the NAA consider payment of the cost of bringing the World's Championship Trophies from Europe to the US, it so ordered. It was reported that the NAA trademark had been copyrighted. It was requested to check on the possibility of making FITA contributions tax deductible. The Board passed a motion that the FITA qualifying date for the 1963 World's Championship will be in June under the sponsorship of the Royal Archers Assoc. at Oak Brook, Ill. The World's Championship will be at Windsor, England in Aug. The Board designated the 1963 NAA Annual Tournament was to be in July but we would deferred naming a location at this time, meeting adjourned.

Board Meeting at Oak Brook, Ill. Aug. 8 later in the day. The Team leader for the World Championship team was announced. The proposed contracts were given to both TAM and the Bowhunting magazines. TAM stated they could not hold to a 10 day deadline on NAA news. The Bowhunting Magazine stated they could meet the 10 day deadline for NAA news. The Board had a lengthy discussion on the matter of the official NAA publication. The decision was to send a complete synopsis to all Board Members for their vote on a decision. The question of the 1963 National Championship site was tabled, meeting adjourned.

Annual Meeting of the NAA Aug. 9 at Elmhurst College, Ill. A financial report was given and accepted as read. A membership report was given that the NAA had 924 members. It was stated that the Board was considering bids for the 1963 tournament from 6 firm bids and the site will be made in the near future. A display was presented of the Sustaining Membership Plaque and announced this membership is available to anyone at the cost of $25. Bids were accepted for the purpose of taking over the administration of the NAA. After thorough investigation it was decided that the National Sporting Goods Assoc. should be awarded the administrative responsibilities of the NAA. Nominees were announced for Regional representatives. Ballots may be cast by active members who are present at this meeting, no proxy votes. Ballots were distributed and the results announced. They announced the Monster Club to raise money for the US FITA Fund. It was asked why the NAA did not conform to the FITA rules on field glasses and it was suggested a Double FITA be shot at the Nationals. The proposals must be submitted in regular form prior to the meeting. It would be placed on the agenda for the next Board Meeting. It was announced the 1963 Qualifying Tournament for FITA will be held at Oak Brook, Ill. It was stated that the By-Laws would be amended so the word professional will replace the word non-amateur. It was announced the NAA has officially asked for permission from the USOC to use the word Olympic to be used in a Junior Archery program. It was announced that the site of the 1965 FITA World Championship has not been determined. There was a report on the question of a handicap archer. The new ruling was read to the effect that aid could be given to such a shooter. It was the shooters responsible for providing his own assistance. A proposal by the Eastern Archery Assoc. to consider a 2 1/2 inch aiming spot to be placed on the target center in national competitions. Discussion followed and it was rejected. meeting recessed until the banquet.

Results: Women's Pro Champ Margaret Tillberry 3722, Women's Amateur Champ Nancy Vonderheide 3577, Men's Pro Champ Bob Pender 3583, Men's Amateur Champ Charles Sandlin 3568, Inter. Girls Carol Ann Strausbuy 3373, Inter. Boys Ed Hansel 3281, Jr. Girls Dolly Anne Hamilton 1837, Jr. Boys John Theodore Lemanski 2864 and Cadet Boys Roger Chapdelaine 2452. Flight (Longest only) Women Frances Lederer 370 yds., Men Charles Pierson 809 yds., Inter. Girls Sandy Beers 129 yds., Inter Boys Trent Niemeyer 541 yds., Jr. Boys John Levings 434 yds. and Cadet Boys Chuck McCormick 238 yds.

1963 NAA Board Meeting at Chicago, Ill Jan. Letter from two absent Board members were requesting they be made a part of the meeting. A committee was made to study the procedures to make recommendations for the NAA Winter Indoor League. A discussion on publishing of high scores each month and the Board decided the top ten in each category should be published in the magazine. It was suggested that a list of All Time Tournament records and National Records be prepared and a draft would be submitted to the Board. It was suggested this list include World Championship records. There was a new Executive Secretary of the NAA elected. Minutes of the Oak Brook Board Meeting were read and with two corrections approved. It was asked by the Chairman that a listing of inventories and assets be requested from the National Sporting Goods Assoc, NSGA be completed as soon as possible. The Board was advised that each person joining or renewing their membership receives a decal. There was a request that new stationary be prepared with the location of the National tournament be added. Envelopes would be sent with the new stationary. A letter was read from Helsinki, Finland that the World's Championship was to be in July. The NSGA had found that there was a substantial amount of work to be done and that a fee of $200 per month was inadequate. They are requesting an increase to $400 per month. It was decided to pay the increase until the next Annual Meeting. The meeting would be adjourned for the AMADA banquet and reconvene later.

Continuation, It was decided the 79th Annual Championship was to be at the UCLA Campus, Los Angeles, Ca. The World Archery Magazine was to have a registration blank for the tournament in June for preregistration. The announcement was to be in February with the fees stated. It was decided that the FITA pins be earned only at major tournaments and Championship tournaments and not club shoots.

NAA Board Meeting at same location Jan. 20. It was stated that 3,000 registration blanks would be printed at no cost to the sponsoring club. All money and registration will be sent to the NAA Office. After NAA expenses are paid the sponsoring club would be given $300. It was stated the NAA had been accepted as an Allied member of the Amateur Athletic Union and with an additional $50 could become a voting member. It was announced that the USOC had granted the NAA use of "Olympic" word for use in our Junior Archery program. The subject of the 1965 World's Championship in the US was discussed. It was stated the NY World's Fair Committee that they believed they can handle the housing situation for your nationals. Agreed money from the FITA Fund will be used for the FITA World's Archery Championship in the US. Other places have expressed interest in this tournament to be host. It was stated that only one organization must be responsible for the project. A US Team leader for the trip to Helsinki was appointed. The FITA Qualification tournament will be held at Oak Brook, Ill. in June. There was a discussion on the interpretation of the word amateur, non-amateur and professional. The NAA stated they used the terms Amateur & Professional and would continue with them. It was stated the permanent records kept at the NAA office for amateurs were issued an amateur card also stated that non NAA members may obtain an amateur card for 50 cents. The amateur affidavit pledge would be filed at the NAA office. There was a committee appointed to help develop the NAA Junior Olympic Archery Program and to submit a report at the next Board Meeting. A nominating committee of three was appointed as will as a budget committee. They then established a $3.50 membership fee for youth under 18. There were two new members added to the Eligibility Committee, meeting adjourned.

NAA Board Meeting at Los Angeles, Ca. July 30 at Sproul Hall, UCLA. This was to set an agenda for a meeting later in the day to discuss; Scopes & sights, Winter League, Amateur & Professional situation, Jr. Olympic program, FITA report, Inter Collegiate tournaments, weeping sheets and a general discussion on arrangements for the tournament, recessed until later in the day.

Board Meeting later in the day same location. The first subject was FITA Rules. It was stated 25 copies of the FITA Constitution were ordered. Letters were sent out to archers shooting 1000 points on the FITA round with a form to fill out to receive the FITA Star pin. A letter was received from Scientific Sports Equipment explaining their Telescopic Bowsight. They felt it was inadvisable to rule against the sight, no action. A report was given on the trip to Helsinki. It was also reported a desire of European countries in regard to the use of the sight with a bubble. It was moved that the NAA approve the use of the bubble, motion passed. At the last Nationals Women using bubbles were requested to tape them but the men were not? There was one man requested to remove a prism sight, no action on the prism. It was felt communication between the board members on all matters concerning NAA matters be better. It was suggested the FITA Rules be included in the NAA Official Rules Book. Anything addressed to the Board will be copied and forwarded to all Board Members. A new Chairman was appointed to the Eligibility Committee. There were protests about Intermediate shooters using prisms, no action. A minimum distance for the target face off the ground was passed. It was suggested an exception be made for schools, camps and colleges, meeting recessed.

Board Meeting same location July 31. It was stated that no firm bids of the 80th National from the Eastern part of the US. The NY World's Fair invited the NAA to have our Nationals at their fair grounds. It was found not to have proper space. A report was given on the Winter League tournament. It was considered to eliminate the Instinctive class from Intermediate down, motion tabled. It was stated it is too difficult to be an amateur and many archers just give up trying to be an amateur. It was expressed being an amateur only to compete in Olympics or FITA World Championships, it was pointed out that this is not the only idea in holding an amateur standing. There was a proposal to change Flight rules concerning Overdraws, forwarded to the Flight Committee. The Board discussed reducing the number of medals & trophies for awards. The Winter League could replace medals with printed certificates, sent to committee. There was discussion on Weeping Sheets, no action. There was a general discussion of the expenses of current services memberships received, awards and the possibility of a budget, meeting recessed.

Board Meeting reconvened Aug. 1 same location. New members appointed to the Junior Olympic Committee. Consideration on the 1964 Nationals site to be made in 90 days. It was moved to look into an NAA Indoor Championship probably shooting an American round. NBC wanted to televise one hour if the NAA sponsored the indoor tournament, motion carried. Florida has offered to run an NAA sponsored shoot during the winter months. It was stated that the 1000 FITA pin could only be obtained in only two NAA tournaments. The NAA will set a criterion for a "major" tournament, meeting recessed.

Board Meeting reconvened Aug. 1 later in the day. It was decided by the Board that a new rules book be printed. A discussion on giving awards to **Bare Bow Divisions**. The archers name shall be put in location on the weeping sheet where they belong, add BB after the name and no award be given, there are to few shooters, passed, meeting adjourned.

1963 NAA Annual National Tournament at Los Angeles, Ca. Annual Business Meeting Aug. 1 at Sunset Room, Sproul Hall, UCLA. It was announced the Detroit was being considered for the Olympics' 23rd Annual world's Tournament hosted by the NAA. If Detroit is the host city, archery will definitely be included. There was a new chairman appointed to the Eligibility Committee. Ballets for the Board of Governors was passed out and collected, the results were announced. It was announced that Florida would like to host a winter NAA tournament, no action. The Board suggested a 450 pin for NAA members only shooting the International Field Round, approved. There was a request to arrange for a scoreboard for the Nationals. It was also suggested that archers wear a number on their back, but we hesitate to ask archers to wear numbers. It was reported that the last Nationals the ladies were on the field from 8:30am to 6:30pm and they were tired. It was suggested that only two be assigned to a target, to be considered later. It was suggested that if possibility of supervised practice, meeting was recessed to the Awards Banquet.

Annual Meeting reconvened Aug 2 at El Miramar Hotel, Santa Monica, Ca. It was announced that there were 185 archers attending the Nationals. The archers attending the World Championship at Helsinki had come directly to the NAA Nationals, meeting adjourned.

Results: Women's Pro Champ Jewel Hamilton 3508, Women's Amateur Champ Nancy Vonderheide 3738, Men's Pro Champ Ed Rohde 3609, Men's Amateur Champ Dave Keaggy Jr. 3568, Inter. Girls Loy Volkman 3305, Inter. Boys Terry D. Witt 3489, Jr. Girls Nanette Mihalik 2364, Jr. Boys Ron Smethurst 2898 and Cadet Boys Duke McCormick 1877. Flight (Longest only) Women Marge Payne 440 yds., Men Harry Drake 669 yds. and Jr. Boys Pat Hailey 240 yds.

1964 Board Meeting at Holiday Inn, O'Hare, Schiller Park, Ill. Feb. The 1963 National Tournaments report stated the sponsoring organization furnished everything but the target faces. The FITA Fund was paid $721. The FITA Qualifying Tournament was discussed. It was explained all FITA expenses were paid by check so there is a voucher for any expense. It was stated that having a detailed report from each sponsoring club on their National Tournament is a very good policy to follow. It was suggested that a list of sustaining members be printed in Archery World to interest more companies in becoming sustaining members. It was stated that the NAA is ready to go forward and is doing so. The last 5 years were disappointing but there will be improvements in the future. The location of the 80th Championship at Jones Beach was discussed. The New York World's Fair Exhibition Tournament is definite to be held on the World's Fair Grounds. There was discussion on pre-registration and last minute registration. Discussion to discontinue Clout Championship for Women, no action. Suggestion of a 2, 3 and 4 awards in all divisions, that is 2 must compete to give 1st place, 3 must compete to give 2nd place awards and 4 must compete to give 3rd place awards. When there is no competition there will be no medal given. Registration fees were set for the up coming Nationals. It was stated that $2 of each registration will go to the NAA. The subject of insurance at the Nationals was discussed. If the TV rights are exercised a scoreboard is to be used for TV and all competitors should wear back numbers for the TV. The 10 highest amateurs and 10 highest Professionals will be invited to participate in the World's Fear Exhibition Tournament. There was much objection to making a loud and clear distinction between amateur and professional shooters. They shall all be called archers. The exhibition is to be held after the NAA Nationals. Schedule for the 80th NAA Nationals was made. Discussion on the location of the 1965 FITA World's Championship. It was stated the World's Tournament should precede the NAA Nationals. A tentative date for the FITA qualification to be in June. The NAA Junior Olympic Archery Development program must be approved by the USOC in order to use the Olympic name of the program. Archery will be taught in the Cincinnati Schools this winter using the program, a Junior Tournament will be held in May. The AAU Junior 12-14 and Intermediate 15-17. Membership and club promotion discussed. Scorecards to verify new record scores, properly signed by the Field Official and one or more witnesses on the same target. A petition from the Buffalo Archers was presented to make their Buffalo Round consisting of 24 arrows at 60 yds., 36 arrows at 50 yds. and 48 arrows at 40 yds. a Six-Gold tournament. Decision not to recognize the round as a Six-Gold tournament. Report given on the Helsinki FITA Tournament. It was suggested that the NAA send 12 archers to the 1965 FITA World if held in the US, also that the word qualifying be changed to try-outs. It was stated that a 16mm film was available of the FITA Tournament. The subject of amateurism was discussed with reference to the Olympic Rules Article26. It was suggested that any World Champions appearing in public or on TV should report on expenses and any money received and disposition of the money. There was a suggested resolution pertaining to the obligations of NAA members making public appearances concerning archery. It was suggested that the Board members of the Midwest work on a location for the 1965 tournament. It was suggested that the NAA send a letter to the Mexican and Canadian Archery Associations. The letter written to encourage their games and offer any assistance from the NAA. There was a remark that the NAA should promote all archery. It was stated that there is a group who are not amateurs and do not wish to be called professional be classified as semi-pro. After much discussion the proposal was to be a mail vote of the Board of Governors. The Eligibility Committee will be informed of the resolution. It was suggested the NAA request an NFAA member to work with the NAA committee on the Junior Archery Program, no action meeting adjourned.

Board Meeting at Jones Beach State Park Aug. 1. It was announced that there was not a quorum so the meeting was for information only. The Archery World proposed a fee increase to the NAA membership subscribers. There was questioned an increasing in NAA membership dues to cover the cost of subscriptions, the matter was to be held over. It was explained to the Board of difficulties with the World Championship of 1964. The Chairman had met with the US State Department and the fact remained that the NAA should not be used for political purposes because of the entry of East Germany. It was stated he was continuing work with the International Archery Federation in hopes a decision would clear the air. The tournament was promised to Philadelphia in July of 1965. The Board was advised that Philadelphia International Center would help with visitors from other nations. It was stated the NAA did not approve of the attempts of American Excelsior Co. to be recognized as the official target mats of the NAA. It was stated the NAA was recognized as the "Sports Governing Body of the US" by the State Department and twenty two other bodies of the USOC and AAU. It was stated that in order to publish an international field round it would be referred to as the FITA Field Round, meeting recessed.

Board Meeting reconvened Aug. 2 same location. The purpose of the meeting was to review the position of amateur versus professional in archery. The NFAA was to be present but was unable to attend. It was asked of the NAA if the term "open" was used and the answer was yes. Discussion on reinstatement of amateur status. If the professionalization had been done in some sport other than the one in which he wished to maintain his amateur rank. The question of professionalism by "contamination" in AAU rules as long as the competition is sanctioned by the approved ruling body of that sport then the competitions are protected. Discussion on changes of amateur rules, IOC rules were used, further discussion is needed. It was stated regarding an inaccurate score that the lowest score would be accepted and anyone submitting an inaccurate scorecard would be disqualified. It was stated that the individual is responsible for their score and the archer must sign their scorecard. The question of use of a prism, it was decided that no prism would be allowed. The question of using a bubble, decision of the Board that no bubbles would be allowed. Stabilizer, sling and clicker were considered permissible. The equipment is to be inspected on the line. Target assignments are to be A, B & C for three shooters on a target with indicating cards to show which person is to be on the line shooting. It was requested areas for officials be established to enforce rules on spotting and coaching on the line be strictly enforced. The matter of the 1965 National location had not been resolved but five possible locations were possible. The possibility of conducting the National Championship & FITA Qualifications at the same time was discussed but no decision was reached. It was stated that their seemed to be an apparent lack if interest in flight competition and that the Flight Competition be held at Oak Brook, Ill but would still be considered an NAA Championship, permission was granted, a recess was called.

Board Meeting reconvened Aug. 3 same location. It was advised that the NAA had a bid from the Baynton Beach Chamber of Commerce in Florida. It was decided by the Board to delay a decision. It was decided to host the FITA Qualification Tournament and the NAA Nationals as separate events. There were prices submitted for printing of the NAA Handbook, it was submitted to that committee. It was stated that a proper program of activities was necessary for the NAA prestige to be maintained. The NAA should not sacrifice funds for the World Championship but seek funds from voluntary contributions. the Board appointed a tournament director for the World Championship. The increase per subscription per member for the year was approved. It was discussed and pasted to develop an NAA flag by next year. There was a new Executive Secretary appointed to continue activities with the National Sporting Goods Assoc. They were advised that the Boy Scouts at Valley Forge had archery instruction for over 23,000 Boy Scouts during their National Meeting attended. Their was a reminder that the Board should make their selection for the President & Vice-President for the coming year before they leave Jones Beach, meeting recessed.

Board Meeting reconvened Aug. 4 at Jones Beach Hotel. The Board was advised the AP, UP and the New York Times had people on the scene to report the tournament. It was stated that a sustained public relations program is a necessity for the NAA and that some funds be set aside for this purpose, tabled. There was a report of the Inter-Collegiate Tournament in the last year that 96 teams participated. It was suggested that a questionnaire be sent to colleges requesting information on participation and what they felt necessary to encourage archery at the collegiate level, NAA office so directed. A team captain for the 1965 FITA Championship was appointed. The Board was to establish a Sportscaster Award, a resolution for recognition for enhancement of the sport of archery was printed by the NAA Office, Meeting recessed.

Board Meeting reconvened Aug. 5 at the East Bath House. It was announced that the 1965 FITA Qualification tournament was to be held at Oak Brook, Ill. There was a discussion on the use of the FITA Funds. The NAA is responsible for awards and local transportation. It is necessary to establish a tentative budget to bring before the annual meeting. The NAA is obligated to run this tournament and financial support its activities as well as being responsible for any losses sustained by the tournament. It was discussed of having a flight event during the World Championship, no action. It was stated that the NFAA had eliminated their amateur classification and had no program for the protection of the amateur archer and that the NAA engage in a bowhunting & field program, motion tabled. It was stated that FITA had their International Field Round to be used, meeting recessed.

Board Meeting Aug. 6 at Gilgo Pavilion. Announced that 154 archers had registered. The National Sporting Goods Assoc. was changing banks and they needed NAA permission to transfer NAA funds, passed. Volunteers from the Board to prepare awards for the Banquet were assigned. A payment of $700 was authorized to the host club, meeting recessed until the Banquet.

Results: Women's Champ Vicki Cook 3753, Men's Champ Dave Keaggy Jr. 3648, Inter. Girls Carol Hinckley 3120, Inter Boys Max Lingo Jr. 3559, Jr. Boys H. Ward 2980 and Cadet Boys M. Butler 2431. Flight (Longest Only) Women Fran Lederer 418 yds., Men Major F. Levings 691 yds., Pro Men Harry Drake 732 yds. and Inter Boys John Levings 579 yds.

1965 NAA Board Meeting at Holiday Inn, O'Hare Jan 15. There was much discussion on the handling of NAA funds by a new Board member. It was suggested that a gross income and expense report be prepared with a separation of statements for the Winter League, FITA Fund and the National Tournament, good idea no motion it was left to the hands of the Finance Committee. A membership report was given and after some discussion it was noted that it did not reflect extra family members at $1 each. This breakdown was to be made. It was stated that the club membership plan offers individual membership for $4 and family memberships for $5, if six or more names are submitted with the club application or renewal. This was to be strictly adhered to. This $1 reduction applies only through club applications. It was asked why at the Annual Meeting at the Nationals is not held all at one time? It was said that members did not get there all at one time. It is difficult to schedule meetings ahead of time because of various duties by the Board to help in many places where the host club did not have the personal to do so. It was stated that the Board spends too much time discussing details on every item, really. Motion that a Board member in each region be appointed as liaison officer to be responsible for proper tournament activities, approved. Motion that a certificate be given for new record scores after approval for the NAA office, passed. A report was read from the National Crossbowmen thanking the NAA for its support and they have increased their members now in 25 states, meeting adjourned.

Board Meeting Jan. 16 same location. Discussion on the word "sanctioned" for tournament awards. An NAA sanctioned tournament must be registered in advance with the round shot specified and affirming it is run under NAA rules. A letter of approval must be on file at the NAA office. It was suggested that the name "FITA Fund" gradually be changed to "USA Team Fund". It was discussed that the Flight competition wants there own tournament in 1965 to be held in the West. It was stated the NAA wanted the Flight competition as part of the NAA National Championship, no decision. A motion and discussion that any NAA affiliated club may sponsor a Qualifying Tournament for a fee of $25 to be put in the FITA Fund. There was a report that we still are not sure where we stand as far as archery in the Olympics. There was a motion to actively pursue the possibilities of entering the Pan American games in 1967, passed. Motion that anyone wishing to compete in the 1965 World Championship Events be qualified and certified and must contribute $850 to the US Archer Fund on or before July to cover expenses from New York. It was stated the request for the 1965 Championships being turned down was a refusal to recognize East Germany. It was determined by FITA the US was being discriminatory because of political affiliation. It was stated that the NAA is planning to go to the FITA administration council to see whether we have a valid reason for attesting the decision but that we needed a 2/3 vote. Motion to shoot 6 arrows at 50 & 30 meters at the FITA Qualifying tournament at the discretion of the tournament officials, passed. The 1965 Tournament Committee reported that the Purdue University was ready for the NAA Nationals. University Club rooms are available at $7.50 for single and $10 for double. There was a motion to add the 300 Indoor Round to the NAA Winter League and keep the Chicago Round, motion passed. Suggestion that the FITA Team take time to stop for exhibitions and public relations work with archery clubs in a couple of countries, thought it was a good idea. A discussion to the question of whether a committed pro status eliminates the possibility of a person returning to an amateur status. It was stated that by the AAU a period of three years must lapse before an amateur status can be considered. Amateur competition rules were discussed. Bills were presented for $200 for the USOC, $50 for dues in AAU and $25 for FITA, bills paid, meeting adjourned.

Board Meeting Jan. 17 same location. Discussion of the relationship between the NAA and the National Sporting Goods Assoc., there was a new Executive Secretary appointed. It was mentioned that all NAA correspondence the NAA should refer itself as the "Sports Governing Body". A report was given on the Junior Olympic Program showing adult exposure as well. There was consideration of chartering junior clubs but a program has not been developed sufficiently at this time. The Secretary was to credit the NAA with 25 cents for every amateur card issued. That there shall be eight qualified archers and a team leader be entered in the World FITA Championship and paid for out of the FITA Fund, meeting adjourned.

Board Meeting Aug. 1, 9am at West Lafayette, Ind. Purdue University. It was discussed of a possibility of target royalty on all official NAA target sizes other than just the 48" face. Target scoring rings were discussed, it was determined that rings score different in the FITA and American Rounds was confusing, no action. It was stated that the differences between the NCAA and the AAU still curtail operations of sorts in the governing bodies. It was suggested a Junior Archery Tournament be held in the three NAA regions. The TV Agency Lester Lewis Assoc. would pay all expenses to bring 24 finalists to New York for a televised shot off, vote to pursue this. It was stated there is still a difference between the NAA & NFAA on Amateur versus Pro status. It was reported that there are 185 archers registered for this Nationals. An Opening Ceremonies should be a part of the National Tournament. It was reported that the NAA had 172 clubs affiliated with 2,496 individuals involved. It was voted to finish the NAA Handbook. A copy of the Junior Olympic Archery Program was presented an approved for finial study by the NAA Board. The 10 ring scoring system is to be used for all Target rounds & that a double FITA Round be shot at the Nationals. It was felt by the Board, not to change at this time. The Flight Committee discussed their be a separate competition from the NAA Nationals, this was to be discussed at the Annual Meeting, recessed.

Board Meeting reconvened Aug. 1, 7:30 pm same location. It was proposed a central location for a National Indoor Meet, no decision. The FITA Congress voted that the US could register 10 FITA tournaments to keep records and shoot for FITA awards, one to be the NAA Nationals, meeting adjourned.

Board Meeting Aug. 6 same location. To decide on the National Championship, an Australian shot the highest score at the tournament. It was decided the Australian be named high score but the award for National Champion go to the Highest US Amateur. There was a protest that a women and Inter. Girl became ill and was allowed to make up their scores missed. The Board agreed that the full score shot be allowed minus the three ends that were missed, meeting adjourned.

Results: Women's Amateur Champ Nancy Pfeifer 3746, Men's Pro Champ George Clauss 3745, Men's Amateur Champ George Slinzer 3559, Inter. Girls Cathi Towner 3397, Inter. Boys Gerry Koelke 3461, Jr. Girls Maureen Bechdolt 2532, Jr. Boys Tom Herrin 3109 and Cadet Boys Stuart Broeren 2300. Flight (Longest only); Women Amateur Norma Beaver 497 yds., Women Pro Monica Wildenburg 449 yds., Men Amateur Fred Lederee 549 yds., Men Pro Chris Wildenburg 593 yds. and Jr. Boys Dale Parker 303 yds.

1966 NAA Board Meeting Jan. 14 at O'Hare Inn, Chicago, Ill. It was noted that the NAA membership dues exceeded $10,000 for the first time, the NAA financial status was very good. The Board Chair attended two USOC Meetings. The USOC was schedule to select the City for the 1972 Olympics. The AAU assured the NAA that they would do everything possible to promote the NAA Junior Olympic Archery Program. It was reported the NSGA has entered into a contract for automation of its records. This will help in cutting down the time spent on detail work for membership, mailings and so forth. The NAA secretary submitted a form to be used to challenge another's amateur status. The Boards opinion was that the NAA is not a police force. Any recognition at a tournament should be held up until a challenge has been satisfied. There was to be a Canadian & US Archery competition but the schedule, location and financing had to be worked out, approval given. It was reported that Colt-Sahara & Ben Pearson Tournaments asked for NAA sanction. The NAA should name observers for protecting amateur status in this type of tournament, meeting adjourned.

Board Meeting reconvened Jan. 15 at same location. A letter was written to the Chamber of Commerce of Flagstaff, Az. requesting tournament preparation for the NAA National

Tournament. The shooting time of 2 1/2 minutes on the line was questioned, how to speed it up. It was the general feeling that the Tournament Committee should set times. It was suggested that Inter. boys be allowed to shoot the men's FITA Round. If an Inter. moves into the senior men's division he would not return to the Junior Round. The Flight Committee had set up there Championship in Ca. This would be acceptable if they registered the tournament. The Flight Committee offered to have a demonstration in Flagstaff. There was a report read from the Crossbow Committee, it was accepted. There was a brochure presented from Valley Forge State Park for the 1969 World Championships but other sites might be considered, meeting adjourned.

Board Meeting reconvened 1 pm same day and same location. There would be 20 to 30 nations attending the 1969 World Championship. **FITA target faces** are now122cm for the longer distances and 80cm for the shorter distances, with the scoring lines on the outside of the colors. The lines must be touched to count the higher scores. Report on the 1966 Winter League with changes suggested for 1967, no action. It was suggested to replace inactive Board Members with someone from the same area. It was suggested to have an archery exhibition in Mexico for the 1968 Olympics. We could invite people from the Mexicana International Sports Federation to our National Tournament, approved. All Olympic donations offered the NAA to be earmarked for the "US Olympic Fund". There was discussion of the International Field Round Championship stating it was not too popular in other FITA countries, tabled. There was a report on US Team Uniforms being ready for the World Championships, meeting adjourned.

Board Meeting reconvened 8pm same location. Motion that FITA Funds being used by the NAA office be in a separate account, motion lost. It was suggested the "Monster Button" be called the "US Team Button", accepted. It was stated additional funds will be needed for the Pan American Games events. It was stated the US Team Travel Fund used just for FITA events. It was suggested this fund be renamed "NAA Team Travel Fund" and used for other events, passed. It was decided a decal would be made along with the buttons, passed. There was discussion about the US Team Captain, no action. There were 9 location around the US selected to host FITA Star Tournaments, meeting adjourned.

Board Meeting reconvened Jan 16 at 8am at the same location. Further discussion on the 9 FITA tournaments for 1966. It would be best if these tournaments moved around the US in 1967. A motion that the NAA pay for the FITA Star Pins earned in 1966, passed. Detroit will be submitted to the IOC for consideration for the Olympic Games. The NAA Handbook was discussed. Discussion on a NAA Archery Camp program but it was felt there needed to be more work on it before the Board could sanction such a program. A fee of $8.50 was set for affiliating a JOAD club and it would include a subscription of the official NAA magazine be included. There was much discussion on the proposed JOAD program for schools, changes were suggested and it was felt the Board needed more information, tabled and meeting adjourned.

NAA Board Meeting July 8am at Americana Motel, Flagstaff, Az. A letter had been sent to FITA by Ben Pearson on amateur regulations and was referred to the NAA. The JOAD program was discussed and it was felt more time was needed. The Chairman attended a

USOC meeting and the NAA received $1000 for the promotion of the Youth Archery. It was stated there was a membership drop and a membership drive was needed. Motion passed to present a certificate to State & Regional Tournament Champions for amateur men, women and freestyle divisions if the tournament is registered but no barebow distinction be involved. There were letters of criticism about the Winter League the Board voted to keep the rules as is. A motion was passed that the Chair has the authority to appoint State & Regional NAA Representatives, meeting adjourned.

Board Meeting reconvened 6pm same location. A study on establishing the "Ambassador Cup" tournament between Canadian & US archers near Niagara Falls, motion approved. Date set for the US Tryouts in 1967 but no locations bid. Steps must be taken to secure a site. There were no bids for the 1967 National Championship to date. It was suggested the International Field Round be sanctioned and that any NFAA sanctioned field rounds would be included. A NAA Indoor Championship was approved, no date or location established. Changes of FITA Rules suggested by the NAA: that bubbles be permitted, that the prism be permitted and that the arrow must cut the line for the higher score. The Board decided to postpone the election of Board President & Vice President. Board recessed until the Annual Meeting.

1966 Annual Meeting Aug. at Americana Motel, Flagstaff, Az. It was stated that no bids have been submitted for the 1967 NAA National Championship. It was reported the USOC Development Committee had awarded the NAA $1000 for the promotion of the JOAD program. It was announced a new 900 Round was established scoring 10 center to 1 point for the outside ring. It was discussed that a new site for the 1967 US Tryouts was needed. It was announced the Ambassadors Cup was to be held at Niagara Falls between Canadian & US archers. It was stated the new NAA Handbook was available for $2 from the NAA office. It was announced that Archery World magazine would become a newsstand issue with 6 pages for the NAA news. Suggestions for FITA Rules changes will be submitted to the FITA council. The NAA Board is considering promoting an Indoor Championship. There will be certificates for State Champions, approved. The results of the election for Board of Governors were reported. The results of a questionnaire on changing the Championship Rounds was 50% were satisfied and 0% were not familiar with the rounds. The question was raised why the NAA does not recognize Barebow divisions. It was stated the NAA has recognized Barebow since 1955. It's a case that freestyle is dominate and barebow is not as prominent. The question was raised why there is no competition in a division with less than 3 shooters. Standing NAA rules state certificates are awarded but not medals in this case. It was announced that the archery exhibition in 1968 in Mexico was not to happen because archery has been considered a major sport in the Olympics of 1972, meeting adjourned.

Results: Women's Amateur Champ Helen Thornten 3682, Women's Pro Champ Faith O'Neill 3304, Men's Amateur Champ Hardy Ward 3582, Men's Pro Champ Victor Leach 3549, Inter. Girls Donna Wesson 3242, Inter. Boys Chuck McCormick Jr. 3544, Jr. Girls Maureen Bechdolt 2484, Jr. Boys Dennis Israel 2904, Cadet Girls Deborah Rogneby 1409 and Cadet Boys Bill Glackin Jr. 1907. Flight (Longest only); Amateur Women Norma Beaver 818 yds., Non-Amateur Women Monica Wildenburg 535 yds., Amateur Men Cy Newcomb 772 yds., Pro Men Harry

Drake 1100 yds., and Inter' Girls Diane Godsey 534 yds. NOTE: after the Flight tournament it was discovered the measuring tope was off, awards were given but no official Record were established.

1967 NAA Board Meeting Aug. 6. There was a report of a Board Meeting held Jan. 1967 but I couldn't find a record of it. There was a report on the World FITA Meet. It was reported that FITA had changed the International Field Rules and established a new target face. Requirements to participate in the Annual Tryouts were to be established. It was approved to use the 900 round for the Indoor Championship. It was reported "The Archers Handbook" was doing OK but their needed to be a proofread before the next edition. Dates were set for the 25th World Archery Championships and the 1st World Field Archery Championships to be held in 1969. It was stated a committee to advise on teaching programs and preparation of teaching archery was needed, approved. It was reported that FITA did not accept the NAA proposal to change the scoring. There was a report that there were 64 JOAD clubs. There was a 500 pin to be made for the Freestyle and a 450 pin for Barebow Divisions for the International Field Round shot on 28 targets, meeting adjourned.

NAA Annual Meeting Aug. 10 at Greene Central School, Greene, NY. It was stated a Collegiate Committee was formed and the 1st US Inter-Collegiate Tournament was to be held in Nov. It was announced the 25th World Championship and the **1st World Field Championship** was to be held at Valley Forge in Aug. of 1969. The dates for the Winter League were given. It was stated the establishment of the 450 pin for Barebow and the 500 pin for Freestyle divisions to be earned shooting the 28 target International Field by NAA members. It was announced that FITA has established an 1100 & 1200 pin for their outdoor round. There was an NAA representative at all USOC meetings. It was announced the NAA had 3000 members. The meeting was recessed until the Banquet later the same day. The highlights of the National Tournament were shown on closed circuit television, meeting adjourned. Results: Women's Champ Ardelle Mills 3769, Men's Champ Ray Rogers 3824, Inter. Girls Kristie Kaiser 3536, Inter. Boys Mike Grey 3691, Jr. Girls Bruceen Goodrich 2650, Jr. Boys John C. Williamsn3055, Cadet Girls Cheryl Stauffer 2177 and Cadet Boys George C. Ruth 2464. Flight (Longest only); Women Norma Beaver 881 yds., Amateur Men Fredrick Lederer 783 yds., Pro Men Harry Drake 1048 yds. and Crossbow 1359 yds.

1968 NAA Board Meeting Jan. 12 at Howard Johnson Motor Ledge, Chicago. It was mentioned at a USOC meeting there was some controversy between the National Collegiate Athletic Assoc. and the Amateur Athletic Union. There was a boycott against the USOC by some athletes because of race, creed or color. There processing of membership list was working satisfactorily with few complaints. A report was given that the NAA had 146 Clubs and State Assoc.'s, 73 JOAD clubs, 3100 members with 203 Junior members. There was a committee formed to raise funds for the NAA Team Travel Fund. There was a committee formed for the establishment of an Archer's Hall of Fame. A schedule was set for the 84th Annual NAA Championship: Mon. Team Shoot and practice, Tues 90 & 70 meters for the men and 70 & 60 meters for the women, Wed. 50 & 30 for men and women with Clout, Thurs. American Round for men and women and Fri. 900 Round for men and women. There was a report on the Ambassador Cup held in Montreal. The ten FITA Star Tournaments were approved with the NAA Annual Championship to be held at Tahlequah, Ok. There was a request to consider the release aid and the compound bow for NAA competition. The Board refused approval because FITA would not permit their use. It was passed that if a youths birthday occurred after March they shall be permitted to compete in the lower age group until Oct. of that year, meeting recessed.

Board Meeting Jan. 14 same location. There was a committee appointed to certify shooting records. A 300 pin was approved for the 300 Indoor Round. It was approved to establish a certified Archery Instructor Course at a fee of $8.50 per person, meeting adjourned.

Board Meeting Aug 4 at Tahlequah, Oklahoma Chamber of Commerce. Reported the NAA Archer's Handbook was in reprint because of demand. There was a report about the NAA Instructors Course that 86 certificates had been awarded at three locations. It was approved the 80th Annual Championship to be held in Portland, Or. in 1970. The 1969 Tryouts would be at St. Louis, Missouri. Their was a report on the Pan American Games. The Olympian Award was added to the JOAD program. There was a report on the 25th FITA World Championship, meeting adjourned.

Results: Women's Amateur Champ Vectoria L. Cook 2650, Women's Pro Champ Marva Goodman 2529, Men's Amateur Champ Hardy Ward 2789, Men's Pro Champ Earl H. Hoyt Jr. 2641, Inter Girls Cynthia E. Slade 2535, Inter. Boys Dennis Israel 2637, Jr. Girls Pamela Slade 2484, Jr. Boys Judd Myers 3090 and Cadet Boys George B. Ruth 2476. Flight (Longest only)

Women Diane Godsey 528 yds., Non-Amateur Women Monica Wildenburg 581 yds., Men Don Brown 811 yds., Non-Amateur Men Harry Drake 807 yds and Inter. Girls April Godsey 337 yds.

1969 NAA Board Meeting Jan. 10 at Howard Johnson Motor Lodge, Chicago. The USOC is interested in the FITA World Archery Championships and the inclusion of Archery in the 1972 Olympic Games. The Archer's Handbook and Official Tournament Rules were revised and reprinted and were being sold. There was a letter read from Portland, Or. asking to be relieved of the responsibility of hosting the 86th NAA Nationals, motion approved. A report was read on the Team Travel Fund, meeting recessed.

Board Meeting Jan. 11 same location. There was a report read on the All American Intercollegiate Championship. A budget was submitted and accepted for the 25th FITA World Championship, fees were set. A Team Captain was appointed for the 4th Annual Ambassador Cup. It was approved to host the 2nd US Amateur Field Championship in June. The fees were set for this years NAA Nationals at Valley Forge with a schedule for Junior & Cadet shooters; Thurs. Aug 21: Juniors will shoot 36 arrows from 50 & 40 meters at a 122cm face, Cadets will shoot 36 arrows from 40 & 30 meters at a 122cm face; Fri. Juniors will shoot 36 arrows from 30 & 20 meters at a 80cm face, Cadets will shoot 36 arrows from 20 & 10 meters at a 80cm face; Sat. Juniors will shoot 30 arrows from 50, 40 & 30 yds. at a 48" face, Cadets will shoot 30 arrows from 24 arrows from 40, 30 & 20 yds at a 48" face; Sun. Juniors will shoot 30 arrows from 50, 40 & 30 yds at a 48" face, Cadets will shoot 24 arrows from 40, 30 & 20 yds. at a 48" face. The dates for the FITA Star Tournaments were set, meeting recessed.

Board Meeting Jan. 12 same location. York, Pa. was awarded the 2nd US Amateur Field Championship with a fee of $10. The US Tryouts were to be held at St. Louis, Missouri. A report was given on the advantages of Miami University as a permanent site for the NAA Annual Championships. It was approved to hold the 1970 Annual Championship at Miami University. A Team Leader was appointed for the 1969 World Championships, meeting adjourned.

Results; Women's Champ Doreen Wilber 2629, Men's Champ Ray Rogers 2768, Inter. Girls Beth Flannery 2154, Inter. Boys Stephen Lieberman 2677, Jr. Girls Pamela K. Slade 2502, Jr. Boys Mark Hall 2939, Cadet Girls Jodi Crawl 2492 and Cadet Boys Don Dabelow 2949. Flight (Longest only) Women Diane Godsey 603 yds., Men Vern Godsey 790 yds., none Amateur Men Earl Rozer 567 yds., Jr. Girls April Godsey 468 yds. and Inter. Boys Bill Mendels 647 yds.

1970 NAA Board Meeting Jan. 23 at Stouffer Inn, Cincinnati, A proposal from the Athletic Institute to pay $500 for an amateur who might perform for them to demonstrate archery, motion approved. A resolution was passed to allow an amateur archer to give a demonstration provided he receives no other remuneration than actual expenses. It is necessary to notify and receive NAA approval. It was approved to recognize the barebow class. There was a report on the Eagle Cup Tournament in Mexico City last Dec. It was passed to send a letter to FITA to organize the 2nd World Field Archery Championship held under their rules. It was passed to hold a JOAD Tournament. The FITA Star Tournament location were approved. A 300 Outdoor Round was approved shooting 20 arrows each from 60, 50 & 40 yds. scoring 5, 4, 3, 2 & 1 using a 48" target face, with a perfect score of 300. The Jr. 300 round would be shoot from 50, 40 & 30 yds. It was approved to build a booth for use at various sports shows. There was a nominating committee appointed. There was a brief report on the Hall of Fame Committee, meeting adjourned.

Board Meeting Aug. 3 at Student Union Building, Oxford, Ohio. A report was read that stated 217 shooters had registered for the Nationals. It was approved to hold the 1971 US Tryouts in the 26th FITA World Championship at St. Louis in June of 1971. A new Flight Committee Chairman was appointed and the Crossbow division was dropped. There was a report by the Public Relations Committee on magazine having an NAA Membership application and a proposal for publishing an NAA News Letter sent out, meeting recessed.

Board Meeting Aug. 4 same location. There was a manufacturers promotional plan proposed, no action. A motion was passed to accept the definition of Archery Equipment set forth by FITA for target archery, motion accepted, meeting adjourned.

Board Meeting called on the shooting field Aug. 7. A new Board Member was approved. It was approved to hold the 4th Annual Field Championship at Miami University. Moneys were transferred from the NAA General Fund to the Team Travel Fund, meeting adjourned.

Results: Women's Amateur Champ Nancy Myrick 2712, Women's Pro Champ Betty McKinney 2552, Men's Amateur Champ Joe Thronton 2811, Men's Pro Champ earl Hoyt

Jr. 2748, Inter. Girls Irene Lorensen 2347, Inter. Boys Raymond Wade 2751, Jr. Girls Jody L. Brown 2456, Jr. Boys Michael Trogone 2668, Cadet Girls Jodi Crowl 2474 and Cadet Boys Don Dabelow 2864. Flight (Longest only); Women Ruth Godsey 596 yds., Men Vern Godsey 781 yds., Non-Amateur Harry Drake 1861 yds., Inter. Boys Bill Mendels 567 yds. and Jr. Girls April Godsey 417 yds.

1971 NAA Board Meeting Jan. 15 at Marriott Inn, Cincinnati. It was stated the Nominating Committee had no report. There was a new contract with Archery World. The Public Relations Program was tabled for a lack of funds. A report was given on the Ambassador Cup, the Eagle Cup, the Field Tryouts, the World Field Championship, the 3rd Annual US Field Championship and the 86th Annual Target Championships. There was $100 per month approved for the JOAD program, meeting recessed.

Board Meeting Jan. 16 at same location. A report was given on the Hall of Fame. There were guidelines for selection & nominations for the Hall of Fame made. Efforts for 501 C3 tax exempt status were continuing. The Board approved a College Committee to promote a College Program. A motion passed to present a resolution to FITA to elimination of the Barebow Division in the World Field Archery Championships. Another resolution to FITA was to approve a North American Archery Championship. It was approved to combine the Ambassador & Eagle Cup tournaments into one event known as the North American Championship. A report was approved for the Permanent Site for the Annual Championship to be Miami University. It was approved to add the 900 & 300 Outdoor Rounds for classification to all archers with AA, A, B & C classifications in each round. The committee for selecting top-ranking archers gave their report, meeting recessed.

Board Meeting Jan 17 at same location. Locations for the FITA Star Tournaments were approved. A "National Standard Achievement Awards" was approved for FITA, 900, American, 300 Outdoor and International Field Rounds. The award will be available from the NAA Office after an application is submitted for said award, meeting adjourned.

Annual Meeting Aug. 9 at Student Center, Oxford. It was passed that the Team Travel Fund be a separate account from the General Fund. There was a protest by some in having two archers on the line shooting the same target at the same time. Board approved shooting two at a time in A & B then C & D rotation. A report was read that the 4th US Field Championship had 67 shooters and our Target Nationals had 270 shooters registered. An invitation was received from the National Archery Assoc. of France offering to pay all transportation cost for one NAA archer to attend their French Championship, motion approved. The Board approved the US Team Manager & Coach for the World Championship. An approval to hold the Olympic Tryouts was given with conduct according to present rules & regulations. There was a report on the FITA World Championship at York, England. It was stated FITA approved the North American Championship. FITA elected George Helwig as a member of the Technical Commission and Clayton B. Shenk as a member of the Jury for the Olympic Games in Munich, Germany, Sept 1972, meeting adjourned.

Board Meeting Aug. 12 in the Towers Room at Miami University Union Center. Nominations for the Board of Governors was presented, meeting adjourned.

Results: Women's Amateur Champ Doreen Wilber 2766, Women's Pro Champ Ann Weber Hoyt 2567, Men's Amateur Champ John Williams 2871, Men's Pro Champ Philip Grable 2724, Inter. Girls Janet Kemmerer 2477, Inter. Boys Kevin Erlandsen 2788, Jr. Girls Annette Demos 2649, Jr. Boys Barry Wilson 2921, Cadet Girls Jodi Crowl 2896 and Cadet Boys Christopher Powers 2803. Flight (Longest only); Women Frances Lederer 492 yds., Men Vern Godsey 811 yds. and Non-Amateur Men Harry Drake 786 yds., Footbow 2028 yds.

1972 NAA Annual Meeting Aug. 3 at Student Union Building, Miami University. There were reports on the 25th FITA World Championship in York, England, the Mid-Winter meeting in Jan. (I have not found) and the recent Olympic Trials. The Olympic Team members were introduced with the Team Leader and Coach. Men: Ed Ediason, Dennis McCormak, John Williams; Ladies Maureen Bechdolt, Linda Myers, Doreen Wilber; Team Leader George Helwig and Coach C. R. Fowkes. The 1973 NAA Championship would be at Oxford, Ohio in Aug. The 4th NAA Indoor Championship will be at Harrisburg, Pa. in April of 1973. The 6th US Field Championship will be at Seven Springs, Champion, Pa. in July 1973, meeting adjourned.

Board Meeting Aug. 8 at Miami University Center. Motion passed approving sending eight archers to the 3rd World Field Championship in Udine, Italy in Sept. 1972. Tryouts for the Championship of the Americas were to be held at Ft. Lauderdale, Fl. in Oct. and to send a US Team to Mexico in Dec.

Results: Women's Amateur Champ Ruth E. Rowe 2701, Women's Pro Champ Nancy R. Brown 2319, Men's Amateur Champ Kevin Erlandson 2842, Men's Pro Champ Edward S. Brown 2699, Inter. Girls Louise Grondin 2636, Inter. Boys Darrell Pace 2859, Jr. Girls Jodi Crowl 2752, Jr. Boys Larry Merdock 2940, Cadet Girls Robin Craig 2575 and Cadet Boys Tom Stevensen Jr. 2910. Flight (Longest only) Non-Amateur Women Monica Wildenburg 540 yds., Men Vern Godsey 776 yds. and Non-Amateur Men Chris Wildenburg 666 yds.

1973 NAA Board Meeting Jan. 5 at Holiday Inn, Bridgeton, Mo. A report was given by the College Division that indicated 55 member Colleges affiliated and there were plans for the Intercollegiate Tournament was scheduled for May. A report from the Ranking Committee for Target & Field was given. A report was given about the 1972 Olympic Games stating John C. Williams and Doreen Wilber had won Gold Medals. It was passed to hold a FITA Round and two 900 Rounds in the 1973 NAA Championship. There was a motion to declare State Team Champions for men & women as reported, then printed in Archery World. The 1973 4th Annual Indoor Championship is to be held in Harrisburg, Pa. along with the Pennsylvania State Indoor. It was reported that the Archery Hall of Fame was established by the American Archery Council, meeting recessed.

Board Meeting Jan. 6 same location. a Motion passed to send a men's & women's team to the 27th FITA World Championship. Fifteen FITA Star Tournaments were approved as scheduled. An invitation was accepted form the South African Archery Federation to attend their International Championship with all expenses paid. Approval for a Team patch to be given all members of said teams with the words "National Archery Assoc." included in the design. An "Official Rules & Regulations Interpretation" committee was formed, meeting adjourned.

NAA Annual Meeting Aug. 5 at Student Union Hall, Miami University. Report on the Jan. Board Meeting. Report on the College Division that 34 colleges competed in the Annual Interscholastic Championship held at East Stroudsburg, Pa. An oral report on the JOAD program was given. It was reported the Internal Revenue Services Article 501 (C3) had not been approved. It was reported that 190 to 200 registrations had been received for the 89th Annual Championship. It was reported that 495 archers participated in the NAA Annual US Indoor Championship. It was reported the 1st Field Championship of the Americas is to held at Walt Disney World near Orlando, Fl. It was accepted for the Palmyra Sportsmen Club to host the Tryouts for the Field Championship of the Americas, meeting recessed.

Annual Meeting reconvened Aug. 6 same location. The AAC voted to permit the compound bow in competition. The NAA does not approve the use of compound bows in Sanctioned Tournaments. It was approved to publish a book commemorating the 1st 100 years of the NAA by Robert Rhode. The publishing of an Instructors Manual was given to the College Division. It was passed to change the distances of the Clout Round. It was approved to count rebound or pass thorough as 7 points when the holes are not marked after arrows are scored and drawn from the target face. It was approved to use the FITA 18 meter or the FITA 25 meter indoor rounds in the Winter League Mail-In, meeting adjourned.

Annual Meeting reconvened Aug. 9 at University Center of Miami University, Oxford. Report that the 90th Annual Championship is to be held at Miami University, Oxford. The 91st Annual Championship is to be held at Valley Forge State Park, Pa. in 1976 this is to be a part of the US Bicentennial celebration. It was reported that FITA had refused to allow the peep in the bowstring or stabilizers in the Barebow Divisions. The Nominating Committee announced nominees for the Broad of Governors and the results were reported at this meeting, meeting adjourned.

Results: Women's Amateur Champ Doreen Wilber 2833, Women's Pro Champ Ann Hoyt 2612, Men's Amateur Champ Darrell O. Pace 2958, Men's Champ Earl H. Hoyt Jr. 2791, Inter. Girls Jodi Crawl 2746, Inter Boys Richard Bedner 2868, Jr. Girls Janet McCullough 2809, Jr. Boys Don DaBelow 2917 and Cadet Boys Tom Stevenson Jr. 2974. Flight (Longest only) Non-Amateur Women Monica Wildenberg 522 yds., Men Vern Godsey 786 yds. and Non-Amateur Men Harry Drake 710 yds.

1974 NAA Board Meeting Jan. 18 at Ramada Inn, Bridgeton, Mo. The Treasurers report showed income for 1973 was $59,726.56, expenses were $55,883.70 stating the NAA was doing well. It was reported that the Palmyra Sportsmen's Cub hosted the Field Championship of the Americans Tryouts at no cost to the NAA. It was reported the NAA was making a continuing effort to acquire tax exemption status. A report was given on the College Division. The Ranking Committee reported 43 men & 35 women were listed in the Target Division and 20 men & 13 women were listed in the Field Division. There was a brief report on the Achievement Award Committee, meeting recessed.

Board Meeting Jan. 19 same location. The American Archery Council was to hold the 1974 Archery Hall of Fame Banquet in Oxford, Ohio. It was reported the 4th Edition of the Archers Handbook was updated and was to be printed. An archer wishing to establish a class must compete in an archery tournament registered and sanctioned by a member club of the NAA, Men's classes for the 900 Round are AA-775, A-675, B-575 and C class under 575. Women's classes for the 900 Round are AA-725, A-625, B-525 and C class under 525. There was to be 2 ends of 3 sighter arrows and 1 end of 5 sighter arrows permitted preceding the 1st official scoring of all NAA tournaments. Tie's will be broken 1st by the most number of hits, 2nd by the most hits in the highest scoring zone, 3rd by the most hits in the second highest scoring zone, if the same for both the archers it will be declared equal. An archer on the shooting line shall not receive any assistance or information from anyone while on the line shooting. Visual aids may be used between shots for spotting arrows. For Target shooting a bow shall be limited to 80 lb. pull, for indoor shooting a bow shall be limited to 50 lb. pull. 12 FITA Star Tournaments were approved as scheduled. Palmyra Sportsmen's Club will host the Annual US Field Championship in July. A team was to be selected to be sent to Zagreb, Yugoslavia for the 4th Bi Annual World Field Championship. There was to be a team to be sent to Puerto Rico for the 2nd Bi Annual Target Championship of the Americas. Passed that a registration fee and a cut-off date must be established for all Future Tryout Tournaments sponsored by the NAA. Schedule for the 90th Annual NAA Championship was established: Mon.-Team event, Tues.- 1st half of the FITA Round, Wed.- 2nd half of the FITA Round plus the Clout Round, Thurs.- the 1st 900 Round and Fri.- the 2nd 900 Round. All official Target faces will have the patented FITA & NAA emblem must appear on each target face. It was announced that money was available to invite archers from the USSR to an International Archery Match in 1975, details to be established later. It was announced the 3rd Bi Annual Target Championship would be held at Valley Forge State Park in 1976. The 28th World Target Championship was scheduled for Switzerland in 1975. Archery is schedules for the 1976 Olympic Games, meeting adjourned.

Annual Meeting Aug. 4 at Morris Hall, Miami University, Oxford, Ohio. Team leaders for the 4th World Field Championship in Yugoslavia and the Annual Target Championship of the Americas in Puerto Rico were approved. Archers wishing to enter US Tryouts must establish qualifying scores; Target-Men 1100, Women 1050 for Field- Men Freestyle 450, Women Freestyle 400 and Men Barebow 400, Women Barebow 350. Tryout for the 28th World target Championship will be at St. Louis in May. The Annual US Field Championship will be held at Lebanon, Pa. in July, also to be used as the Tryouts for the World Field team. A report was given in the Certified Instructor Workshops, meeting adjourned.

Annual Meeting Aug. 8 at Towers Room, University Center, Miami University. It was announced the 91st Annual Championship is to be held at Miami University in 1975. It was announced the JOAD program would use the metric system in all events beginning Jan 1975. It was stated the College Division had 62 colleges or universities associated with the NAA. There were 200 archers at the 1974 Intercollegiate Championship in Deland, Fl. and the 1975 Annual Intercollegiate Championship was to be held at Cerritos College, Norwalk, Ca. It was announced that Bear Archery Co. paid for the printing of 1500 Archery Instructors Manual. It was announced that the Team Travel Fund benefitted from several archers appearance on national TV and contributions were being accepted. The Olympic Trials would be held in Oxford in June 1976 for the US Olympic Team. As of Jan. 1975 shooting equipment rules of the **NAA shall be changed to correspond with those of FITA**. Resolution passed that the NAA Championship be a Double FITA Round with the Board to review if it should be continued for the future tournaments, Meeting recessed until the Banquet.

Results: Women's Amateur Champ Doreen Wilber 2856, Women's Pro Champ Marion Rhodes 2662, Men's Amateur Champ Darrell Pace 2997, Men's Pro Champ Victor Berger 2861, Inter. Girls Jodi Crowl 2754, Inter. Boys Richard Bedner 2790, Jr. Girls Janet McCullough 2858, Jr. Boys Mike Gerard 308 and Cadet Boys Donald Wrocklage 2967. Flight (Longest only); Women Frances Lederer 515 yds., Men Vern Godsey 800 yds. and Non-Amateur Men Harry Drake 789 yds.

1975 NAA Board Meeting Feb. at Ramada Inn, Bridgeton, Mo. Oral report was given on the World Field Championship in Zagreb, Yugoslavia. There was a report on the Target Championship of the Americas. The Pan American Archery Federation was formed with the purpose of promoting Archery in the Western Hemisphere to get Archery into the Pan American Games. The French National Archery Assoc. requested permission to reproduce the NAA Instructors Manual. This is copyrighted material and that a fee was expected. The Educational Committee reported that there were 71 colleges using their Archery Instructor Certification Shop. The cost for the Team Travel Fund and the cost of sending a representative to the FITA Meeting was discussed. The Ranking Committee gave their report using aggregate scores for all sanctioned NAA annual tournaments for the year to establish their list. A report was given on the JOAD program and the National JOAD Championship was scheduled for March at Wyandotte, Mich. with the eastern JOAD Championship at Harrisburg in April. It was stated Official NAA Target face should be used in all JOAD events. It was announced that 14 FITA Star Tournaments were approved as scheduled for 1975. It was stated that Flight Shooting Rules follow International Flight Rules. A registered flight meet must be shot on a different day than a sanctioned NAA meet. There were two resolutions sent to FITA for approval: 1 a definition for a peep hole in the bowstring, 2 a definition of a stabilizer and a maximum limit of four attached to the bow. A motion was passed to purchase a medal detector and a timing lights for the field. It was announced the US Indoor Championship at Harrisburg was in April and the US Field Championship was to be in July. The US Indoor would consist of one FITA II and one 900 Round. It was passed that all future NAA Tournaments include US Team Tryout tournaments with a separate fee but no shooters will be eligible for the Tryout unless qualified before the event, meeting adjourned.

Board Meeting Aug. 3 at Morris Hall at Miami University. A report from the Educational Committee recommended a minimum of 60 hours for the NAA Certified Instructor's Course to be held over eight days, motion passed. The College Division stated the Annual US Collegiate Championship in May would be at Brevard Community College, Cocoa, Fl. It was stated that 384 archers had registered for the NAA Annual Target Championship. A motion passed to award 1ˢᵗ, 2ⁿᵈ & 3ʳᵈ places in all NAA Tournaments regardless of the number of competitors in al divisions, meeting recessed.

Annual Meeting Aug. 7 at Towers Room, Miami University. It was announced the 92ⁿᵈ Annual Championship would be at Valley Forge State Park. A report was given on NAA participation in International archery events for Field & Target. Report on the efforts of the USOC Archery Sports Committee and that there were 155 JOAD clubs. Resolutions approved: shooting may not begin if it is raining or an electrical storm is present, tryouts to select World Championship Teams shall be conducted in the same manner as any NAA event. A slide show took place from the 28ᵗʰ FITA World Archery Championship, meeting adjourned.

Results: Women's Amateur Champ Irene Lorensen 2867, Women's Pro Champ Judi Webber 2711, Men's Amateur Champ Darrell Pace 3032, Men's Pro Champ John C. Williams 2923, Inter. Girls Sandra Van Kilsdonk 2781, Inter. Boys Richard Bedner 2894, Jr. Girls Susan King 2876, Jr. Boys Tim Weaver 2990, Cadet Girls Sandra King 2750 and Cadet Boys Marty Sliwenski 2985. Flight (Longest only); Women Myrna Amber 649 yds., Men Bruce Odle 922 yds., Non-Amateur Men Arlan Reynolds 744 yds., Inter. Boys Kelly Reynolds 667 yds., Jr. Boys Bob Ambler 311 yds., Compound Women Arlan Reynolds 720 yds., Compound Broadhead Women Myrna Amber 193 yds., Compound Broadhead Men Bruce Odle 405 yds. and Recurve Broadhead Arlan Reynolds 399 yds.

1976 NAA Board Meeting Jan 30 at Fiesta Inn, Tempe, Az. There were eight NAA Instructor Schools planned and a rewriting of the Instructor Manual was in progress. The NAA had representatives at the FITA International Judges Committee in Italy paid for by the USOC. There was a consistent routine developing: College Division report, a JOAD report, a Ranking Committee report and scheduling of sectioned tournaments with fees to be set. The 92ⁿᵈ Annual Target Championship was to be in Aug. at Valley Forge State Park. The NAA had the obligation to establish World Team members. Robert Rhode reported on the progress on "The First 100 Years of the NAA". The Archery Hall of Fame dinner would be held in connection with the 92ⁿᵈ NAA Championship at Ursinus College. It was announced that 19 FITA Star Tournaments were approved including FITA I & FITA II Indoor Rounds. It was passed that the NAA affiliation of State Archers of Ohio and refusing affiliation of the Ohio Archers, two state organizations was to be studied. The requirements to earn **the Six Gold pin was changed to six arrows in the 10 ring** as accepted by FITA. It was passed that present International Judges formulate a criteria for selecting US NAA Judges, meeting adjourned.

NAA Annual Meeting Aug. 6 at the Chapel of Ursinus Collage, Pa. It was announced the 93ʳᵈ NAA Annual Championship would be at Miami University. Reports from Committees were read and accepted. The NAA was proud to know Luann Ryon & Darrell Pace had won Gold at the 1976 Olympic Games. It was reported in the 3ʳᵈ Target Championships the US Women's & Men's Teams won individual 1ˢᵗ, 2ⁿᵈ & 3ʳᵈ place medals plus they both won Team events with record scores. There was a question asked why the NAA could not change rules in FITA and why certain clothing had to be worn, reply given that the US only one vote, meeting adjourned.

Results: women's Amateur Champ Luann Ryon 2497, Women's Pro Champ Marian Rhodes 2260, Men's Amateur Champ Darrell Pace 2576, Men's Pro Champ John Williams 2454, Inter. Girls Patti Iske 2307, Inter. Boys Tim Weaver 2315, Jr. Girls Cindy Vezzetti 2235, Jr. Boys Martin Sliwinski 2467, Cadet Girls Terri Pesho 2534 and Cadet Boys Carson Wilsey 2158. Flight (Longest only); Women Myrna Amber 554 yds., Women Non-Amateur Arlyne Rhode 675 yds., Men Bruce Odle 1077 yds., Men Non-Amateur Harry Drake 836 yds., Compound Women Arlyne Rhode 612 yds., Compound Men Bob Rhode 885 yds., Amateur Compound Men Bruce Odle 977 yds., Compound Broadhead Women Arlyne Rhode 333 yds. and Amateur Compound Broadhead Bruce Odle 496 yds.

1977 NAA Board Meeting Jan. at Howard Johnson Motel, Tempe, Az. Reports from Committees were read and accepted with tournament schedules approved. There was a brief report about archery at the Olympic Training Center in Colorado Springs. It was reported the Archery Hall of Fame was active but were searching for a place to establish a location for the museum, Miami University expressed an interest. 15 sites were scheduled for FITA Star tournaments as scheduled. A crossbow event was added to the US National Indoor of 1977. It was passed the 1977 Annual Mail-in Winter League be cancelled. It was approved that each State may have one Archery Assoc. affiliated with the NAA. It was requested that each member of an International Team be given eight NAA pins to trade with other national teams, tabled, meeting adjourned.

Board Meeting Aug. 1 at the Student Center Building of Miami University. Reports from Committees were read and approved with the scheduling of tournaments approved. It was passed to hold the NAA JOAD Indoor Championship at Cobo Hall in Detroit in 1978. It was approved that any Rounds now using yds. be changed to meters Jan. 1, 1978. It was approved to have the members vote on the raising of dues, meeting adjourned.

Annual Meeting Aug. 5 at the Student Center Building of Miami University. Reports from Committees were read and announcement the approval of tournaments scheduled. A celebration for 1979 with the Mayor of Crawfordsville, In. recognize the 100th year for the NAA. A new scoring system for US Field Archery would go from 5, 3 to 5, 4 & 3. A number of questions were asked and answered. It was suggested only NAA members be on the Leader Board at any NAA Tournament, no action. It was indicated an increase in NAA dues were needed, motion passed. Space was donated to house the current Archery Hall of Fame in Graying, Mich., meeting adjourned.

Results: Women's Amateur Champ Luann Ryon 2463, Women's Pro Champ Ann W. Hoyt 2189, Men's Amateur Champ Richard McKinney 2586, Inter. Girls Robin Wools 2365, Inter. Boys Lee Nicholas 2374, Jr. Girls Becky Liggett 2040, Jr. Boys Martin Sliwinski 2504, Cadet Girls Rhonda Liggett 1789 and Cadet Boys Bobby O'Neal Jr. 2279. Flight (Longest only); Women Diana Child 607 yds., Non-Amateur Women April Moon 810 yds., Men Bruce Odle 1071 yds., Non-Amateur Men Bob Rhode 1008 yds., Inter. Girls Arlane Reynolds 677 yds. and Inter. Boys Bob Bahr 894 yds.

1977 NAA Board Meeting at O'Hare Hilton Hotel, Ill. There was a report in July of a meeting at Colorado Springs (I could not find any record). Report from Committees were read and approved. It was stated that John Henry Co. of Lansing, Wagaman Bros. of Lititz and Maple Leaf Press of DeWitt had signed contracts and paid royalties to produce Official NAA Target faces. A more detailed dress code was to be made. Three US National Judges applied for FITA International Judge status. There was interest in a classification system using achievement award scores for class breakdown, need study and report later. Robert Rhode presented his books but it was not to be sold before 1979. The USOC offered space free at the Olympic Training Center in Colorado Springs, offer accepted. A 100 year celebration was approved. Team leader and Coach were approved for the 1979 World Target Championship. The NAA approved using FITA Barebow rules. There was a discussion of the Olympic Tryouts for the 1980 Olympic Games. The NAA Mail-in Winter League was reestablished, It was reported there was $35,169 on hand Jan. 1978. Income for the year was $125,121 with expenses being $142,944 for a $17.345 loss, meeting adjourned.

Results: Women's Amateur Champ Luann Ryon 2487, Women's Pro Cham Ann W. Hoyt 2157, Men's Amateur Champ Darrell O. Pace 2569, Men's Pro Champ John Williams 2455, Inter. Girls Robin Wools 2255, Inter. Boys A. Robert Kaufhold 2389, Jr. Girls Becky Liggett 2364, Jr. Boys Jerry Green 2525, Cadet Girls Debbie Engelke 2124 and Cadet Boys Brad Liggett 2193. Flight (Longest only); Women Sherrie Reynolds 569 yds., Non-Amateur Women Arlyne Rhode 1113 yds., Men Jeff Dandridge 970 yds., Non-Amateur Men Don Brown 1117 yds., Inter Girls Arlane Reynolds 734 yds. and Inter. Boys Bob Bahr 839 yds.

Summery to Today

Everything is set in place for participation in today's NAA format and programs. The NAA Office is still in Colorado Springs, there are more Star Tournaments sanctioned, the JOAD program is very active, World Teams are still picked and the Annual NAA Championship is still going on. The rest is from my memory; We did not send a US Team to the 1980 Olympic Games, big disappointment. The 1984 Olympic Games held in LA, which made money, the profit which was distributed as over $1,000,000 to each National Governing Sports Body in The US. The NAA as a National Sports Body put that money into a Trust Fund to be awarded as Grants to promote Archery across the US. Up to now the Olympic Archery had been an individual competition. In 1988 an Olympic Archery Team competition was established. In 1991 the NFAA applied to the USOC to be the National Governing Body in the US because they were the larger National Archery organization plus a US National Team should represent all of the US not just the NAA. The following year the NAA & NFAA signed a reciprocal agreement, that a members in either archery organization may compete in the others Sectional/ Regional and National Archery Tournaments, which is enforced today. The Compound was a division at an NAA Indoor Sanctioned Tournament in 1993 using the regular scoring at Colorado Springs. The following year the compounds was scoring the X ring or inter 10 ring. In 1995 FITA included the compound division in all it's championships and the NAA accepted the Compound Bow as a division in their JOAD competition as well but the compound was left out of the Olympic Games. Today the NAA is known as the United States Archery Association, USAA and FITA is known as World Archer Federation or just World Archery. The International Olympic Committee, IOC includes Archery but has been a struggle to remain in the Olympic venue. Archery competition format has changed from a archery tournament to a head to head elimination competition.

CHAPTER 11

➤➤➤ ▼ ◄ ◄◄

An NFAA Instructor
Certification Program
(from the 1980's with test)

The program covered a brief history of Archery, the NFAA & NAA as well as equipment being shot and rounds of competition. Bowhunting is an important part of the NFAA. Bowhunting isn't just shooting well but showing respect for the animal hunted and knowing when to shoot at a live target for a clean kill. The instructor program was to identify a well rounded experienced individual who knew archery and would represent the NFAA with a good image.

There was a problem of protecting ones amateur status for to possibility of Olympic competition, especially for youth. Today it is not a issue, the Olympic Games is open competition. There was a need to understand Target & Field rounds and Indoor & Outdoor shooting as part of the program. An individual must understand difference in shooting styles and the equipment used. Archery equipment must be set up and you need to know how fine tune that equipment for optimal arrow flight and grouping. An instructor must make a first good impression, be positive, observe your students anticipation and teach students to shoot against themselves. Don't explain what your student is doing wrong, just explain how to do it properly one shot at a time, always be positive. An archery instructor must use proper terminology, know the difference between safety and courtesy. It is your responsibility as an instructor to help people to get into archery for the fun of it, not to make them champions, that is in their effort at archery. Explain how archery is a good general exercise, a great hobby, great therapy for concentration and a life sport.

True and False

1. Using a trainer bow or mimetic is recommended in group classes.
   true or false

2. Beginner archers can't be expected to recognize faults or shooting errors.
   true or false

3. Checking for the dominant eye can determine if an archer should shoot right or left handed.
   true or false

4. Beginners should not start out with a sight, although some who can't judge distance or alignment will need one later.
   true or false

5. Basic shooting form or technique should be taught in a shot sequence, one step at a time to complete the shot.
   true or false

6. It is OK to shoot straight up into the air or see how far you can shoot if if you are alone.
   true or false

7. A backstop or safety area is not necessary if you can hit the target every time.
   true or false

8. Never run to or from a target or run with arrows in your hand.
   true or false

9. Shooting a frayed bowstring or a cracked or bent arrow is acceptable if you can't afford a new bowstring or arrows.
   true or false

10. When looking for lost arrows or missed arrows behind a target have one person stay in front of the target.
    true or false

11. A Compound Bow is more accurate for hunting.
    true or false

12. A stabilizer on a bow is an anti-torque rod.
    true or false

13. It is best to start beginner archers is a class format shooting a compound bow.
    true or false

14. Buying better equipment will make you shoot better.
    true or false

15. If your bowstring slaps your wrist when shooting, then the brace height is too low or the bowstring is to long.
    true or false

16. One style of shooting has no score advantage over another.
    true or false

17. An archer should always shoot to win in a tournament.
    true or false

18. An archer should have in writing his or her; brace height, nocking point location, etc, etc. (equipment set up) as a permanent reference.
    true or false

19. There is only one method of fine tuning archery equipment for better performance and good groups in the target.
    true or false

20. Arrow clearance out of the bow isn't critical if you can shoot good group in the target.
    true or false

Multiple Choice: fill in the most appropriate answer.

1. The range should be ready and the equipment checked out and ready before the _____ starts.
   (CLASSES, SHOOTING, ADVERTISING)

2. The best distance to start beginners shooting is at _____.
   (20 YDS., 10 YDS., 10 FT.)

3. For the first time beginners should shoot at a _____.
   (BIG TARGET, SMALL TARGET, BLANK BUTT)

4. In group archery classes it is best to have students shooting only _____ arrows per end.
   (6, 3, 1)

5. Each bow should be numbered on the face of the lower limb so the _____ can identify the equipment.
   (INSTRUCTOR, GALLERY, STUDENT)

6. If alone an archer should place his or her _____ in front of the target face to indicate a person is behind the target butt.
   (SHIRT, BOW, QUIVER)

7. If your not sure it is safe to shoot, don't _____.
   (SHOOT, LEAVE, COMPLAIN)

8. Always use matched arrows for your bow weight and draw length, never shoot an arrow that is to _____ for you.
   (HEAVY, COLORFUL, SHORT)

9. Make sure of your target, never shoot at something that can _____ an arrow or cause a ricochet.
   (EAT, DAMAGE, DISCOLOR)

10. The _____ should not be to big or to small for your bow weight or arrow nock.
    (BOWSTRING, ECCENTRICS, ARROW REST)

11. The _____ is the only thing that affects arrow porpoising in flight.
    (PLUNGER TENSION, NOCKING POINT, ARROW REST)

12. Finger protection, tab or glove, is also designed to gave you a _____.
    (GOOD APPEARANCE, SMOOTH RELEASE, FINGER TIP RELEASE)

13. Recurve or longbow bow tiller is generally _____ more on the top limb of the bow.
    (1", 1/2", 1/8")

14. In bowhunter styles of shooting in NFAA competition the sight may have a maximum of _____ fixed references.
    (3, 5, 8)

15. _____ shooting teaches you about equipment and shooting technique that can help your bowhunting shooting.
    (STUMP, SILHOUETTE, COMPETITION)

16. Archery is a combination of equipment _____ an the physical and mental control of that equipment.
    (DESIGN, COST, SET-UP)

17. The difference between a good archer and an excellent archer is _____ on aiming, tension and follow-through.
    (PRACTICE, CONCENTRATION, PHYSICAL REFLEX)

18. The NFAA was started in 1939 because _____ archery didn't satisfy the needs of the bowhunter.
    (TARGET, ROVING, BACKYARD)

19. The United States is divided into _____ Sectional districts for NFAA membership representation on the NFAA Council.
(8, 12, 50)

20. The NFAA equipment restrictions on competitive bowhunter styles apply to _____ championships of the NFAA.
(STATE & LOCAL, INDOOR & OUTDOOR, TARGET)

There was also Arrow diagrams for hunting and target plus five Bow diagrams with Alphabet letters on each part of the five bow designs and two arrows designs that had to be matched to a list of names as the parts.

Answers: 1, 2, 3, 4, 5, 8, 10, 12, 15 & 18 are TRUE
Answers: 6, 7, 9, 11, 13, 14, 16, 17, 19 & 20 are FALSE
Multiple Choice: 1. Classes, 2. 10 yds., 3. Big Target or Blank Butt, 4. 3, 5. Student, 6. Bow, 7. Shoot, 8. Short, 9. Damage, 10. Bowstring, 11. Nocking Point, 12. Smooth Release, 13. 1/2", 14. 5, 15. Competition, 16 Set-Up, 17. Practice or Concentration, 18. Target, 19. 8 and 20. State & Local or Indoor & Outdoor.

CHAPTER 12

Archery in General Today

Archery has been around for thousands of years. Archery is very diverse today and can be complicated to non archers. In the 1970's some NFAA Archery clubs made life size styrofoam animal target as a novelty round for their bowhunters, a more realistic hunting round from unknown distances and life size animal targets, no target butt. The NFAA couldn't make the round standard for their members in 1983 at their annual Board Meeting. A standard format throughout the US, so they left it alone, no action. But there were already 3-D animal targets commercially available and major 3D tournaments being shoot in the Midwest drew a lot of shooters, so in 1984 the International Bowhunters Organization, IBO was formed. In 1986 a 3-D group, Archers Shooters Association, ASA in Georgia was formed from 3D shoot on a TV sports show shooting for money. The Boy Scouts and 4-H have archery programs, a few used the JOAD program but their archery is isolated within their group. Flight shooting and Crossbow competition are separate archery organizations for there groups today. Crossbow is back in the NAA National tournament program. Flight was shoot at a separate location but still part of the NAA.

In 2000 the Genesis Bow was used in the Archery in Schools Program in Kentucky. The Genesis Bow was patented in 2002 but was used before the patent was finalized. Now many states promote The Archery In The Schools archery program is generally through that states Department of Natural Resources. This program is growing and has more competitive archers than any archery group in the US. But it is only for Elementary, Middle School and High School groups. There equipment isn't used in other archery competitions, what do they due after they graduate school? The Genesis bow is rarely used in other archery competitions. The NFAA has created a division for their equipment but it is rarely used.

Some Scout Groups and some 4-H groups use the Junior Olympic Archery Develop program (JOAD) sponsored by the USAA (NAA). It is to promote Olympic style shooting (recurve only) but it has a Compound bow division also. Even thou the compound is not in the Olympics. The NFAA has some 20,000 members with 2000 participates at some national indoor championships. The NAA has some 6000 members with 1000 participates in some national championships. The IBO & ASA have some 14,000 members each with some 2000 participates at major tournaments. The are many 3D shooters that shoot in both organizations tournaments. Most 3D shooters still don't use their hunting equipment in their 3D competition. Their are a lot of shooters that participate in USAA & NFAA tournaments, in more then one style of archery. Very few compete in USAA and NFAA competitions. There is Paralympic Archery competitions, mostly at the national level.   Many states archery organizations have a Paralympic class but not with all their divisions. Archery is part of the Wounded Warriors program, not just for physical problems, archery is a mental game. There is a National Seniors Archery program for archers over 50 years of age at state and national level. You have to qualify for the Seniors Nationals through a State competition to participate in their National Competition held every two years. Archery is part of most State Games programs with a national Archery championship for the National State Games Championship every year. There nationals is generally held in conjunction with a state competition. Most archery overseas is Olympic Archery because most countries don't allow public bowhunting but the compound is becoming every popular anyway. In the US some 95% of all archery equipment is sold for bowhunting. If you go to most Sporting Good stores and archery shops they carry what they can sell, Bowhunting equipment. Most bowhunters don't need an archery organization, their state has an Archery only hunting season. Many bowhunter groups lease land to hunt and have smaller groups.

Competitive Archery is a small part of a minority sport bowhunting in the US. Proper Bowhunting equipment and Competitive archery equipment are not the same. Target, Field and 3D archery equipment is not the same. Competitive archery equipment is hard to find and learn to use properly. It is hard to find archery in any form, even harder to find archery classes to learn shooting archery properly. Everyone has an automatic reflex, their subconscious from past experiences controls some movements without you using your conscious mind. The subconscious only knows what you have taught it and has an automatic reaction as you do something new, not always good for archery. If you have no experience in archery your subconscious will automatically react if not shown proper control and timing of a good shot with the conscious mind. All you want to do is hit the bullseye, not learn proper technique in controlling a good shot sequence, shot after shot for a good group to your arrows, takes time and effort. If you have an interest in learning archery to shoot a bow for personal enjoyment or bowhunting. Take it slow and learn what style of archery you may enjoy before you buy your equipment. Most groups that teach archery supply the equipment to start. There is a lot to consider, but you must make time in your schedule to practice and enjoy your shooting for you to improve your archery skills.

If your serious about improving your control in shooting consistently, you need to shoot a minimum of three times a week to develop good muscle memory, every day would be better. If you try to learn consistent shooting with a bow on your own, it is frustrating and will take a longer time to learn. But who has that much spear time, archery is a great hobby, good exercise and a fun pastime. Learn to shoot against yourself with the time you have available in your schedule. But schedule shooting once a month or once every six weeks can be fun at just shooting, but you must schedule your shooting time to make it a part of your normal routine. You don't have to be Robinhood to enjoy your shooting. Find a friend to shoot with, sharing is more fun, we are social animals. You may never go to an archery tournament, but that doesn't matter if you enjoy shoot your bow. Recreational archery gets little recognition from organized archery groups. You have to shoot the bow & arrow to be an archer, not just shoot in archery tournaments or win something but for the fun of it. Join an ancient endeavor, archery seems to be a secret society, but worth the effort and time. I have made it a life effort and have never regretted it, not once.

2016 Glossary and
Comments of Archery Terms
(this is the most extensive you can find)

AAC – American Archery Council, established to standard archery components and terms.

ACCEPT REALITY – do not fret over things you can not change, one bad shot is not the end of the world, you can not move an arrow after it is in the target, accept your performance and score for that day, in a tournament if your arrow group is not dead center-move your sight.

ACTUAL DRAW WEIGHT (recurve bow) – Recurve bow marked 36 lbs., it takes 36 lbs of pressure to reach a draw of 28". A 1/2" difference in draw length, long or short, will make approx. 1 lbs. in holding draw weight of a recurve bow. The actual draw length is from the bottom of the slit in the arrow nock to 1" past the back of the bow at full draw.

ACTUAL PEAK DRAW WEIGHT - maximum draw weight as a compound reaches top rotation over the axel and starts its drop into reduced holding weight.

ADDRESS the TARGET - to proper your stance in preparation to shoot an arrow.

ADJUSTABLE IRIS – a mechanical aperture that changes visual size looking at the target face through it in which to center your target.

ADJUSTABLE PRESSURE POINT - spring loaded plunger fitted horizontally through the bows riser at exact point where the arrow lies on the arrow rest. absorbs some of the horizontally oscillations of the arrow leaving the bow into free flight.

+

ADULT – 18 years of age and over for most archery competition. NAA senior division is adult 20 yrs. of age & older, NAA masters division starts at 50 & up. The NFAA Male or Female divisions are adult 18 to 49 yrs. old, there Senior or Master Senior is 50 yrs. old & over.

AEROBIC ENERGY SYSTEM -the system that produces energy for a long period of time, a combination of fat, carbohydrate and protein are used for fuel in the body.

AIM – Method of judging elevation and alignment to hit a target with the arrow at different distances (instinctive). Method or system of aiming is using a reference point to hit a target located at variable distances with or without a sight on the bow: Point of Aim, the placement of the tip of the arrow on a particular point (visual location) above and below the target for a given distance. String walking is a system of placing the drawing fingers at different locations on the bowstring to change the visual angle over the arrow to the target face to place the point of the arrow on the bullseye at any distance (need 2 nock locators). An adjustable mechanical sight to superimpose the sight pin or aperture on the center of a target as a visual aiming device for different distances. All systems must be practiced at variable distances to find the right combination to hit your target at that distance.

AIMS – purpose and goals in shooting archery. Setting small goals to help maintain interest in your effort in the sport of archery. You must set aside time for shooting or you will fill your time with something else to do.

AIR BOW – plunger device attached to bow riser and bowstring to absorb shock from a shot bow without an arrow. You can practice shooting without shooting an arrow, not a toy

ALIGNMENT - aligning the bow in a perpendicular position to the target and aligning the bowstring on an identical plane with the bow.

ALUMINUM ARROWS - arrow shaft made from aluminum tubing, light and straight.

AMATEUR - one who qualifies as an amateur under Olympic rules. Not valid since 1987 for archery, some FITA rules must be followed to win cash and be able to compete. One who does not shoot for cash in their sport? (History-Old English) one who does not work for a living at there sport.

AMERCAN ROUND – originally shooting from 40, 50 & 60 yds. scoring 9,7,5,3&1 with 5 colored rings on a 48" target face. Shooting 6 arrows for 5 ends from the 3 distances for an 810 perfect score (original round) takes about 3 to 4 hour to shoot. Today is known as the 900 round scoring 10,9,8,7,6,5,4,3,2&1 on the 122cm 5 multi-colored target face with each color divided into two scoring values shot from yds. and meters depending on the archery organizations rules. Shooting 6 arrows for 5 ends from the 3 distances for a 900 perfect score.

AMO – Archery Manufacturers Organization, today the ATA.

APERTURE – sighting device attached to a sight block or on the bow for aiming. Aiming configuration inside sighting aperture: dot, X hair, glow pin or straight pin.

ALTRA-NOK – (trade name) a metal device attached to the bowstring to act as a nock locator and doubles to align the peep mounted in the bowstring, lots of pressure on the bowstring fiber.

AMERICAN 900 or 900 ROUND – target round shooting 90 arrows, in 6 arrow ends from 60 yds (30 arrows), 50 yds (30 arrows) and 40 yds. (30 arrows) scoring 10, 9, 8, 7, 6, 5, 4, 3, 2 & 1, perfect 900 points, takes about 3 to 4 hrs. for a competition (NFAA round).

ANCIENT ARCHERY – developed during the Paleolithic era (35,000 to 8,000 B.C.) independently developed for hunting and self-defense in many places throughout the world during this time. Archery was artillery, the only accurate long-range weapon man had.

ANCHOR – A combination of points on the face or chin to which the bowstring is drawn, tab ledge and /or index finger are drawn to hold a consistent draw length by touching that spot on the face for every shot holding height and alignment to the target; a particular point or points on the face used to establish full draw and a definite rear alignment, should be able to see the bowstring for alignment on the bow to the target.

ANTI-TOURQUE LOOP - loop attached to the bowstring to use a release aid to draw the bowstring, attached at only one location to the bowstring.

APPLY - use what you learn, never give up, effort and experimentation to learn about yourself and your archery equipment.

ARBALEST – A medieval crossbow that needed a windlass to draw the bowstring back, slow but accurate at closer distances.

ARCHERS PARADOX - flexing of the arrow shaft as it is propelled by the bowstring just after release and flying out of the bow to the target, spine. The heaviest part of the arrow is the point and we apply all the pressure to the back of the arrow with the bowstring.

ARCHERY - the art, practice or skill of shooting the bow & arrow.

ARCHERY CLUB – a group of archers with a common interest who cooperate to establish a safe place to practice and/or hold archery tournaments and archery classes; bowhunters, traditional shooters, JOAD, field, 3-D and/or target shooting.

ARCHERY GOLF – an archery round using a golf course shooting at a 4" rubber ball at the green. Teeing off with a distance shot, towing that arrow and shot until the shooter shoots an approach shot at the ball, every shot counts as a stroke. A normal 9 hole, 72 par golf course is about a 52 par for archery golf. Shot differently around the US, never official nation wide.

ARCHERY HISTORY is a web site – archeryhistory.com
Look at any ancient civilizations and you will find archery history. The different material and design of bow & arrows over the centuries'.

ARROW FLETCHING - a material attached to the nock end of an arrow for air resistance stabilizing of the arrow in flight. Feathers and cotton tied onto the arrow shaft or feathers or vanes glued to the arrow shaft at the nock end of the arrow for stability.

ARROW NOCK - a grove made in the arrow shaft to fit onto the bowstring, a plastic nock fitting into the arrow shaft, an aluminum housing with a post to slide a plastic nock onto (housing fits into the arrow shaft) or a plastic nock that fits directly onto the arrow shaft taper.

ARROW PASS - part of the bow handle or riser against which the arrow lies.

ARCHERY ROUNDS INDOOR-
Freeman Round- 4targets per butt-1 target per archer-20 yds- perfect300
    4 arrows per end - 20 points per end
Flint Round-4targets per butt-1 target per archer-20 to 60 ft.-perfect 280
    4 arrows per end - 20 points per end
FITA I-4targets per butt-1 target per archer-18Meters-perfect 300
    3 arrows per end - 30 points per end
FITA I Champ- 4 targets per butt-1target per archer-18M - perfect 600
    3 arrows per end - 30 points per end
FITA II- 4 targets per butt-1 target per archer-25M - perfect 300
    3 arrows per end - 30 points per end
FITA II Champ-4 targets per butt-1 target per archer-25M - perfect 600
    3 arrows per end - 30 points per end
Indoor 300-4 targets per butt-1 target per archer- 20 yds-perfect 300
    5 arrows per end - 25 points per end
old Vegas -4 targets per butt-1 target per archer- 20 yds-perfect 450
    3 arrows per end - 30 points per end
new Vegas-4 targets per butt- 1target per archer- 18M - perfect 300
    3 arrow per end - 30 points per end
PAA Indoor-4 targets per butt-1target per archer- 20 yds - perfect 300
    5 arrows per end - 25 points per end

ARCHERY ROUNDS OUTDOOR-
American Round-1 target 48"- 40/50/60 yds- perfect 810
    scoring 9/7/5/3/1 for 54 points per end
American 300 - 1 target 122cm - 40/50/60/Meters - perfect 300
    scoring 5/4/3/2/1 for 25 points per end
American 900-1 target 122cm - 40/50/60 yds- perfect 900

scoring 10 thru 1 for 60 points per end

American 900-1 target 122cm- 40/50/60 Meters- perfect 900

    scoring 10 thru 1 for 60 points per end

Classic 600- 1 target 92cm- 40/50/60 yds-perfect 600

    scoring 10/9/8/7/6 for 50 points per end

NFAA Field- 4 size targets- 20" to 80 yds- perfect 280

    14 targets scoring 5/4/3 for 20 points per target

NFAA Hunter- 4 size targets- 11 to 70 yds- perfect 280

    14 targets scoring 5/4/3 for 20 points per target

NFAA Animal- 3 size targets- 10 to 60 yds- perfect 280/294

    14 targets scoring 20/16/12 - 1st, 2nd or 3rd kill -center spot +1

International Round-3 size targets- 20 to 65 yds- perfect 300

    10 targets scoring 5/4/3 for 15 points per target

NFAA 15 Field-4 size targets- 20" to 80 yds- perfect 300

    15 targets scoring 5/4/3 for 20 points per target

NFAA 15 Hunter-4 size targets- 11 to 70 yds- perfect 300

    15 targets scoring 5/4/3 for 20 points per target

NFAA 15 Animal- 3 size targets- 10 to 60 yds- 300/315

    15 targets scoring 20/16/12 - 1st, 2nd or 3rd kill-center spot +1

3D Round- different life size targets-up to 55 yds- 200/240

    20 life size animal target to distance 10 points with 12 spot

Archery Golf- 4" ball- 9 holes- 150 to 550 yds- 1 stroke per shot

(on a par 71 Gold Course, par for archery is 51)

Clout - 1-15M target on ground at 185/165/125M score 180 perfect

    scoring 5/4/3/2/1 for 30 points per end

Outdoor FITA-1target 122cm-30/50/70/90M- perfect 1440

    scoring 10 thru 1 for 60 points per end

Chicago Round- 1 target 48"- 40/50/60 yds- perfect 864

    scoring 5/4/3/2/1 for

Perfect Round- 3 size targets- 10 to 80 yds- perfect 0

    scoring 0/1/2/3 for hit

PAA outdoor- 3 size targets- 20 to 65 yds- perfect 150

    scoring 5/4/3 for 15 points per target

York Round- 1 target 48"- 60/80/100 yds- perfect 864

    scoring 9/7/5/3/1 for 27 per end

Wand Round- 2"by6' soft wood post- 100 yds- first hit

ARROW RACK - a device for storing arrows to prevent their damage when not in use. Could be in a ground quiver, side quiver or back quiver.

ARROW REST - the location where the arrow rests at full draw either on the hand or on the bows window shelf. A device plastic or rubber mounted in the bows window that the arrow rests on at full draw. A device with a wire arm extending for the arrow shaft to rest on, can be stationary or collapsible. A medal strip extended upward with a "V" slot to hold the arrow in place, a launcher arrow rest. A mechanical device that is mounded in the bow window that can be raised to hold the arrow and collapses upon release of the bowstring.

ARROW SHAFT - material or tubing used to form the body of the arrow, wood, reed, bamboo, aluminum, carbon or a composite of materials.

ARCHERY WAR – first military history in 2,340 B.C., when Sargon of Akkad in northern Babylonia conquered the Sumerians of southern Babylonia with an infantry made up mostly of archers. From that time on, many ancient peoples used the bow & arrow in warfare in varying ways and with varying degrees of success.

ARCHER - (old French archier) Latin arcarius, from arcus (a bow); one who shoots with a bow, hence archery, shooting with a bow.

ARMGUARD - a guard worn on the inside of the archers forearm to catch the blow of the bowstring on the arm; if you hit your bowarm with the bowstring you have poor shooting form, is a good idea if you make a mistake. (Japanese) in releasing and revolving the bow in the left hand a guard is worn on the outer side of the forearm to catch the blow of the bowstring.

ARMING - the action of placing a projectile point on the arrow.

ATLATI - American term or name for the arrow or spear thrower.

ARROWS – a shaft (possible cresting), fletching, nock and point made to shoot from a bow. A traditional arrow is made of (different) woods with feather flitching. The possible parts are the pile or head, barb-piece, foreshaft, shafe or stele, feathering, nock and seizing. Modern arrows can be made of aluminum, carbon tubing or a combination of same with variable spine and feathers or vanes as fletching.

ARROW A/C/C - Aluminum/Carbon/Competition arrow shaft made of multiple layers of carbon graphite fibers in an epoxy resin wrapped over a high strength aluminum shaft (0.2mm thick), a parallel tubing shaft. The code numbers printed on the shaft indicate its size: eg. 3-71/300 where 3 in the number of carbon layers, 71 is the last two digits of the core aluminum shaft's thickness in thousandths of an inch (0.271") and 300 is the spine of the arrow in thousandths of an inch. There are specific types of points and nocks for this arrow shaft.

ARROW A/C/E – Extreme/Carbon/Extreme arrow shafts made much the same as the A/C/C arrows, except the shafts are 'barrel-shaped', being thicker in the center of the shaft and tapered at each end. The code numbers printed on the shaft indicates its size: eg. 1206G/370 where 12 is the diameter of the aluminum core shaft measured in 64th of an inch, 06 is the aluminum shaft's thickness measured in thousandths of an inch, G indicates the model series and 370 is the spine of the arrow in thousandths of an inch. There are specific types of points and nocks for this arrow shaft.

ARROW CEMENT - substance used in fastening the arrow-head or fletching to the shaft (historical) A few tribes used glue or cement in making the sinew-backed bows.

ARROW CENTERING - adjusting the position of the cushion plunger and arrow rest so that the tip of the arrow point is correctly aligned to the target.

ARROWHEAD - the part of the arrow designed to penetrate a target or produce a wound. (historical) The parts of the arrow-head are the tip or apex, sides or edges, base, shank or tang, primitive stone arrow-head and facettes.

ARROW LENGTH - measured from the cut end of the shaft to the bottom of the "V" in the arrow nock, not including the point. Arrow length is not the draw length.

ARROW PLATE – A plate, adjustable or fixed, to which the arrow rest is attached. An attachment in the window of the bow riser to give a single point of arrow contact and provide smooth arrow passage.

ARROW POINT (pile) – Metal or stone inserted into the end of the arrow shaft. A wooden shaft fits inside the point, also some carbon shafts fit inside.

ARROW RACK – a device for storing and moving arrows safely with a central location resting place for the arrow to be drawn and shot from, must hold the arrow in place and give adequate arrow clearance as the shaft passes the bow riser into free flight. Should be adjustable for tuning, can be one piece or mechanical.

ARROWSMITH – One who is skilled at making arrows or a person who makes metal arrowheads.

ARROW SPEED - average: longbow - up to 185 ft. per. sec.
    recurve - 180 to 200 ft. per. sec.
    compound - up to and over 300 ft. per. sec.
(ASA, IBO & NFAA have a speed limit of 280 fps for their competitions.)

ARROW STRAIGHTENER – device to counter bend bent arrow shafts to re-straighten that shaft to a degree acceptable for shooting. A piece of bone, horn, wood or ivory with perforation to serve as a wrench in straightening a wood arrow shaft.

ARTHUR YOUNG – First to film hunting big game with the bow & arrow in 1936. Hunting companion of Dr. Saxton Pope, the two are considered the fathers of modern bowhunting.

ASA – Archers Shooters Association, a 3-D archery organization,
    Web site – asaarchery.com

ASSUMPTION – To take or accept as true. I hate the 50 yard target, you will shoot poorly!

ATTENTION - the intake of information and control of the body.

ATA – Archery Trade Association, web site – archerysearch.com

ATP - Adnesinetriphosphate, anaerobic energy system.

ATTITUDE – with regard to a persons action and emotion towards his or her shooting the bow & arrow. Positive attitude is required for enjoyment and improvement. Negative attitude affects everyone around you poorly and takes away from an enjoyable time shooting. We always root for the underdog, why do we enjoy an upset, must remain positive.

AWARD – trophy, medal or plaque given for shooting the highest score in your division and style of shooting within an archery competition or archery tournament, must be earned to have value to the winner.

AXLE – The bearing pin holding the wheel or eccentric in the limb of a compound bow.

BACK of BOW - The surface of the bow furthest from the archer when at full draw. The surface of the bow farthest away from the bowstring of a braced bow, the surface facing the target.

BACKED BOW - A bow consisting primarily of wood but having a strip of material, fiberglass, rawhide, bone, sinew or cord glued or attached to the back of the bow limb plus leather or snakeskin for decoration. Its purpose is to strengthen the bow and to improve its cast or clasticity.

BACKING - a reinforcing material attached or bonded to the back of a bow limb, purpose is to prevent breakage and to improve the bow's cast.

BACK MUSCLE TENSION - pull to full draw to align the shoulders to pivot and use the rhomboids muscles of the pulling arm, front shoulder blade against rid cage, bone on bone, shoulders in sockets.

BACK YARD ARCHER - an archer shooting his own location to practice usually doesn't shoot formal archery tournaments.

BALANCE (arrow) - Slightly off center mid point of an arrow, generally 7 % to 9% to the point of the arrow.

BALDRIC - the strap supporting a quiver or sheath being worn over the shoulder, across the breast and under the opposite arm.

BARB-PIECE - a piece of ivory, etc., on some arrow heads attached to the true arrowhead and having barbs on the sides.

BAREBOW - art of shooting a bow without a sight.

BARE SHAFT – an arrow of a matched set without fletching for tuning the bare shaft method. A bare shaft will fly just as the bow pushes the arrow into free flight without the influence of any fletching. Shoot a group, bare shaft low- nocking point high; bare shaft right- spine weak.

BALLISTA – A very large medieval crossbow used by an army attacking the walls of a besieged town or castle. This crossbow was capable of firing large rocks and spears a long distance.

BALLOON FEATHERS (flu- flu) - a parabolic cut feather glued to the rear of the arrow shaft.

BARB - a projection on the arrow point for fishing and/or hunting (arrowhead) that prevents easy withdrawal.

BARE SHAFT TESTING - the use of a non-fletched arrow at 10 to 20 yards for adjusting the nocking point and cushion plunger stiffness or arrow rest centering on a recurve bow, can be used on a compound bow without a cushion plunger. Shoot three arrows for a group, then shoot your bare shaft for comparison of flight.

BAREBOW – The discipline of shooting without a bow sight. Shooting style, which does not include a bow sight; but with a finger release, sometimes using the string walking system (sightless shooters). Bow without any accessories attached to aim with.

BARRELED SHAFT - an arrow shaft which is thicker in the middle an tappers to the ends.

BASE of an arrow - tip or arrowhead, the portion which fits into the shaft.

BASE LIMB STABLIZER - an extended weight on a rod that screws into the top and bottom of the bows handle or riser at the base of the bow limbs.

BASIC TECHNIQUE - systematic method or sequence of using a bow to propel an arrow accurately into free flight at a target. The elements of shooting, step by step, to shoot one good shot with consistent execution and timing. Fundamental shooting form to fall back on when anxiety or confusion accrues less complicated.

BASIC TUNING – Finding proper arrows, a good arrow rest and adjusting the nocking point for a consistent strike pattern on the target.

BEST GOLD (target archery) - arrows shot the one judged to be nearest the center.

BBF – Bare Bow Federation, a group of sightless shooters (archers that do not use sights on the bow) that socializes together within the NFAA.

BEGINNER – trying something new; one who is trying a phase of archery unfamiliar or has minimum resource and experience in. Get help from books, the web or take archery lessons. Not consistent enough to fine tune their archery equipment.

BELLY of the bow – the inside surface of the bow nearest the bowstring when braced. Now called the "face" of the bow. Self bow the belly is usually rounded.

BLINDS – used for scoring judges in OR round, also a concealment used by bowhunters to hunt from.

BLUNT POINT – Arrow point with a flat tip designed not to let the arrow penetrate a target or tree, usually a conical rubber arrow point. Used for hunting small game bowhunting, judo point, some times called a butt-shaft.

BLANK BALE – target butt without a target face, shooting close range without aiming to feel the flow and timing of your shot, eyes closed can help you feel the shot, should not shoot more than 10 or 12 shots in a row.

BODKIN – A medieval type of arrowhead designed to shoot through protective chainmail, usually worn by Knights.

BODY ALIGNMENT – a balanced T-stance, to determine body angle and shoulder alignment before, during and after a well executed shot. Body weight should be balanced on both feet. After setting your feet for a shot, raise your bowarm and draw the bow to anchor with your eyes closed. When you open your eyes the bow should be aligned on the target face, adjust feet for alignment change.

BODY COMPOSITION - the relation of fat content to lean body mass.

BOLT – A short arrow used in a crossbow.

BOUNCE OUT (bouncer) – an arrow that rebounds from the target face's scoring area. NFAA re-shoots the shot or accepts group members' verification of scoring hit. NAA marks all the arrows holes as shot, so you can score the unmarked hole in the target face for the value or scoring of the rebound arrow.

BOSS - target usually made of compressed straw. BOW - a device made of flexible material with a bowstring or cable system connecting two workable limbs to store energy that can propel an arrow with a bowstring, longbow, recurve and compound. A bow is defined as having two working limbs. Indian bows, backed bow, grafted bow, build-up bow and self bow.

BOW ARM or HAND - The arm or hand that holds the bow, proper alignment enables a smooth consistent shot, with the elbow turned to the outside and the arm relaxed but locked. Pressure from a drawn bow should be into the stub of the bowarm, through a relaxed bow hand and wrist to the shoulder.

BOW CASE – Case or container for transport of archery equipment, bows and accessories for storage on short and long trips. A long bag or case of wood or plastic, leather or cloth in which the bow and accessories are kept when not in use.

BOW EFFICIENCY - the percent of stored energy in a bow which is transferred to the arrow at release.

BOWFISHING – using a barbed arrow with an attached line to shoot legal fish with the bow & arrow. Only rough fish may be shot and you need a fishing license, shark, gar, carp, etc.

BOW HAND - the hand holding the bow riser.

BOWHUNTER – a person who hunts game animals with the bow & arrow. 95% of all archery equipment sold in the US is for bowhunting.

BOWHUNTER EDUCATION – IBEF, International Bowhunter Education Foundation; instruction given on bowhunting accessories and bowhunter technique with trained and certified instructors.

BOW HANGER – a device to hold your bow by hanging, so it is ready to shoot while hunting or storing safely when not in use at an indoor or outdoor archery range.

BOW HOIST – device to haul up your bow into a tree stand or blind.

BOW LIMB DAMPENERS - a soft rubberized material attached to the bow limb between the bow nock and the bow riser. Can be mounted between split compound limbs.

BOWMEN – another term for an archer.

BOW PRESS – a device to relax pressure of the bow limbs of a compound bow to change cables, bowstring and/or maintenance on the bow parts.

BOW RACK - a device used to hold bows when not in use, can be permanent or portable.

BOW SCALE - a mechanical device the measures the draw weight of the bow at any stage of the draw.

BOW SHOT - the distance to which an arrow flies from a bow.

BOW LIMB TIP PROTECTOR - a piece of rubber or other material designed to slide over and protect the lower limb tip and holds the bowstring loop in place.

BOW TUNING - system of adjusting the mechanics of the bow to get the best arrow flight and grouping pattern for your system of shooting.

BOW WINDOW - a cutout section of the bow riser to get to center shot through which the archer may sight.

BOW WOOD - the substances used for bow making, generally a hard wood but horn, antler, bone have been employed to reinforce the bow, leather or snake skin use to decorate.

BOW QUIVER – device that attaches to the bow riser that holds hunting arrows safely to be used for carrying and shooting at game, should practice with all the bow accessories set the same way you are going to hunt.

BOWYER – a person who makes and repairs bows.

BOW RACK - a device to hold bows safely when not being used, or while not shooting in a tournament or practicing.

BOW REEL – A device attached to the bow to hold coiled string or line attached to a bowfishing arrow to retrieve shot fish. Most rough fish can be legally taken with the bow & arrow.

BOW SIGHT - a mechanical or stationary device attached to the bow riser, that can be seen through the bow window and which allows the archer to sight directly on the intended target at variable distances with a visual reference; fixed pins and moveable sights (single pin). Parts: extension bar, slide bar, sight block and sight pin or aperture; some have a clutch and/or micro block adjustment, vertical and windage.

BOW SLING - a restraining strap or cord that encircles the bow riser and the archer's hand to prevent the bow from falling after you release a shot, finger and wrist sling. It is a mental crutch to know the bow will not fall when the archer shoots a relaxed grip on the bow.

BOWSTRING - the string or cord used to brace a bow that transfers the energy from the bow limbs to the arrow when pulled back and released, an artificial material with a sufficient number of strands to use for the bow's design and peak bow weight.

BOWSTRING SERVER – device with adjustable tension for smooth thread flow serving a bowstring, center serving and bowstring loops.

BOW SOCK – A camouflage cloth sleeve which fits over the bow limbs when hunting.

BOWSTRING WAX – moisturizer applied to keep bowstrings from drying out. Apply wax and rub to heat the bowstring, to protect and make strong.

BOW STRINGER – A cord with two dissimilar size pockets or one pocket and one saddle, used to string and/or unstring a recurve bow safely. Any device which aids an archer in bracing their bow.

BOW STAND – A device that sticks in the ground or sits on the ground and holds the bow safely off the ground and keeps ready to shoot behind the shooting line. A platform used by bowhunters to hunt from.

BOW STAVE – A piece of wood used to make a self-bow or laminated limbs for a bow riser, must be properly cured or dried to keep from cracking.

BOWSTRING LOOP – a small woven or served loop at the center serving to hold contact with a release aid for shooting.

BOW SCALE – a hand held bow scale that measures the bow's draw weight and holding weight, compound and recurve. A wall scale is used for the same purpose of weighing the pressure stored by the bow limbs.

BOW SQUARE – T-shaped device to measure brace height and nocking point location on the bowstring. Can be used to measure bow tiller, peep location and/or kisser button location.

BOW VICE – clamp to attach and hold the bow upright for working mostly on a compound bow and can be used for leveling accessories, like the sight.

BOW WEIGHT – The number of pounds of energy required to pull a bow to 28-inchs. You will have 1.5 to 2 lbs. per-inch difference in marked draw weight, shorter less and farther more than marked. It is peak draw weight for a compound bow, not holding weight.

BOW WAX - a wax used to keep bowstrings from dehydrating.

BOWYER – One who makes bows.

BRACED - the bow with the bowstring in the nocks of the bow limb and ready to shoot, like a recurve or longbow braced.

BRACING (stringing) - to string or brace the bow so it is ready to shoot. Bending the bow and putting the eye loop of the bowstring over the upper and lower nock in the bow limbs.

BRACED BOW – a bow which is strung and ready for shooting. A compound bow is strung all the time, draw weight can be adjusted.

BRACER (wrist-guard) - a contrivance for protecting the archer's wrist from being galled by the bowstring for low brace height bows.

BRACE HEIGHT - the length of a perpendicular line from the bowstring to the arrow's point of contact with the bow (arrow rest or pivot point). The length of a perpendicular line from the bowstring to the back of the bow's surface used by most manufacturers for the brace height. With Longbows it is the archers fist with the thumb extended so the hand touches the bow and the thumb tip touches the bowstring.

BREAK OVER - the lessening of pull weight after peak weight is reached of a compound bow pulling to full draw.

BRIGHT EYES – brand name for reflectors that stick to trees to mark a path to and from a bowhunting stand or bowhunting area.

BROADHEAD - a sharp metal cutting bladed arrow point used for bowhunting, 2 blade, 3 blade, 4 blade and folding or hidden blades.

BRUSH BUTTONS – A globular rubber object attached to the bowstring, touching the bow limb when braced; preventing twigs and such from lodging between the bowstring and bow limb.

BUBBLE – Leveling device for shooting the bow, attached to the sight or bow riser.

BUILD-UP BOW - a bow made by gluing pieces of elastic wood and other substances together, as in Asiatic examples.

BULL'S EYE - the area on the target face with the highest scoring value, usually dead center.

BUSS CABLES – Cable or string fibers that wrap around the eccentric and is attached to the opposite limb axle, controls the energy being stored and travel of eccentrics and the power stroke, has relaxed tension at full draw.

BUTT – (target butt) – A safe backstop for arrows on which a target face is attached for scoring the arrow hits in the target face. Do not touch any arrows, target face or target butt until all arrows are scored.

BUTT SHAFT - (historical) a blunt arrow for shooting at a butt, the ancient style of target.

BUTT SHOOTING – bowmen (about 1600) aimed at targets mounted on an earthen butt at ranges of 100 to 140 yds. The butt was originally a wooden cask.

BY-LAWS – standing rules governing the regulations of internal affairs and competition of an archery club or archery organization.

CABLE EXTENSION - the length of cable or string which wraps around the eccentric wheel and is attached to the bowstring.

CABLES – A steel cable or multi-fiber string that connects the cams or eccentrics to the opposite bow limb of a compound bow, called buss cables.

CABLE GUARD – large rod attached to the riser of the bow to offset the buss cables of the compound bow for arrow clearance so the arrow can pass without interference.

CABLE SLIDE – device on the cable guard that the buss cables move through to minimize cable wear and maintain cable alignment.

CALORIE – a unit of energy used to measure the energy value of food.
What do you require to control your bow during and through a competition.

CAMS – the shape of an elliptical wheel or eccentric (not round) at the end of the compound bow limb that controls the force-draw curve of the bow or the energy stored by the system of the bow. There are many different designs; soft cam, hard or radical cam and single-cam (mounted on lower bow limb).

CANT - to tip or hold the upper bow limb to the right or left of vertical while at full draw. The reference to right or left is determined by the position of the upper limb being plum to the target.

CARBON/ALUMINUM ARROWS - an aluminum shaft arrow wrapped with carbon for strength on the outside.

CARBON GRAPHITE ARROWS - composite arrows made of carbon and graphite.

CAN DO – there should be nothing negative, stay positive. You may wish to be on the Olympic team. You can do anything you wish to work at, you may not wish to work that hard. Set small goals and add new ones as you meet goals.

CASE – carrying case to hold bows, arrows and accessories, both hard and soft sides.

CAST - The ability of a bow to project an arrow down range, trajectory; generally determined by the bows power stroke, bowstring travel after release.

CENTER GUAGE – a device that measures the alignment of the bowstring to the sight aperture, in relationship of the bow riser.

CENTER SERVING – The protective winding at the center of the bowstring where the nock locator is attached and the arrow is nocked for shooting.

CENTER STABILIZER - an extended weight on a single rod that screws into the handle or riser of a bow, extends straight towards the target.

CENTERSHOT - the right/left placement in the sight window or riser that allows for the placement of an arrow rest above the grip or head placement in the handle +to hold the arrow at the center of the bow limb alignment.

CERTIFIED ARCHERY INSTRUCTOR – meeting minimum requirements and completing and passing required tests on material to certify minimum knowledge to teach archery under an archery organization's authorization.

CHANGE – the only thing consistent in archery is change. Most archery clubs that lease land move every 5 years. Rules and regulations of archery organizations change every year, if not more. Changing styles of shooting is a positive change. Archery is diverse. Archery has about a 30% turnover in membership every year; most archers are in and out of the sport in about 2 ½ years.

CHEST PROTECTOR – a device made of stiff material that attaches around your upper body protecting the chest area from the bowstring at full draw and release.

CHIPPING HAMMER - called also hammer stone, a stone used for knocking off chips or spalls in making stone arrowheads.

CONCENTRATION - the mental ability to focus on each step of the shot sequence to execute one shoot as a time the same every time.

CHOOSE – to select from a number of possibilities; Target, Field or 3-D; Instructive, barebow, freestyle limited or unlimited. Most new archers only have a perceived choice to shoot a better score, not to learn what modern archery has to offer. Most do not know there is a choice except accessories.

CHRYSAL - a pinch or faulty line across the grain on the belly of a self bow, generally of wood..

CLASSIC FORM - a method of shooting with as little deviation as possible from normal body position.

CLASSIFICATION - grouping for competition by skill level, scoring average or shooting style, different for each organizational competition.

CLEARANCE – arrow passing the bow riser and arrow rest without any part of the arrow contacting with either, for consistent arrow grouping in the target. You need bowstring clearance of the archer's clothing at the bowarm and chest area at full draw before and after release.

CLICKER – a device that makes a "click" sound when an archer pulls his or her bow to full draw and the device falls off the end of the arrow. Usually a small strip of metal mounted in front of the arrow rest giving precise indication of full draw by falling off the end of the arrow and making an audible click.

CLOCKING - calling the arrows location on the target where they strike.

CLOSE BACKED - a composite bow with a covering over the assembly of all bow materials.

CLOUT - An archery contest where the aim is to hit a target laid out horizontally on the ground with 5 scoring rings and a visible aiming flag at the center of the scoring area. The English shoot the clout in yards today men compound shoot 185M, Recurve bow and Crossbow shoot 160M, Youth shoot 110M are also shot by different divisions, an FITA/NAA competition, scoring is 5, 4, 3, 2 & 1, also see FITA rule book, the round takes about 2 hrs. for a competition, was originally 180 yds.

CLOSED STANCE – the position of the archer's front foot is forward of an imaginary line from the archer's back foot to the center of the target being shot.

CLUB – A group of people meeting at a location to shoot or practice the sport of archery. Generally promote common rule and host archery competitions for members and the public. Good place to learn about the sport with other interested participates of archery.

CLUB OFFICER – person voted to run a club. A club needs volunteers to operate and promote our sport as a group in a club format. These are thankless positions that need dedicated archers there is no training except experience.

CLUTCHING - condition usually developed in the bow hand upon release or grabbing at the bow upon release.

CHRONOGRAPH – Device that measures the speed of an arrow in feet per second when shot through.

CHRYAL - a pinch or faulty line across the grain in the wood on tehe belly of a self bow.

CHOKER – in reference to an overly tight grip on the bow handle, does not allow the bow to efficiently align for consistency.

CLOUT ROUND - a type of archery round of shooting where archer's shoot to a large ringed target laid out on the ground shoot from a long distance depending on their age classification.

COACH – One learned in the skills and disciplines of archery and teaches for a fee this knowledge to individuals. The NAA & NFAA have formal training for different levels of certified archery knowledge.

COCK FEATHER – The feather or vane set at a right angle to the slot in the nock, now called index fletch on a 3 fletched arrow. Some launcher archery rests require the cock fletch when nocked point straight up or support rod arrow rest requires the cock fletch to be nocked straight down when nocked on the bowstring for the arrow to pass without deflection.

COLLAPSE - a pulling to full draw and relaxing your muscle tension, loss of muscle tension at release; drawing hand moves forward at release, no follow-through.

COMFORT ZONE – as we practice and develop a comfortable and consistent shooting routine, we develop certain expectations. We know our average scores and when we score above that average we know it or are told about it and have self-doubt. The vast majority of our shooters will have a few bad shots to get back into their comfort zone. You must believe there is no limit and do your best, every shot, one at a time.

COMPETITION – a gathering of archers shooting a standard round to compare scores. Competition using defined divisions and styles of shooting using rules and regulations of an archery organization. You need to compete against yourself, do the best you can. There is value learned that can be used in everyday life. To find the best archer everyone needs to shoot his or her best.

COMPLAINERS – some people are never happy, some people feel cheated. Some people consider those who just shoot (not workers) are the complainers. But the some archery workers complain about the these shooters?

COMPOSITE LIMB – A composite limb in made of two or more layers of compatible material for better straight and cast, loose and laminated.

COMPOUND BOW – a metal or cast riser with short stiff bow limbs with eccentrics, cams or idler wheels mounted in the ends of the bow limbs which use a cable system of pulleys, these cams leverage as they turn over to reduce holding weight at full draw. Most modern compound bows have a 65% let-off from peak draw weight to full draw (holding weight), some compound bows have an 80% let-off. Some organizations have a speed limit of 280 fps and a maximum draw weight to be legal in their competition. Some archers who just bowhunt have bows set up to shoot 350 fps. The compound bow is less efficient at recovering stored energy than the longbow or recurve bows, but it stores a lot more of energy. (historical) bow made of two or more pieces of wood, bone, antler, horn or whale bone lashed or spliced together.

COMPOSITE BOW - a bow of different designs made from a number of materials laminated together to increase the power, consistency and longevity of the bow.

COMRADERY – alike, sharing something in common, a relationship established by a common activity. Archery is best shared. Shooting alone you only think about score or how well you are doing. Shooting with a friend you enjoy the sport of archery.

CONCENTRATION - sub-conscious control of the shot sequence to completion (focus on a single task). Not allowing distractions to effect or interrupt your sub-conscious control (the flow or execution) of one good shot. Ability to stop the shot sequence when a distraction allows a deviation, do not shoot a shot you know to be bad.

CONDITIONING – comprehensive planning of your meals, exercise, imagery, practice and mental conditioning to improve physical and mental control of executing one good shot.

CONSTITUTION – is to state purpose and write down the structure and principles of a club or organization.

CONTROL - the ability to mentally control the shot sequence while aiming accurately before the release and follow-through.

CORE LAMINATIONS - any material, wood, fiber or plastic used between the back (tensile) and belly (compressive) surface laminations of the bow limb.

COURSE APPROVAL – any official or sanctioned tournament must be shot on a course or range that has been inspected and approved as being acceptable under the rules that apply for that organization, for awards or scoring records.

COVERING - covering or sealant over a bow to keep out moister or dampness, snake skins, leather, membrane, shellac and Indian bows with birch back used.

CUSHION PLUNGER – Shaft incased with adjustable spring tension mounted in the bow riser through to the bow window so the arrow shaft rests at the horizontal center of the shaft to absorb the oscillation of the archer's paradox as the arrow is leaving the bow. A part of fine-tuning for better arrow flight, a must for finger shooters sometimes called pressure plunger.

CREEPING - any forward movement of the drawing of the bow, before or after reaching full draw or at release, called a collapse of shooting form. Usually caused by loss of shoulder and/ or back muscle tension.

CRESTING - identification marks on an arrow, usually painted rings below the feather or flitching.

CRAFTS – to make unique objects requiring special skills like quivers, armguards, tabs, arrows; accessories for archery.

CROSSBOW - a bow attached to a wood stock with a mechanical lock and trigger, shoots bolts. Competitive crossbows use recurve limbs, maximum 95 lb. draw weight, most be hand cocked. Hunting crossbows use compound and recurve limbs with 200 lb. pull or more. They use a cocking device to bring the bow limbs to full draw.

CROSSHAIR SIGHT - a sight with a circular aperture with two fine lines crossing at right angles, the intersection of the lines is aimed at the target.

CRESTING – Painted colored bands applied to the arrow shaft in front of the fletching used for unique identification of arrows.

CROSSBOW – A bow mounted horizontally on a stock with a triggering device from braced position. Competition crossbows must be hand chocked. Hunting crossbows use chocking devices because of their heavy draw weight, both recurve and compound limbs are used.

CUT OFF TOOL – adjustable length saw to cut modern arrow shaft material squarely to best fit the arrow point.

DACRON – A synthetic material used to make bowstrings, used on older bow designs that need to stretch upon shooting. Using a no stretch bowstring material on an older bow can damage the older designed bows.

DEAD RELEASE - a release of the bowstring in which the drawing hand stays at the anchor point, as the fingers straighten, no extended tension, called a static release.

DEEP HOOK - gripping the bowstring with three fingers in the first joint of the fingers or even deeper behind the first joint of the fingers.

DECAL – a picture or logo on specially prepared paper or plastic for transferring to metal or glass.

DEFLEX – A deflex bow, when unbraced, is bent toward the bowstring.

DEHYDRATION – condition resulting from excessive loss or restriction of fluid. Should not drink a lot of water 20 minutes before a competition but once you start shooting drink lots of water.

DENTAL FLOSE – A flat waxed linen strip use to clean between the teeth. Used to serve over the bowstring serving to make the arrow nock fit properly. Used to serve over loose bowstring serving to delay proper repair.

DISTANCE MARKERS - marker or line placed on the field or target to indicate the distance from the shooting position and the target.

DIVISIONS – separation in archery competition by age and sex; master, senior, adult and youth in male and female for presentation of awards after a completed tournament.

DOINKERS – A rubber vibration dampener fitted to the ends of stabilizer bars. The stabilizer weights are fitted onto the doinker.

D-LOOP- loop added to the bowstring to accommodate a release aid.

DOMINANT EYE - your stronger eye that automatically aligns objects, It is best to start shooting with your dominant eye, right eye dominant – right handed shooter, left eye dominant – left handed shooter. 10% of right handed and 10% of left handed people are opposite eye dominant.

DOUBLE SCORING - process by which two archers keep score at a target to eliminate errors in scoring.

DINAMIC TILLER - tiller measured at full draw.

DIRECTOR of SHOOTING – (DOS) The official in charge of a FITA archery tournament, controls the timing of ends and flow of the tournament.

DOMINANT EYE - the stronger or dominant eye preferred by archers in sighting at their target.

DRAW – Pulling the bow back to store energy to shoot an arrow. The act of bending the bow limbs by drawing the bowstring to full draw while holding the bow steady on target, never stop pulling even if you're not moving back, build into the follow-through.

DRAW ARM – the arm that draws the bowstring to full draw.

DRAW CHECK – A device fitted to a compound bow so the archer can maintain a consistent draw length. Can be a "clicker" but usually two small blocks, one fitted to each buss cable to block pulling or drawing the bow back. Is a clicker on a recurve bow that the arrow fits under and clicks as the arrow is drawn to anchor.

DRAWING ARM - the arm that pulls back the bowstring to your anchor.

DRAW FORCE LINE - should be a straight line through the point of pressure on the bow handle, the nock of the arrow and the point of the drawing elbow at full draw.

DRAWING HAND – The hand which draws the bowstring back to full draw. Hand which holds the release aid that draws the bowstring back to full draw or into the stops.

DRAW-FORCE LINE – it should be a straight line between the point of pressure on the bow handle (pivot point), the nock of the arrow and the point of the drawing elbow at full draw.

DRAW LENGTH ADJUSTMENT BRACKETS - a pylon mounted near the lower and upper ends of the handle riser used to adjust the draw length on a four-wheel compound bow.

DRAW LENGTH – determined by archer's body structure; distance from your anchor point to the back of the bow at full draw (manufacturer) or distance from your anchor point to the pivot point of the bow at full draw. Because you can break over a compound bow does not mean it is a proper fit for your draw length. It takes an outside view to determine proper body alignment for your draw length.

DRAW WEIGHT - the force required to draw a bow to full draw. Poundage marked on bow a recurve bow is at 28"draw. Recurve and longbow is holding weight at full draw. A compound bow has a peak draw weight and a relaxed holding weight at full draw. NAA has a 60# peak bow weight for their competitions.

DRESS CODE –World & USAA archery has a dress code for all its official championships. Most all other archery organizations do not have a dress code for their competitions just a conduct code.

DRIFT – a natural deflection of an arrow from true flight to the target due to the effect of wind, a poor release or other outside influence.

DRYFIRE - releasing the bowstring from full draw without an arrow, this can damage a bow.

DROP AWAY ARROW REST – device attached to the arrow support that moves or allows the arrow support to drop away as the bowstring is released.

DRAW STOP – a block on each buss cable that meet and stop cable movement for consistent draw length. A module on the eccentric that stops movement as it meets the cable.

DUOFLEX – A bow design which incorporates both deflex and reflex bends.

DURATION of EXERCISE -the work load maintained over a period of time.

DYNAMIC DEFLECTION - the amount of bow limb bend at full draw.

DYNAMIC TENSION - constant pulling of the back and shoulder muscles which allows the archer to remain at a constant full draw without creeping.

EARN – For our effort to have value and take pride in an award, we must earn it with an honest effort to make it worthwhile. Youth should be given a participation award; unless their scores are 1st, 2nd or 3rd over all, trophies to all youth shooters is wrong and confusing to them. It is not earned.

EARS - the recurved extremities of a composite bow limbs.

EAR PLUGS - used to eliminate sound distraction while you are shooting.

ECCENTRIC – a metal or plastic wheel or cam (non-round) that controls the draw length and force draw curve of a compound bow by its shape and turnover, the larger the eccentric the longer the draw length. The turnover of the eccentric causes a decrease in the holding weight of the bow at full draw.

EFAA – English Field Archery Association

EFFICIENCY - in a bow it is the amount of energy output over the energy input expressed as a percentage.

EFFORT – archery should be a pleasant pastime, a diversion to every day life, not a second job. Our effort should be the best we can do with the time we have to put into it. You can try too hard, expect too much too soon and create frustrations, archery's dropout attitude. If you can't have fun at it? You will build confidence and self-discipline over time and effort.

ELECTOMYOGRAPHY - an instrument that records and measures electrical changes in a muscle in use, used in coaching not competition.

ELECTROLYTE – an inorganic salt that, in solution, conducts an electric current, trace element in the human body.

ELEVATION ADJUSTMENT - generally a mechanical sight mounted on the bow so it can be seen through the bow window to aim at a target. Can be lowering or rising to arrow alignment instinctively to hit a target. Can be using the tip of the arrow as a visual reference higher or lower to hit the target. Can be walking the bowstring or walking your face to use the tip of the arrow on the targets center.

ELECTRONIC DEVISE - a sighting devise with a light as the aiming point on the target, cab be a electronic release aid.

END - a specified number of arrows shot before scoring and retrieving, Generally an end has some timing control per shot or per end, different for rounds shot and organizational rules.

END LOOP – the part of the bowstring that fits over the bow limb nocks or cable end tear drops.

ENGLISH ARCHERY – first became an important weapon of war for the English at the Battle of Crecy (1346) and later at Poitiers and Agincourt. From 1330 to 1414, English kings banned all other sports in England because they diverted time from archery practice. A royal decree of 1363 required all Englishmen to practice archery on Sundays and holidays

ETHICS - actions showing respect for our fellow archers and their equipment and the wild game we may hunt, abiding by the right and wrong of actions. Learn and respect the rules and regulations of the different archery organizations in competition. Cheating in any way shows disrespect to yourself, the sport and your competition.

EQUIPMENT LINE – a line 3 meters set behind the shooting line, behind which all archery equipment is to be placed when not in use.

EQUIPMENT RULES – different archery organizations have restrictions on types of archery equipment that is acceptable for their competitions; equipment inspections may be required.

EXCUSE – reason for missing; the wind, the sun, to much noise, to quit, etc. An accuse is never needed for a bad shot, it is easy to shoot a bad shot.

EXECUTION – a sequence of steps from stance to follow-through in the exact same sequence and timing to complete one good shot. Must have self-confidence and discipline to execute one good shot under any condition. The execution of a well-run tournament is enjoyable for all participants.

EXERCISE – any cardiovascular conditioning workout will help, working with free weights is better than machines, cross training helps and flexibility exercises are good but shooting is the only compete workout for archers.

EXPANDABLE BROADHEAD – Imbedded blades in the point's shank that expand when they hit a target, used for better arrow flight when hunting.

EXCELSIOR BALES - white pine material baled similar to a hay bale, used as a target butt for archery. EXTENSION – a variable length sight bar attached to the riser with a mounting block and extends to the sight block.

EYE - the loop of a bowstring which passes over the upper and lower nock on the bow limbs in bracing the bow.

EYE FLINCH - a blinking condition caused by uncertainty as to when to release. wanting to release when the sight is not on the target.

FACE (target) - a non-stretch material in a configuration and size for the archery round to be shoot.

FACE of BOW - the surface or side of the bow facing towards the bowstring, also called belly of the bow.

FACETTES - the little surfaces left by chipping out a stone arrowhead.

FACEWALKING - a technique used in barebow or instinctive shooting involving raising and lowering the anchor point to adjust to the distance being shoot.

FADEOUT - the tip of the bow limb where the bowstring touches the bow limb at rest.

FAIRPLAY – honorable treatment, fare action or conduct during a competition or any situation when you represent archery in a public arena.

FAST – a cry of warning, hold fast to the string and come down. Sometimes about arrow speed, that bow is fast.

FASTFLIGHT – A synthetic material used to make bowstrings. A slippery material with very little stretch, that requires a specific serving to be used for newer bow designs. Not to be used on older laminated bows.

FASTFLIGHT S4 – A composite of Polyester 'Spectra' (Fast Flight) and 'Veteran' materials used to make bowstrings. Due to its strength, less strands are required to make a bowstring, so the bowstring is lighter and faster.

FEATHERING (fletching) - the strips of feather at the butt of the arrow, including methods of seizing or fastening.

FEATHERS - generally turkey feathers used for fletching arrows.

FEE – cost to join an archery club or archery organization, cost to enter an archery competition or clinic.

FEEL GOOD SHOT – The one shot where the timing, execution and feeling was all right to you and the arrow hits dead center, try and do it again.

FIBERGLASS – a material used in the lamination of a composite bow limb. A strong arrow shaft used for beginners, very heavy.

FIELD ARCHERY - a standardized competitive round consisting of 14 target unit for NFAA and 12 target unit for FITA field. Designed for varied shooting distances form 20 ft. to 80 yds for NFAA and 10 to 60 Meters for

FITA field. Generally shot in a wooded area, each target is a different distance. Invented in the US by bowhunters in the 1930's. Two units are shot per day for a competition score, takes about 3 hours per unit to shoot. Also see FITA field rules. Was invented because the current archery rounds of the day where not conducive for practice to bowhunt.

FIELD ANCHOR – Anchor on the face at full draw with fingers holding the bowstring at the cheek or the corner of the month, can be split finger or 3 fingers under.

FIELD GLASSES - a magnifying device to see the arrows in the target face to determine score or placement of grouping of arrows: binoculars or telescope.

FIELD POINT – Arrow point shaped with a shoulder to prevent burying in wood or skipping off the ground, good for roving stump shooting.

FIELD RANGE – has three rounds that can be shot; NFAA distances marked, white stake for the field round, red stake for the hunter round and yellow stake for the animal round. FITA distances are marked for the known distance field rounds, unmarked field round and the forest round with red stakes for recurve and compound, blue stakes for barebow. FITA field uses torturous terrain for their course. NFAA has a much more moderate terrain.

FINE TUNING – Minute adjustments of arrow rest, nocking point, tillering, brace height, stabilized weight plus arrow spine tuning.

FILAMENT REINFORCED LIMB - compound bow limb constructed of modern plastic or carbon materials and reinforced with filaments which run the full length of the limb.

FINGER GLOVE - three leather fingers for the drawing hand held by strapping around the wrist or a whole leather glove, to give finger protection and help with a smooth release of the bowstring.

FINGER PROTECTION - any device that relieves the pressure of the bowstring from the drawing fingers: glove, finger tab, release aid and thumb ring.

FINGER RELEASE - the use of one's fingers drawing the bowstring with a finger protection devise such as a tab or glove placed directly over the fingers and on the bowstring for the purpose of drawing and releasing the bowstring at full draw with 2 or 3 fingers. Can be done without finger protection, not recommended.

FINGER SLING - a small strap that attaches the thumb and index or middle finger of the bowhand to support the bow when the bowstring is released.

FINGER TAB - a flat piece of smooth material or layers of material worn on the drawing hand to protect the fingers of the drawing hand and help with a smooth release of the bowstring.

FISH ARROW – solid fiberglass shaft with barbed point and rubber fletching. This arrow needs a braided line attached to the point and through a hole just under the nock to fly to its target at close range.

FISH POINT – a point with a reversible barb and braided line attached for retrieval after the shot.

FISTMELE – The old English term for Brace Height. Putting your fist on the bow handle with your thumb extended, should touch the bowstring of a braced longbow.

FISH TAILING – a side to side movement of the arrow shaft in free flight to the target; many causes. Study of strike pattern of the arrows in the target face can help. Use paper of bare shaft tuning to correct.

FITA –Federation Internationale de Tir a Arc. Affiliated with the IOC as the international governing body for Olympic archery, known as World Archery today. Founded in 1931 in Poland, it has their own archery rounds shot for world championships, web archery.org. called World Archery today.

FITA OUTDOOR – target tournament where men shoot from 90M, 70M, 50M & 30M, women shoot from 70M, 60M, 50M & 30M; shooting 36 arrows from each distance in 6 arrow ends. Is generally shot over two days, also with youth distances.

FITA I – indoor tournament shooting 30 arrows in 3 arrow ends for 18M Championship round is 60 arrows.

FITA II – indoor tournament shooting 30 arrows in 3 arrow ends for 25M.

FIXED PINS – aiming system using fixed straight stock pins, must be pre-set for different distances. Pins can be painted or fiber optic.

FLAKER - the pointed implement of bone, antler, etc. used for shaping flint arrowheads, spearheads, etc. by pressure.

FLAX-LINEN – A natural material used to make bowstrings. Used in medieval times.

FLETCH – to glue a feather or vane onto an arrow shaft, rear drag for stable arrow flight.

FLETCHING - the feather, vanes or other devices attached to the rear of the arrow shaft, which stabilize the arrow in flight.

FLETCHER – A person who in making arrows puts the fletching on the shaft, akin to fleche.

FLETCHING JIG – A device used to hold the arrow shaft and fletching in place for correct location and alignment until fletching is set or dried.

'FLETCH-TITE' – A clear glue used to attach fletching to the arrow shaft. Also used to apply arrow nocks to the shaft.

FLIGHT ARCHERY – competition based entirely on distance with several classes based on bow draw weight, highly specialized tackle.

FLIGHT ARROW – A light weight tapered arrow shaft used in Flight Shooting (for distance only). Mostly carbon shaft about 16" long.

FLIGHT of ARROW - the arched path of the arrow in free flight to its target (trajectory).

FLIGHT BOW – A bow specifically made and used for flight shooting. Usually with a 'shoot through' overdraw arrow rest with short stout limbs.

FLIGHT COMPENSATOR - metal object under the stabilizers that counteracts any fault in the shoot causing torque.

FLEMISH BOWSTRING – (Flemish twist) strands of fiber to make a bowstring with bow wax and a braiding of the strands to form a loop at both ends. The bowstring is stronger at the loops but harder to get the needed bowstring length, pre-stretched.

FLINCH - to move the bow arm or drawing hand before or at the release; usually caused by anticipation of the release (a fear of missing) or poor shooting technique, indecision as to when to release.

FLOATING SHOULDER (rotated shoulder) - shoulder of the bowarm in a relaxed condition will float in and behind the bow which develops loss of control upon release.

FLU- FLU ARROW - an arrow with large feathers or spiraled feathers used for targets thrown in the air or shooting birds. The arrow can only be shot a very short distance due to the wind drag of the feathers. FINGER GLOVE - three leather fingers for the drawing hand held by strapping around the wrist or a whole leather glove, to give finger protection and help with a smooth release of the bowstring.

FOCUSING - a state of mental set, the one pointedness of the mind.

FOLLOW-THROUGH - the reaction and movement of the body and arms as you release the bowstring holding extended tension until the arrow hits it's target. Building a consistent sequence to the shot, to full draw, to release and the follow-through should be automatic and consistent (finishing the shot or conclusion of the shot).

FOLLOW THE STRING - the bow partially retains the shape at full brace when unstring or not braced or strung.

FOOT MARKERS – Lines, golf tees or other devices to indicate the archer's foot positions at the shooting line, should not be to large or high to interfere with other archers moving or walking to and from the target.

FOOTING - a piece of wood inserted in the shaftment of an arrow at the nock end of the arrow.

FORCE DRAW CURVE - the graph created by plotting the draw weight against the draw length for a bow as it is drawn to full draw with a scale.

FORM - the various elements of an archer's shooting style, consistency is the name of the game.

FORM MASTER- training device to apply pressure to the draw elbow after you release the bowstring, holding back tension, adjustable bands, straps or ridged frame.

FORESHAFT - a piece of hard wood, bone, ivory, antler at the front end of a hollow-shafted arrow to give weight and to serve for the attachment of the head or moveable barb, generally of reed or cane.

FORWARD LOOSE – moving the draw hand forward as the bowstring is released (collapse).

FOOTED ARROW SHAFT - an arrow reinforced at the point end of the shaft with a spliced hardwood to a wooden shaft material.

FOUR H – national youth programs in all most every county in every US state which most programs include archery.

FOUR- WHEEL COMPOUND BOW - a compound bow with an eccentric wheel attached to each bow limb tip and an idler wheel attached near the middle of each bow limb with cabled connecting each wheel to the opposite idler and a draw length pylon on the opposite end of the riser.

4 FLETCH – used by bowhunters for easy nocking an arrow, no requirement to have the index fletch placed properly.

FREESTYLE – A method or style of competitive shooting classification using a release aid to drop the bowstring for shooting the arrow, all accessories legal.

FREEZE – Inability to hold the sight on the center of the target at full draw or the inability to release when sight is on the center of the target. Freezing can happen with any system of aiming an arrow at a target. It is a matter of confidence, get closer and try again, until you can hold on the target and shooting at the center work your way back to longer distances.

FREQUENCY of TRAINING - number of training sessions and length per week.

FRUSTRATION – a mental condition that the archer feels he or she has no control over, defeated; an unresolved problem. Archer thinks they are not trying hard enough, when they are trying too hard. Generally caused by target panic, just keep getting closer until you can hold dead center of the target. Changing anything will help your target panic for a short time; go to an open aperture, a clicker, a back tension release.

FULL DRAW - bow arm extended and set with the shoulder alignment square to the target and the bowstring has been drawn to the archer's anchor point for a consistent draw length and follow-through. Full draw is the exact same distance for every shot.

GAA – Georgia Archery Association founded 1995, affiliated with the NAA as a state Olympic archery organization, web – gaarchery.org

GAME ANIMAL - animals legislated by state laws that may be hunted.

GAPPING – a method of aiming off target to allow for distance or alignment to hit the actual target face. Shooting at an imaginary target below the actual target at close range, or shooting at an imaginary target above the actual target at longer distances.

GAP SHOOTING – An aiming technique of pointing or aiming at an imaginary target or aiming spot above or below the actual target to allow for different distances.

GENESIS – technology of a compound bow with no let off, draw weight is the same poundage stored from 15" to 30" draw.

GEORGIA GOLDEN OLYMPICS – non-affiliated archery competition for shooters 50 years of age and over, web – georgiagoldenolympics.org. Affiliated with the National Senior Games that has national competitions held ever 2 years (odd years). Most states have golden Olympic archery.

GLOVE – A shooting glove is a 3-finger covering worn on the string fingers for protection (usually leather) and a smooth release of the bowstring.

GLUCOSE – the form in which sugars are transported in the blood stream for energy to shoot.

GLYCOGEN – the storage form of carbohydrate in man; found in most tissues of the body, in muscular tissue it is converted into glucose.

GOOSE FEATHERS – The feathers of the Grey Goose were used by medieval archers because of their quality (water resistant) and for good arrow flight.

GOLD – The yellow center (bullseye) of the multi- colored target face for target archery, scoring 10 inner or 9 outer. Going for the Gold.

GRAIN – The unit of weighing archery components, points, inserts, etc. An avoirdupois ounce contains 437.5 grains.

GRAND MASTER BOWMAN - archer who has demonstrated superlative shooting ability at the highest level.

GRAND NATIONAL ARCHERY SOCIETY (GNAS) - the governing body of archery throughout the United Kingdom.

GRAFTED BOW - a species of compound bow formed of two pieces joined together at the handle or grip.

GRASS ROOTS – ordinary archers, the origin of interest in modern archery, but they do not support to organized archery.

GRIP – the area to hold the bow, used in reference to holding the bow. Removable custom handle or grip to fit archer's hand. The handle of the bow held by the archer. The act of loosely holding the bow during a shot, the bow hand knuckles should be at 45 degrees to the bow riser with the pressure into the stub of the bow arm. Your bow arm wrist can be low (relaxed), middle (natural) or high (extended). The same term should be applied to the corresponding part of swords, daggers, etc.

GROUND QUIVER – A medal rod with a loop pushed into the ground or set on the ground to hold arrows or a tube held upright for arrows to be placed in readiness to shoot.

GROUPING - a pattern of arrows close together on a target, indication of consistency in shooting. Strike pattern of the group on the target face can tell you of possible shooting errors in your execution.

GAP SHOOTING – gapping or aiming at an imaginary target below the real target for close shots and shooting at an imaginary target above the real target for long shots to allow for the trajectory and flight alignment of the arrow to the target.

GUNBARREL - a method of aiming with the anchor close to the eye and the archer sights down the arrow shaft to the target.

HALL of FAME – NFAA Archery Hall of Fame, plus Archery Hall of Fame (NAA): there are 2 plus other sports hall of fame, plus state sports hall of fame. Most states have their own Sports Hall of Fame.

HANDICAP – a system of handicapping an archer's score by skill level to even comparable competition scores. NFAA leagues use an 80% handicap. That is 80% of the difference between your scratch score and perfect score. A score classification - the number code by which an archer is graded according to scores shot, ability.

HAND GRIP - point of contact of the bow hand and bow.

HANDLE - part of the riser section held by the archer when shooting. A bow handle or grip can be interchangeable; low, medium or high wrist. Some archers do not use a grip on the bow, but hold directly onto the riser section at the handle section designed to hold a grip.

HANDLE RISER – the center section of a one piece bow, the metal section of a takedown bow or compound to which the bow limbs are attached.

HANGER – an arrow that hangs loose across the target face, generally shooting is stopped to score and remove the hanging arrow. If it falls, it can be considered a rebound arrow.

HANGING ARROW - an arrow that has penetrated the target with the tip of the arrow only and hangs down across the target face.

HANGING BOW SCALE – a device to measure the bow's holding weight, at any pulled distance (usually your full draw) to the design of any style bow. You can use scale readings to make a force draw curve graft.

HEAD – point or tip of an arrow, fishing head, broad head, etc.

HEAD POSITION - with an upright balanced stance squire to the target the head should be rotated to look at the target without moving the head to touch the bowstring, pull to your anchor without movement of the head.

HEAD SET - a device to cover the ears for noise reduction.

HANG-BRACKIT (ON A COMPOUND) - a device to hold the eccentrics at the ends of the bow limb extended towards the archer with a cable or string system connecting each eccentric with the axle of the opposite eccentric.

HEAT EXHAUSTION – a failure of the body's cooling system marked by symptoms of extreme prostration.

HEAT STROKE – the end stage of heat exhaustion when sweating stops, get lot to drink and get out of the sun.

HEAVY TACKLE – bow draw weight or peak weight of the compound acceptable for bowhunting. Most US states require a pull of 45# or more to be legal for bowhunting.

HEELING – Exerting pressure with the heel of the bow hand on the lower part of the handle at release of the shot, pressure applied to the handle below the point of balance, arrow goes high.

HELICAL - fletch placement that places fletch at slight offset from straight fletch and places a slight curvature in the fletching from front to back.

HEN FEATHERS (shaft feathers) – the two feathers or fletch not at right angles to the nock on a three fletched arrow shaft.

HEX KEY SET – Allen wrenches to fit and adjust bow peak draw weight and accessories on the bow, arrow rest, sight, etc.

HIT – arrow lodged in the target face after a successful shot to be scored, an arrow lodged in almost anything.

HIGH ANCHOR - an anchor point at full draw touches the cheek or cheek bone with fingers holding the bowstring.

HIGH BREACH HEIGHT – bowstring too short, loss of power stroke. You lose speed but gain stability.

HIGH WRIST - top of the bow hand wrist in line with the top of the bowhand, pressure flows through the "V" of the thumb and forefinger and bones of the hand into the wrist.

HISTORY FITA (first) - Michal Sawicki - champion 1931 (Poland) only one classification Aug. 1931 Lwow, Poland

HISTORY NAA (first) - Mr. W. H. Thompson, male champion, Mrs. Spalding Brown, female champion Aug. 1879 Chicago

HISTORY PRO (first) - target event - Russ B. Hoogerhyde champion, Minerva Lanzer champion June 1940 Milwaukee - field event - Howard Hill champion, Mrs. Henry A. Bitzenburger champion same year.

HOBBY – pursuing a relaxing activity that you are interested in. Can be serious taking up a lot of time or pursuing your shooting when you can.

HOLDING - maintaining the aim and draw before release or loosing the bowstring.

HOLDING WEIGHT - force exerted to hold full draw. Recurve and longbow is maximum holding weight at full draw. A compound holding weight is 65% to 80% reduction of peak weight.

HUNTING ARROW - an arrow used for hunting game with a blunt or broadhead to harvest legal game.

HUNTING BOW – a bow made and set up especially for bowhunting game. A bow with a heavy draw weight for humane harvesting of game, 45# minimum draw weight.

HUNTING WEIGHT - draw weight sufficient to shoot a heavy hunting arrow to penetrate and harvest wild game humanely; a minimum of 45 lbs. is required in most US states.

HORNS - the ends of a bow called ears.

HYPERTENSION - a condition arising from competitive shooting, usually causing an adrenaline flow throughout the body, possibly a sweating condition.

IBEF – International Bowhunter Education Foundation, formed from NFAA Bowhunter Education program.

IBO – International Bowhunters Organization – a 3-D archery organization, web ibo.net

IDLER WHEEL – a metal wheel mounted to control the movement and alignment of the cable system of a compound bow.

IFAA – International Field Archery Association, original NFAA field archery under an international archery organization formed in the late 1960's.

IMAGE – Outside or individual's perception of our sport. Uninformed people think archery is dangerous? One who does not win thinks they were cheated? You may think the judge was not fair? Archery is a lot of fun?

IMAGERY – a mental process of thinking about shooting form, shooting in a tournament under certain conditions, that last arrow to shoot your best score ever; practicing in the mind. Existing only in the imagination, not real.

INDIVIDUAL – every archer in archery. Individual memberships make up an organization. Grass roots archery is built one archer at a time. Do not try to convert archers, promote archery to new ones.

INDEX – a raised ridge of plastic on the arrow nock that is in line with the index fletch. Since the nock index is in line with the index flitch, the archer can feel it and thus position the arrow correctly on the bowstring without looking. The fletching that is set at a right angle to the slot in the arrow nock.

INDEX FLETCHING (cock feather) – The feather or vane set at right angles to the slot of the arrow nock, also called the cock feather.

INDOOR ARCHERY – self explanatory; indoor rounds are shot under FITA, IFAA and NFAA rules and regulations for local leagues to world championships.

INSTABILITY - in a bow, exaggerates small errors in shooting form, causing them to become a major fault in the shot. usually an unstable bow is in poor setup or poor use of accessories.

INSTRUCTOR – one who teaches what they know to others about shooting archery. One who is certified by an organization that they have proven a certain level of knowledge about teaching archery. You do not have to be certified to teach a sport you love.

INSTINCTIVE SHOOTING – shooting an arrow instinctively without the aid of a mechanical aiming device or point of aim method. usually it is more learning through practice, no sighting method.

INTENSITY of TRAINING - the work level at which an exercise is performed, the number of foot pounds of work per minute expanded in an exercise.

IOC – International Olympic Committee, web Olympic.org.

ISHI – the lone survivor of the Yana tribe of Indians (1911). Ishi strongly influenced the archery of Dr. Saxton Pope.

INTERNATIONAL ROUND – NFAA outdoor round shooting 30 arrows in 3 arrow ends from 20 yds to 65 yds scoring 5, 4 & 3, perfect 150 points. 2 rounds shoot for a competition. Was originally the PAA (Professional Archery Association) round in the 1960's.

JERKING - body movement at release, pulling fingers off the bowstring and stretching in the shoulders effecting the bow arm, trying to help the shot. Let the bow do its job.

JIG - a device for gluing feathers on the arrow shaft, same label is given to the device that makes bowstring.

JOAD – (indoor & outdoor) NAA youth program to promote Olympic style archery founded around the first re-introduction of archery in the Olympic Games. The Junior Olympic Archery Development program included the compound bow in 1995.

JOB – a full time effort. Obsessed with improving one's score, just do the best you can. Not a hobby! Generally a short lived archer.

JOINTED BOW - a two piece bow joined at the middle.

JUDO POINT – An arrow point fitted with spring-loaded wire prongs that will catch on grass or scrub and stops the arrow quickly. Used for hunting small game bowhunting.

JUDGE – a trained official who enforces the rules and regulations of an archery organization in tournaments or competitions. Respect for the job has to be earned. There are different levels of experience; Judge Candidate, Regional Judge, National Judge and FITA Judge. The NFAA has no judges program.

JUMPING THE STRING – Sometimes when an animal hears the twang of the bowstring, they often make a quick, instinctive move; sometimes evading the arrow by chance.

KICK – the recoil of the bowstring and/or bow as the arrow is released, related mostly to longbows.

KICKING - conditioned reflex in the bow arm upon release, you release the bowstring when sighting off center you kick the bow arm towards the center of the target.

KINETIC ENERGY - the product of force over a distance of action, producing a motion that (without friction) is called kinetic energy.

KISSER BUTTON – An indicator or protrusion or disc placed on the bowstring above the nocking point as an additional anchor point reference. Touches the archer's lips, tooth or nose at full draw, usually made of plastic.

KNEE - junction between siyah and working limb on a composite bow.

KYUDO – First practiced in Japan, a ceremonial style of archery, involving Zen meditation to 'become one with the bow'.

KYUDO ARROWS – Traditional arrows used in Kyudo archery, over 1 meter in length, fletched with traditional feathers.

KYUDO BOW – A Japanese longbow, approx. 79 inches long. The 'grip' is about one third distance from the bottom tip of the bow. The bowstring is drawn using a shooting glove fitted with a thumb groove for the bowstring to sit in. The drawing hand is pulled back until over the rear shoulder and the bowstring is released by relaxing the thumb, allowing the bowstring to slip out of the groove.

LACTIC ACID - an acetic build up in the cells and muscle fibers usually developing after prolonged strain, causing aching and soreness,

LADY PARAMOUNT – originally the patroness of an archery meeting, today it is the lady invited to present the awards or is in charge of a tournament.

LAMINATED BOW or BOW - a bow or bow limbs made of several layers of different material glued together, a hardwood or artificial core reinforced with fiberglass and/or carbon.

LAMINATED LIMBS – a bow limb made of several layers of different material, a hardwood or artificial core reinforced with fiberglass or carbon.

LAUNCHER – a style of arrow rest used extensively on compound bows for release shooters that suspends the arrow on top of the launcher for better arrow clearance, angle and/or strength of launcher varies.

LEAGUE – (indoor and outdoor) Comparing scores and competing on a point system by individuals and/or teams (with varying number of team members) on a weekly basis. Number of weeks determined by rotation of team competition, each team should compete against every other team at least once. Round to be shot for the league is up to the shooters or club running it. Mail-in leagues are very popular.

LEFT-HANDED ARCHER – An archer who holds the bow in the right hand and draws with the left hand to anchor under the dominant eye. Harder to find is a left-handed bow. Some left eye dominant shooters, shoot right handed with a patch over the left eye.

LEFT-HANDED BOW – a bow with the sight window cut out on the right side of the bow riser for better arrow clearance while shooting.

LESSIONS – formal or informal training in the use of archery equipment. You can gain the knowledge need on your own, but it is best to contact one of the national archery organizations for locations of their affiliated archery clubs.

LET DOWN - returning from full draw to the undrawn position with control without releasing the bowstring, not shooting a bad shot starting over from the beginning, sometimes even putting the arrow back in the quiver.

LET-OFF - the reduction from peak draw weight to holding weight at full draw, the holding weight of a compound bow at full draw.

LEVEL – a glass level bubble fitted in the bow sight or on the bow to determine vertical holding of the bow while shooting an arrow. Not legal in FITA recurve competition.

LIFE SPORT – sport capable of participating in at almost any age; 6 to 90 yrs. of age. Almost anyone can shoot archery with today's equipment. Must be old enough to have hand eye coordination to learn proper control and consistency. Oldest archer NSG 2001 was 101 yrs of age.

LINE GUAGE – clip on device to determine string alignment to bisect bow limbs and riser with the bowstring to align the arrow rest.

LINE JUDGE – official stationed at the shooting line of target tournaments to control rules or infractions of rules, correct scoring errors and help shooters with the flow of the tournament, equipment failure, rebound arrow, etc.

LINE of MAXIMUM LEVERAGE - a straight line drawn from the axle of an eccentric wheel or cam through the center of the wheel or cam on the opposite side.

LIMB - one of the arms of a bow from riser to tip, the part of the bow that stores usable energy for propelling an arrow. The parts of a bow above and below the handle or grip.

LIMB DAMPENERS – A rubber device shaped like a mushroom attached to the bow limbs to reduce the vibration in the limbs at the time of a shot.

LIMB POCKET – a recessed slot in the top and bottom of the riser, shaped to fit the ends of the bow limbs. This secures the limbs and maintains correct limb alignment when the bow is braced.

LIMB TWIST – A failure of the bow limbs to stay aligned with the bowstring. Limb twist to one side or the other, you can see the bowstring is not aligned with the bow limbs. Not fatal (bow usable) unless the bowstring slips off the bow limb while shooting.

LIVE RELEASE - release style that allows drawing hand to slide back along the side of the neck in a follow-through, also called the flying release.

LOADED BOW – a bow with an arrow on the bowstring ready to shoot.

LONGBOW - straight limb design of a bow; traditional (one piece or self); modern laminated or take down. Self-bow (made of one piece of wood), tradition of the old English bows. A traditional English or Welsh bow design. Considered traditional archery, wood on wood (wood bow and wood arrows).

LOOP – the served loops at the end of the bowstring that fits in the bow limb nocks to string or brace the bow.

LOOSE - to release the bowstring to propel an arrow. A command given to archers to release the bowstring, usually in battles. The act of letting the bowstring slip from your drawing fingers.

LOOSE ANCHOR - using few reference points on the face to anchor the fingers holding the bowstring, doesn't even touch the face.

LOVE OF ARCHERY – to some it is shooting a good score, to some it is just enjoying shooting and to some it is helping others enjoy shooting. Which are you?

LOW BREACH HEIGHT – bowstring too long, bowstring hits your wrist as you shoot. This increases of power stroke of the bow. The arrow is on the bowstring for a slightly longer time. Gain speed and lose stability.

LOW WRIST - bow hand is placed flat against the bow handle or grip, with pressure of the bow flowing directly into the forearm bone.

MAGAZINE – a periodical publication that typically contains essays, stories and illustrations. Most archery magazines are bi-monthly. You receive a subscription with a membership to the NFAA, which is their official publication.

MARK - the object which the archer intends to hit.

MASS WEIGHT – the actual physical weight of the bow and accessories in hand shooting, actual physical weight of a completed arrow.

MATCH - a competitive archery event, sometimes by mail.

MATCH ARROWS - arrows with same spine with same color nocks, fletching and any cresting plus same weight points, matched set.

MATT – A circular disc of woven straw that holds the target and stops the arrows for scoring.

MARKER (stake) – visual location for the distance to be shot at a target face, can be a known or unknown distance.

MASTER – divisions of competition; NAA masters start at age 50, NFAA masters start at 65 yrs of age.

MASTER EYE - the stronger eye should be used to determine right or left handed shooting of the bow, eye dominance.

MATCHED SET - 1. Arrows: consistency of length, nocks, points, fletching and spine for all arrows used by one archer. 2. Arrow to Bow: proper spine matched to the bow's draw or holding weight and the archer's draw length.

MEMBERSHIP – has some restrictions before one is accepted as a member and after membership completes an application and all fees are paid; honorary, life, family, patron, adult and/or youth memberships. You are the organization get involved.

MENTAL FOCUS - concentration on each step of your shot sequence until the arrow hits the target.

MENTAL IMAGERY - the ability to develop an image from experience to study the execution of the shot in your mind.

MENTAL REHEARSAL - the active studying of a series of images.

METHOD – a system shooting point of aim, string walking, fixed pins, unlimited, Olympic, etc.

MICRO HOLE LENSE - glasses with micro holes placed to visually aid in aiming an arrow to the target, can be corrective or plain lenses.

MIDNOCK - a nock tapered down from the nock grove to the base of the nock, giving a smother release from the bowstring.

MINNOWING – Erratic arrow flight leaving the bow to the target. Needs basic tuning, not necessarily fine tuning, but basic tuning can help.

MINOCKING - arrow nock not fully on the bowstring, arrow falling form the bowstring to the ground upon release.

MIS-NOCKED - the arrow falls out of the bow at full draw on the release of the bowstring, this occurs when the bowstring is not all the way in the nock of the arrow. If you let up and draw back again sometimes the arrow nock is dislodged.

MISS – An arrow not scoring, marked on the score card as 0, - or M; not with X.

MODULE – an interchangeable metal plate attached to the eccentric that can vary draw length, a metal plate attached to the eccentric to act as a draw check.

MONGOLIAN LOOSE - the loose used by Asiatic archers where the thumb is hooked around the bowstring, thumb ring.

MOUNTING BLOCK – sight block that slides or screws up and down a sight bar with sight apertures attached to it.

MULTIPLE DRAW ECCENTRIC - an eccentric wheel or cam with two or more slots or pages into which the cable or string can be placed in order to generate different draw lengths.

MUSCULAR ENDURANCE - the ability to repeat muscular contractions.

MUSCULAR STRENGTH - the maximal amount of force that can be exerted for one repetition.

NAA – National Archery Association founded in 1879, today US Archery Association USAA, affiliated with USOC & FITA (today WORLD ARCHERY), the USAA is the NGB (National Governing Body) for Olympic archery.

NAA AMERICAN 900 – target round shooting 90 arrows in 6 arrow ends shooting 60M (30 arrows), 50M (30 arrows) and 40M (30 arrows) scoring 10, 9, 8, 7, 6, 5, 4, 3, 2 & 1, perfect 900 points, takes about 3 ½ hours for a competition.

NADA – National Alliance for the Development of Archery, discontinued 2013.

NASP – National Archery in the Schools Program started around 2000 not active today.

NATURAL STANCE - the position of the feet that allows the archer to come to full draw and aim without bow arm movement with the body balanced until the shot is complete. This stance will allow the raising of the bow arm aligned directly on the center of the target.

NCAA ARCHERY – 27 colleges are affiliated with the NAA to compete in their collage division for NCAA archery titles: champion or all-American.

NEWSLETTER – a written report issued periodically by a club or organization to disseminate updated information to its membership.

NFAA – National Field Archery Association, founded 1939, affiliated with IFAA. An original American archery rounds, field archery shot in yards.

NFAA BOWHUNTING – Art Young game awards to recognize success in hunting with the bow & arrow. Has a land owner agreement and promote fair chase respecting all hunting seasons and conservation.

NFAA FREEMAN ROUND – indoor round shooting 60 arrows in 12 five arrow ends scoring 5, 4, 3, 2 & 1 from 10 yds, 15 yds and 20 yds, perfect 300 points, see NFAA rules.

NFAA INDOOR – indoor round shot from 20 yds with 60 arrows shot in 12 five arrow ends scoring 5, 4, 3, 2 & 1, perfect 300 points.

NFAA 300 FIELD – field shooting 15 target units scoring 5, 4 & 3 in 4 arrow ends, perfect 300 points, web nfaa-archery.org

NOCK - 1.the end of the arrow with a notch in it for fitting onto the bowstring, never to tight or to loose. 2. the grooves in the tips of the limbs of a bow to fit the bowstring for bracing the bow. 3. the act of fitting an arrow onto the bowstring.

NOCK END REPAIR TOOL – smoothes dents and cracks at the tapered end of the arrow shaft where the nock fits.

NOCK LOCATOR – (nock set) a mark or device that indicates where the arrow is placed on the bowstring for each shot.

NOCKING - placing the arrow on the bowstring preparatory to shooting.

NOCKING PLIERS – a device used to attach or move the nock locator on the bowstring.

NOCKING POINT – a consistent place on the bowstring where the arrow is nocked or placed on the bowstring before each shot. Often whipped with dental floss or a nock set, sometimes just a ink mark.

NOCKING POINT HEIGHT - where to properly nock your arrow, the distance the nock locater is placed above square (90 degrees) on the bowstring.

NOCK SET – (nock locator) a small brass attachment or small serving point added to the bowstring to locate the nocking point.

NON-PROFIT – IRS 501-c3 for tax exempt status.

NOOSE- the end of a bowstring which occupies the lower horn of a bow.

NOSE MARKER - a raised location on the bowstring that can be felt on the nose to aid in establishing an anchor point.

NOVELTY ROUND – almost anything you can think up, that is safe; from shooting balloons, tic/tac/toe, or playing poker, etc.

NSGS – National Senior Games Association, web nationalseniorgames.org

NYLON MESH BACKSTOP - nylon material or nylon mesh hung in back of target butts to stop missed arrows.

OBLIQUE STANCE - the positioning of the feet in a 45 degree angle towards the target. the toe of the foot closest to the target is open to point directly toward the target while the rear foot is kept at a 90 degree angle to the target. the feet are under the shoulders and knees are locked.

OFFICIAL – someone in authority to make decisions on infractions of rules and regulations or decisions on arrow's score value in dispute during an archery tournament. Generally appointed and elected not always experienced or trained.

OLYMPIC ARCHERY - reestablished as permanent competitive event in 1972. Was dropped from the Olympic competition in 1920.

OPEN STANCE – the position of the archer's feet at the shooting line that opens the front of the archer to the target. The front foot of the archer is behind an imaginary line extended from the archer's back foot to the center of the target being shot.

ORGANIZATIONS – governmental archery structures to promote their form of archery on a national and world level. Sometimes seems they are self involved and not interested in archery as a whole. You cannot force an archer to join or support your group. An organization must prove it is responsible to earn your support. You are the organization, it you do not like something, get involved and change from within.

OVER ARROWS - arrows shot over the center of the mark and beyond the target.

OVERBOWED – using a bow with a stronger draw weight than the archer can comfortably handle or shoot with proper shooting form.

OVERBRACED - a bow being braced higher than intended by the bowyer.

OVERDRAW - designed to place the arrow rest closer to the archer to be able to use a shorter arrow, less weight, more speed. Can be added to most bows; must have fall off protective shelf - also increases effect of bow torque. Drawing the bowstring further than the bowyer designed the bow for.

OVERDRAWING - drawing the arrow clear past the arrow rest, drawing the bowstring further than the bowyer intended, drawing past your anchor point at the face.

OUTDOOR ARCHERY – Many archery rounds developed over 400 years in many countries for the enjoyment of testing archers' skill with the bow & arrow. Too many to list; but are shot under FITA, NAA, ASA, IBO, IFAA & NFAA rules and regulations.

OVERHAND - shooting overhand is to shoot at the mark over the bowhand, when the head of the arrow is drawn to full draw, system of aiming.

OVERSHOOT - a shoot above and beyond the target.

OVERSTRUNG - a bowstring to short for the bow, bowstring height is thus too great.

PAA – Professional Archers Association founded in 1961, faded out in the late 1980's.

PACKING - leather, snake skin, fish skin or other soft substance used in binding the nocks and the grip of the bow.

PAPER PUNCHERS – archers that enjoy shooting archery rounds that use paper target face for scoring. Name given to tournament archers by bowhunters.

PAPER TUNE – a frame that hold a piece of paper tight so you get a clean tear when you shoot an arrow through the paper into a butt. The tear can be read as to how the arrow is flying. A clean hole with fletching tears is desirable for compound and release aid, by adjusting the nocking point; arrow rest alignment and bow draw weight. With a recurve bow and finger release you don't want or need a clean tear, you want to shoot a good group in the target.

PARADOX – Archer's paradox is a series of diminishing bends of the arrow shaft as it straightens out in flight. The paradox or flex helps clearance for consistent arrow flight.

PARILYMPIC ARCHERY - held two weeks after the Olympic Game at the same venue.

PASS THROUGH - an arrow that is not held by the target butt, passing completely through the target butt.

PATCH – an organizational emblem or club logo of cloth sewn on a shirt, jacket, cap, etc.

PBS – Professional Bowhunters Society

PEAK WEIGHT - a maximum draw weight of a compound bow (about 2/3 of draw length) before reaching full draw to a reduced holding weight. Peak draw weight is at full draw for recurve and longbow.

PEEK – the movement of the head or bowarm in order to see the arrow in flight or where the arrow hits the target after release, body movement is the result, not good.

PEEP SIGHT – Plastic or medal structure with a hole drilled in it and is mounted in the bowstring above the nocking of the arrow to be used as a rear sight for alignment. Needs to be mounted to your shooting form and anchor, not just placed in the bowstring. (sometimes called peep hole)

PENDULUM SIGHT - a hunting sight that adjusts automatically to any angle of the bow when shooting.

PENDULUM SIGHT – a bow sight that moves to stay level as the bow elevation is moved up or down. Designed to use from a tree stand to eliminate multiple sight pins.

PERFECT END - an end shoot in which all arrows land or hit in the highest scoring area on the target.

PETTICOAT – any part of the target face outside of the scoring area. An arrow stuck in the petticoat is scored as a miss. Some older target faces tied onto the target butt with a cloth petticoat attached to wraparound the target butt.

PIECED (arrow) - an arrow of two or more pieces to obtain proper length.

PHYSICAL FITNESS - the basic components of fitness are muscular strength, muscular endurance, flexibility, body composition and cardiovascular fitness.

PILE – a metal tip of an arrow, head of the arrow; any arrowhead may bear the same name, in which case we have a one-pile arrow.

PINCHING – the squeezing of the index and middle fingers of the drawing hand against the arrow nock during the draw and release.

PINCH NOCK - arrow nock with to narrow of a slot for the bowstring, a arrow nock with a narrow slot that widens into a circle at the base of the slot.

PIN SIGHT - a bow sight that makes use of the head of a pin or facsimile to aim with on the target.

PINWHEEL - the dead center of the target.

PITCHING TOOL - knapping tool, a column of antler or other hard substance, used between the hammer and the core in knocking off flakes of stone for an arrow pile.

PIVOT POINT – Contact point between the hand/arm pressure spot and the bows grip or handle. Center of all torque created during the shot.

POINT of AIM - aiming with the point of the arrow, referring the point as a visual reference for elevation, aiming point, not necessarily on the target face.

POINT - a unit of scoring. Highest total points will win an award. Some tournaments keep track of X ring hits to be used to break tied scores. Tip of the arrow.

POINT ON - the distance from a target at which the point of the arrow is centered on the bullseye, corresponds to the arc of the arrow for elevation at that distance.

POKER - a rod projecting from the bow as a form of stabilizer.

POPINJAY - shooting at an artificial bird arranged on a perch at the top of a mast.

PORPOISING - caused by incorrect nocking point location.

POWER TEST - the use of a white spray powder on the fletched end of an arrow or white spray powder on the riser and arrow rest to determine any contact between fletching, arrow rest or riser as the arrow passes into free flight.

PRACTICE BOW - a light draw weight bow used for teaching beginners archery, a bow with a heaver draw weight then normal for pulling to build strength.

PREP LINE - the desirably straight line before drawing of forearm and shaft to full draw, at anchor.

PRESSURE POINT - the spot on the arrow rest or bow shelf plate against which the arrow lies and presses when the bowstring is released.

PRE-GAP - a method of aiming where the aim is established prior to the draw.

PRIORITY – most important, to work on the skills needed to learn and improve along with the proper use of equipment for better arrow flight to improve our best effort in consistency. Setting small goals to show levels of improvement, working towards larger goals for motivation.

PRO SHOP - commercial archery shop where archery equipment may be rented or purchased, some have indoor lanes to practice.

PIVOT POINT – the contact or pressure point of the hand on the bow grip, center of rotation axes of three movements of torque. Arrow rest should be mounted directly above the pivot point.

PLUNGER BUTTON – a spring loaded pressure button mounted in the sight window of the riser so the arrow lies at its center to absorb and compensate for the archer's paradox as the arrow leaves the bow.

PLUCK - pulling the fingers off the bowstring, letting the draw hand move away from the face, generally causes bowarm movement and the bowstring can slip the bow arm.

PLUM – the vertical alignment of the bow when shooting, straight up and down. The vertical alignment of the sight bar in relationship to the bowstring.

POINT – a unit of scoring. Highest total points will win an award, some tournaments keep track of X ring hits to be used to break tied scores, tip of the arrow.

POINT BLANK – a short distance where you could point straight at your target, a close target.

POINT of AIM - system of using the point of the arrow on a visual reference to adjust for arrow trajectory to hit a target, below the target at close range and above the target for shots farther out.

POINT ON – distance where the elevation of the bow places the point of the arrow visually on the center of the target face to hit the target with a good shot.

POPE & YOUNG CLUB – bowhunting organization that keeps records of trophy big game taken with the bow & arrow under the rules of fair chase.

POOR LOSER – someone who blames their equipment or others for a poor score in competition. One who gets mad at self because his or her score did not win the tournament. There is only one thing worse than a poor loser is a poor winner, bragging they are the best and putting others down.

PORPOISE - up and down behavior of an arrow in flight, nocking point needs adjusting.

POST SIGHT - a type of bowsight that makes use of a device that projects at a right angle downward or upward from the mount, the tip of which is held on the target for aiming on the target.

POTENTIAL ENERGY - the loading of an elastic object which stores energy applied within it, this energy is said to be potential energy.

POUNDAGE – amount of pressure to draw a bow back or to full draw. Draw weight of a bow.

PRACTICE - time used to perfect technique in shooting and tuning of equipment for improved arrow flight and building confidence in shot execution, work on one thing at a time. Just shooting to perfect bad habits takes a long time. You must learn self-discipline to practice regularly.

PRE-AIM - a method of placing the bow, point of arrow or sight pin at an aiming position (on target) just before you reach anchor and full draw. Refine aiming as you pull into your anchor and full draw.

PRECEPTION – a possible image or conclusion perceived by others. Judges must be perceived as fair. Clicks should not be perceived within an archery club. The image of self-promotion is detrimental to unity of any group, etc.

PREGAME MEAL – should be 2 or 3 hours before the event for competition.

PRE-GAP – a method of pre-aiming to establish approximate aiming location of the bow arm before reaching full draw.

PREPARATION – design a training routine for you and your equipment to peak at a major competition, you must know yourself and what to improve on, you must be prepared to do your best.

PRESSURE - stress, shooting a tournament, worry about score, thinking about winning; just not concentrating. All pressure comes from within, see concentration.

PRESSURE POINT- that spot on the arrow plate against which the arrow is pushed at the instant of release, also in the bowhead.

PRIDE – a feeling of gratification or accomplishment, must be earned.

PRISM - a sighting devise of glass that refracts the sight image so as not to lower the sight to aim at the target, available in various degrees of refraction.

PROFESSIONAL – one who shoots for money. NAA has no Professional Division; NFAA has a Professional Division, ASA has a Professional Division and IBO has a Professional Division.

PROMOTER – there are many dedicated archers who represent our sport with dignity and positive image. Every archer should be a promoter of our sport, it is time consuming.

PROTOCOL – traditional customs, regulations, precedence and etiquette to host and run an archery tournament or activities.

PUBLICATION – brochure is a pamphlet or leaflet to bring before the public an announcement. Advertise your invitational tournament schedule and club activities.

PULL - act of removing arrows from a target and butt.

PULLING - to remove the arrows from the target after scoring, or to shoot a another end.

PULL WEIGHT - the number of pounds required to draw a bow to full draw, generally 28". Ascertained by suspending the bow at its grip and drawing with a spring scale.

PUSHING the BOW - the act of moving the bow toward and usually to the right side of the target during the act of releasing the bowstring and follow-through.

PUSH-PULL METHOD - method of shooting whereby the bow arm is pushed forward toward the target and the release arm is pulled back through a combination of muscles in the back and shoulder structure.

PYKING (BOW LIMB) - recurving of bow limb tips away from the archer. generally a steaming of the wood bow limbs.

QUARREL – a crossbow bolt.

QUICK DISCONNECT – device that mounts in the riser and connects the center stabilizer with a twist.

QUIVER - a device to hold and carry arrows and some accessories. Varying forms are back, belt, bow and ground quivers.

RANGE - a location or course for shooting archery safely, for tournaments or practice. A designation for the shooting different distances or rounds.

RANGE FINDER – a device used to measure the distance from the archer to his target, helps in relocating the sight pin to aim properly for that distance.

REBOUND – an arrow that bounces off the scoring area of a target face.

RECURVE BOW – a bow that uses recurve limbs of different degrees. One-piece recurve laminated bow with large beautiful riser sections, a take down recurve bow, shorting the working part of the bow limb and acting as levers to help cast to the arrow..

RECURVE LIMB – the end of the bow limbs that bend or curve away from the archer when shot and uncoil as drawn to create a double hinge in the bow limbs that store energy.

REINFORCEMENT - splints of a rigid material built into a composite (compound) or sinew backed bow.

REFERENCE SHAFT CHART – computer calculated shaft size selection chart, to determine proper shaft size for best arrow flight by using type of bow, peak draw weight of the bow and the archer's draw length, 90 % accurate.

REFLECTIVE TRAIL TACKS – tacks that are placed on a trail to and from a hunting location that glow when hit by a light and can be followed safely in and out in the dark.

REFLEX – A reflex bow, when unbraced is curved away from the bowstring.

REFLEXED - the bow reverses itself to some extent when unstrung or relaxed, the opposite of following the bowstring.

REINFORCEMENTS - Fiberglass or carbon to laminate bow limbs, splints of a rigid material build into a compound or sinew-backed bow.

RELAXED - the bow when it is unstrung and at rest.

RELAXATION at FULL DRAW - no more muscle tension used then is needed to control the shot sequence until the arrow is in the target.

RELEASE - 1.the act of letting the bowstring leave the fingers. 2. a mechanical device used to let go of the bowstring, loose the arrow. You should never have to think about the release, concentrate on aiming and the release should happen when everything is right. (historical) 1) Primary release, thumb and first joint of forefinger pinching the arrow nock. 2) secondary, thumb and second joint of forefinger, middle finger also on the bowstring. 3) tertiary, thumb and three fingers on the bowstring. 4) Mediterranean, index, middle and ring fingers on the bowstring. 5) Mongolian, thumb on the bowstring with or without a thumb ring.

RELEASE AID – a mechanical device hand held for releasing the bowstring, which is temporarily attached to the bowstring and used to draw and release the bowstring. Wrist held release aid using index finger to trigger the releasing of the bowstring. Hand held release aid, can be triggered with thumb or pinky; hand held release aid can be a back tension release by hand rotation alone through just pulling.

RESPONSIBILITY – of actions; a burden of obligation, chargeable with being the source, reliable and dependable.

RETRIEVE – to return with your arrows after scoring. Hold target face and place hand as close to the target on the shaft and pull straight out. Arrow in the grass when found should be pulled back out the way it went in. Arrow in wood or a tree should be rotated slowly at the base of the shaft, sometimes a screwdriver driven into the wood near the base of the shaft will relieve pressure on the shaft.

RETRIEVING ARROW (barbed arrow) - one with a barbed head designed for retrieving fish or burrowing game.

RETURN CABLE - the length of cable or string which attaches a eccentric to the axle of the opposite bow limb.

RIBAND - a term applied to the stripes painted on the arrow shafts. (historical) ribands have been called clan marks, owner marks, game tallies.

RIGHT-HANDED ARCHER – an archer who holds the bow in the left hand and draws the bowstring with the right hand to bring the bowstring back to the anchor point.

RIGHT-HANDED BOW - a bow with the sight window cut out on the left side of the bow riser for better arrow clearance while shooting.

RING SIGHT - a circular pin or hood is used to aim with, the internal pin is removed to aim at the target, open aperture in sighting on the target.

RISER - the center section of a takedown bow, generally wood or metal.

ROBIN HOOD – a term given when a second arrow shot embeds into an arrow already in the target face, arrows are end to end: NFAA award if lodged in the bullseye during a tournament. A bandit archer of legend who lived in Sherwood Forest, near Nottingham, UK. Said to have unsurpassed skill with the bow & arrow. Also robbed the rich and gave to the poor.

ROUND - a defined structure of course and # of arrows: determined number of arrows at a specified target face or faces for a determined score value on a prescribed course or target from set distances for standard competition. A 3-D round has no standard distance for target size. "Rounds" are given names, usually of the towns or cities, in the country of origin or total score.

ROVING – the predecessor of modern field archery. Grew out of casual hunting, targets in the woods of various shapes and sizes, simulating small game, were chosen and shot at by a small group of bowhunters at unknown ranges over rough ground.

ROYAL TOXOPHOLITE SOCIETY – archery club formed in 1787 under the patronage of the Prince of Wales (later George IV).

RULES – a principle or regulation governing conduct and procedure for an archery competition, dependent on sanctioning archery organization.

SCI – Safari Club International

SAFETY - a non-dangerous condition required for an enjoyable outing, mostly common sense.

SAFETY AREA - area around a archery range designated off limits during any shooting.

SAFELY BELT – a harness and/or safety strip used in a tree stand.

SCHOLARSHIP FUND – both NAA & NFAA have scholarship funds that you may contribute to and apply for school monies.

SCOPE – target: telescope with tripod or binoculars to view arrows in the target face. Field/3-D: carrying binoculars to view arrows in the target face.

SCORING - the value of an arrow hitting a target face with divided line with value, an arrow touching a dividing line shall count the higher value.

SCORING AREA - that part of the target face made up of scoring rings.

SCORE CARD – card with places to record value of arrows that are embedded in the scoring area of a target face, cards are distinct to the round being shot.

SCOUTS – both boy and girl scouts promote archery merit awards.

SCRITCH – leave a tournament before it is over, quit or not show up.

SEFIN - see, Thumb ring

SELECTIVE ATTENTION - what a person chooses to concentrate on.

SELF – to make an effort for yourself, learn something new. Learning self-confidence in your effort and improvement. Learn commitment and structure to follow the rules and compete. The only opinion that counts is yours.

SELF ARROW - an arrow made entirely of one piece of wood.

SELF CONFIDENCE – faith in your ability to perform, to do your best under any condition.

SELF BOW - a bow made of one piece of material, usually wood but also possibly steel, aluminum or fiberglass, as compared with a composite bow.

SELF DISIPLINE – the training of one's self to improve, a discipline to schedule practice. To learn your capability and limits, know your routine and timing to peak performance.

SELF RESPECT – proper esteem or regard for the dignity of one's character. To know with your experience and knowledge you can make the right decisions for the sport of archery.

SEMI-RECURVE BOW - a bow that is neither straight limb or fully a recurve limb.

SENIOR – division of competition; NAA adults are called seniors, IFAA/NFAA seniors are 55 and older. Golden Olympics competitors start at 50 yrs of age. NAA over 50 are called Master.

SERVING – the wrapping of thread on the bowstring at its center and loops to protect the bowstring material from damage or fraying.

SERVING TOOL – device with variable tension on treads to rotate around the bowstring to serve and protect from wear.

SET – a bend in the wood bow limbs that develop towards the bowstring after considerable use or storing improperly. A loss of efficiency, less of stored energy is the result.

SET ARM DRAW - the method of reaching full draw by first extending the bow arm and then drawing the bowstring to full draw.

SETUP - the preparation of tuning your archery equipment to achieve it's top potential performance.

SHAFT - the main body or tubing part of an arrow, the portion behind the head or point. (historical) anciently an arrow, in a foreshafted arrow the lighter portion behind the foreshaft.

SHAFT ARM – the arm that draws the bowstring back to full draw.

SHAFT GROOVES (historical) - furrow cuts along an arrow shaft from the head backward, they have been called blood grooves or lightning grooves.

SHAFTMENT - the part of an arrow on which the feathering is laid.

SHALLOW HOOK - allowing the bowstring to roll out to the meaty tips of the fingers, creates muscle tension in the hand.

SHANK - the part of the arrowhead corresponding to the tang of the sword blade.

SHELF - a place on the bow for a rug or arrow rest, lower surface of the bow window.

SHOT – the drawing and release of the bowstring to propel an arrow. This term in connection with the stake number, i.e., "4th shot", shall be used in referring to the different shots on any course.

SHOOT AROUND ARROW REST - an arrow rest which requires the bottom most fletching of the arrow to pass to the outside of the support arm of the arrow rest.

SHOOT SEQUENCE - a sequential sequence to control one shot process from trance to release of the bowstring, exactly the same every shot.

SHOOTER – one who supports participation in archery tournaments. One who uses the bow & arrow as a hobby in his back yard. There is a learned value in shooting that can be used in everyday life. It is the shooter's responsibility to learn the rules and regulations of the organization's round to be shot.

SHOOTING ERROR - a mistake in control, judgment or attitude causing a bad shot. We must learn from mistakes and not repeat them, always concentrate on a good shot; not your errors.

SHOOTING LINE - line parallel to the target butts from which archers can shoot their arrows safely.

SHOOTING RULES – rules and regulations established by the sponsoring archery organization for the round being shot.

SHOOTING SPECTACLES - sunglasses or for optical vision correction.

SHORT ARROWS - those which fall short of the mark or fall off of the arrow rest before you reach full draw.

SHOT SEQUENCE – Stance, nock an arrow, hand into the bow, fingers set on the bowstring, pre-draw to your anchor, pre-aim, settle into anchor and square shoulders as you pull with your draw elbow to full draw, aim, hold tension, release the bowstring and follow through until the arrow hits its target.

SHOOTING DIVISION - age grouping and by sex for archery competition, NFAA, Cub (under 12), Youth (12-14), Young Adult (15 - 17), Adult (18 - 49), Senior (50-59), Master (60-69) and Master Senior 70+. USAA, optional Yeomen (under 8), Bowmen (under 12), Cadet (12-14), Junior (18-19), Senior (20-49), Master 50+, Master 60+ and Master 70+.

SHOOTING GLOVE – 3 leather finger covers with straps to fasten around the wrist.

SHOOTING LINE - an imagery or marked line at a uniform distance form a target from which all archers shoot.

SHOOTING STOOL – 3-D seat that holds arrows and accessories, carried on the range.

SHOOT THROUGH ARROW REST - an arrow rest which requires the bottom most fletch of an arrow to pass between the support arm or arms of the arrow rest and the riser.

SHOOT OFF – to break tied scores for the championship after regular competition is complete. NFAA shoots 3 additional ends or targets, if still tied, arrow for arrow (inside out) until tie is broken. Olympic round is arrow for arrow for 3 arrows, with the 3rd arrow being closest to the center of the target breaks the tie.

ARCHERY STYLE - NFAA Traditional, Barebow, Bowhunter, FITA Olympic, Freestyle Limited, Bowhunter Freestyle Limited, Freestyle (Open), Bowhunter Freestyle, Crossbow, Professional.

NAA (USAA) Longbow, Barebow, Recurve, Compound, Crossbow, Masters Compound Limited.

SHOOTING TAB – a leather device used to protect the shooting fingers and helps in a smooth release of the bowstring.

SHOOTING TECHNIQUE - step by step sequence from stance to follow-through executing proper control and timing to complete each shot.

SHORT ARROW - those which fall short of the mark, arrow to short to allow the archer to reach their full draw and shoulder alignment.

SHOULDER QUIVER or BACK QUIVER – a device worn over the shoulder and back to hold arrows to be shot.

SINKING - the gradual loss of a bow's power.

SIDES of an ARROWHEAD (broadheads) - the sharpened portions between the apex and the base, also called the edges.

SIGHT – a device using a visual reference mounted within the bow window to put on the center of a target so the arrow hits the center of the target. A sight must be adjustable or multi sight pins can be used for varying distance and windage.

SIGHT ADJUSTMENT – move aiming device in the direction the arrows are hitting off; (arrows right) move sight to the right, etc.

SIGHTERS - unscored arrows shot for practice before a round is officially started, to make adjustment for sighting for that distance.

SIGHTER ARROWS – practice or non-scored arrows shot before a round to check and/or adjust sighting marks.

SIGHT EXTENSION – adjustable bar that can be moved in or out to which the sight is attached.

SIGHT BLOCK – the movable part of the sight that holds the sight pin, aperture or scope.

SIGHT WINDOW - the cut out portion of the riser section above the grip.

SIGHTING MARKS – position mark on sight bar for sight block placement for actual distance being shot. Number scale on sight bar that can be used to position the sight block for a specific distance to be shot, can be point of aim marks in the ground.

SILENCER - a clump of yarn, leather or rubber attached to the bowstring to reduce vibration and bowstring noise, usually used for bowhunting.

SINEW - bow limbs whose elasticity is increased by use of sinew along the back of the bow limb, either in a cable (as among the Eskimo) or laid on solid by means of glue.

SINEW BACKED BOW - a bow whose elasticity is increased by the use of sinew along the back, either in a cable or laid on solid by means of glue, wedges, bridges and splints are also used.

SINKING – the gradual loss of a bow's stored energy, older designs; due to heat, self bows; due to use; they just wear out.

SIX-GOLD – An award to archers for shooting a perfect end of six tens.

SKI ARCHERY – a combination of Nordic skiing and archery with a 12 km course for men and 8km for women, during the circuits 12 arrows from 18M are shot. There is just a hit or miss, for each miss a 300M's is added at the finish.

SKILLED – An archer consistent enough to fine tune their archery equipment for better performance in a tournament. This effort may take a year or two, depending on time and practice.

SKIRT - the part of the target face outside the scoring zones.

SKY SHOT – Pulling the bow to full draw with your bowarm pointed into the air. This is dangerous, if you misfire. Mostly compound release problem (over bowed).

SLEIGHT - the facility with which an archer releases his bowstring.

SLING – strap or cord fastened around the bow and archer's wrist to prevent the bow from falling when shot, also a finger sling. This allows shooting with a relaxed bow hand.

SNAKE - act of an arrow disappearing under the grass.

SNAP SHOOTING – releasing the bowstring without reaching full draw or anchor point or releasing without pausing to aim. A fault in which the archer releases prematurely before they hold and aim carefully.

SPIRAL FLETCH - feather or vanes which are attached to the shaft in a spiral manner, either right or left winged.

SPLIT CABLE - configuration of buss cables on a compound bow.

SPLIT LIMB - design of two smaller bow limbs that work together instead of one solid bow limb.

SPOT - number of targets on a face, one spot, three spot or five spot targets. To observe or call the hit of an individual arrows in the target.

STANCE - foot position to control the relaxed stance aligning of the trunk and shoulders to the target until the arrow is in the target, should be the same every shot. Square, open and closed are variances.

STATIC TILLER - measured on equipment as braced not storing energy from pulling or at full draw.

STRAIGHT LIMB BOW - a bow with straight limbs, having no reflex or recurve built into it when manufactured.

STRESS MANAGEMENT - the conscious control of the physiological functions of the body within the shot sequence.

STRING ALIGNMENT - placing the bowstring between the sight aperture and the riser while at full draw aiming.

SPRINGY - a small curled spring used as an arrow rest, substituted for a cushion plunger.

STYLE - classification used for competition or practice by equipment and accessories used.

SOFT SHOOTER - describes a shooter that uses a soft relaxed bow arm with a bent elbow.

SOLID BOW – common reference to a bow made of solid fiberglass or plastic.

SOUND SHOT – Not seeing your target and shooting at a sound in the brush. This is wrong and dangerous.

SOURCE – the origin of equipment, from which something comes, information from a book, person, document or film.

SPALL - a large flake of stone knocked off in blocking out arrow heads.

SPECTATORS LINE (target archery) - line at least 15 meters behind the shooting line.

SPEEDNOCK - a nock that has been molded with an index on the nock to locate the index feather by feel.

SPIDER – When an arrow hit the center if the X in the target face making little legs outside the arrow shaft, making it appears as a spider.

SPINE – the arrow's resistance to bending, a measurement of the amount of arrow shaft flexibility. The stiffness or amount an arrow bends when shot from a bow. Spine measurement: hang a 2 lb. weight at the center of a shaft suspended on supports 26" apart and measure the amount of bend in the shaft, low profile and light weight.

SPINWING – a type of fletch made of Mylar that uses tape the adhere to the shaft.

SPIRAL FLETCH – feathers or vanes attached to the arrow shaft in a spiral manner, extra wind drag.

SPLIT FINGER - Mediterranean hold of fingers on the bowstring, index finger above the arrow nock with two fingers under the arrow nock.

SPORTSMANSHIP – a competitor who exhibits qualities of fairness, courtesy and grace in winning and defeat. Showing a respect of others and their equipment.

SPOT or X RING – center aiming mark inside the highest scoring ring recorded as an "X" next to the score of that target or end to be used as a tie breaker at the end of competition.

SPOTTER – an observer with scope or binoculars that identifies the value of the score for that arrow just shot.

STABILIZER – an extension by a light rod mounted to the bow that holds a weight used to minimize vibration and minimize the torque dampening that accrues during the release and follow through as the arrow leaves the bow. Dampens of the bow on the three axes of torque centered at the pivot point.

STABILIZER WEIGHTS – screw-in weight or weights to be added to the stabilizer system.

STACKING – a characteristic of bow performance where the force draw curve increases more rapidly over the final part of the draw to anchor, unpleasant increase in draw strength necessary to complete to full draw.

STANCE - the physical alignment of the body in relation to a target while shooting with feet in the same position. Open stance, Squire stance and Close stance in a upright, balanced with extension control are required for a good shot and follow through, aligns the shoulders to the target.

STATIC DEFLECTION - the degree of limb bend before the bow is drawn,

STATIC RELEASE (dead) - releasing the bowstring without any back tension, release hand or release aid doesn't move backwards, static or moves forward towards the target.

STATIC TENSION - an archer who comes to full draw and locks into position so that their back and shoulder muscles develop into a tight and static condition which doesn't allow free movement on release.

STAVE - a piece of wood, destined to be shaped, into a bow after curing.

STELE (stale, shaft) - the wooden part of an arrow, an arrow without feather or head (point).

STORED ENERGY - the amount of recoverable energy contained in the bow limbs when the bow is at full draw.

STRAIGHTNESS – shaft tolerance, best + or - .001"

STRETCH – horizontal movement of the bow hand and drawing elbow at the bowstring release, follow through is on this horizontal plane; not straight forward and straight back until the arrow hit its target.

STRETCHING BAND – large rubber band to warm up by pulling and holding before practice or scoring, warm up.

STRIKE PATTERN – if an archer is shooting consistently you can tell errors or needed corrections from the group pattern of the arrows in the target. Good group low or high, move sight. Group near center one arrow left of center, forced shot, stretching in the shoulders. Group near center one arrow right of center, no follow-through, collapsed shot.

STRING – to place a bowstring on a bow – multiple strands or cord to brace a bow for shooting. Endless – one constituent strand whipping to form the loop of the bowstring. Laid in – loops are formed by splicing to make one bowstring.

STRING ALIGNMENT - the visual placement of the bowstring in relationship to the bow when at full draw for consistent right and left placement of the arrows hitting the target.

STRING ANGLE – bowstring pinch, the angle formed by the bowstring at the nocking point when the bow is at full draw.

STRINGER – a device to aid in stringing or bracing a bow; cord stringer, wall stringer or box stringer. (historical) a maker of bowstrings.

STRING FINGERS – the fingers used to draw back and hold the bowstring, placement can vary depending of purpose and style of shooting. The two or three fingers used to draw and release the bowstring.

STRING JIG – an adjustable frame used to make bowstrings.

STRING PATTERN - the relationship between the bowstring and the sight aperture.

STRING NOTCH - the grooves at the ends of each bow limb into which the loops of the bowstring fit for bracing the bow.

STRING WALKING - system of aiming by moving or walking different placement of the holding fingers on the bowstring so you can aim with the point of the arrow on the bulls' eye from any distance.

STRING HAND – drawing hand, the hand used to pull the bowstring back.

STRING HEIGHT - brace height or fistmele, distance from the pivot point to the bowstring of a braced bow.

STRING PEEP – plastic or metal hole mounted in the bowstring to use as a rear sight alignment, peep sight.

STRING SILENCER – A small attachment to the bowstring for reducing the noise from the bowstring twang.

STRUNG BOW – a braced bow ready to shoot.

STYLES – different archery equipment setup, with different scoring capability in different archery organizations to attempt fair competition.

SQUSRE STANCE - a foot position on the shooting line in which a line to the target runs from toe to toe.

STABILITY - the ability of a bow to absorb small errors in your shot sequence.

STABILIZER - additional weights extended in front of and at each end on a rod from the bow riser, to eliminate torque and absorb the shock of the release.

STRUNG BOW (braced) - a bow ready to shoot.

SUMMER YOUTH CAMPS – most camps offer archery but have no connection with organized archery, some require certified archery instructors, most do not.

SWAYING - a condition which exists primarily from a straight or squire stance where the archer is not firmly balanced and the body sways from toe to heel.

SYSTEM – an ordered and comprehensive scheme or plan of organizational procedures or shooting sequence of a shot. A national archery organization with its structure of states & clubs affiliates to promote competition. A style of shooting the bow and arrow that has unique aiming procedure; instructive, bare bow, string walking, freestyle limited or unlimited for longbow, recurve or compound bows. A round of archery used to compare scores, with its rules and regulations. Clubs organized to promote a phase of archery.

TAB – A flat pad to cover the three shooting fingers for protection and a smooth release. Some have can't pinch levers and ledge to help a more consistent anchor.

TACKLE - an inclusive term for archery equipment and related accessories for shooting archery, all equipment used by an archer.

TAKE-DOWN - a recurve bow designed to disassemble into a smaller size for storage or travel. Some longbows are two pieces laminated under the handle. A 3-piece bow that has a metal riser with laminated recurve limbs.

TAPER TOOL – device, like a pencil sharpener; that cuts accurate taper on wood shafts, 5 degree.

TARGET BUTT – an object at which the archer shoots, paper target face with scoring rings or 3D game animal. A disk of straw covered with canvas skirting with a target face on it, can by portable or stationary.

TARGET ARCHERY - a competitive round with archery traditions over hundreds of years, Olympic archery a new form of modern archery.

TARGET ARROW - a wooden or light weight arrow of aluminum or carbon for outdoor shooting.

TARGET CAPTAIN – the archer who decides who is to call the value of the arrows in the target face, and who records the scores and interprets the rules for that group.

TARGET CARD - a card to record score.

TARGET DAY - day officially set aside by an archery club for formal shooting or practice.

TARGET FACE - a sheeting material that is attached to the target butt for scoring which indicates the scoring area for a specific round for each archer to shoot at, can be one target face or multiple targets on one face.

TARGET PANIC - to release the bowstring prematurely or before final aiming procedure is achieved, cannot stop the sighting device on the center of the target. Believed to be a mental condition causing a loss of control in shooting form, inexperienced or lack of confidence.

TARGET STAND – a frame made to hold the target butt can be stationary or portable made of suitable material to stop and hold the arrow.

TASSELL – pieces of fabric or yarn used to clean the arrow shaft if wet or dirty, usually hung from the belt or quiver.

TEACHING ARCHERY – do not have to be certified, sharing your knowledge of archery with an interested person seeking such knowledge. Sanctioned course procedure with material from an archery organization and after satisfactory completion they certify your ability to teach under their approval.

TEAM – an indeterminate number of archers per-team for competition by organization. FITA & Olympic teams have 3 team members shooting 9 arrows in 3 ends. IFAA teams have 8 team members, one of each shooting style & total accumulative score in competition. NFAA Pro-Am team competition held during their national tournament schedule, There are up to 4 non-pro members shooting with a professional archer. The Pro and each non-pro shooter make up a team.

THUMB RING - a ring of bone used to protect the thumb of the drawing hand when using the Mongolian release.

THREE FINGERS UNDER - place the drawing fingers of the drawing hand on the bowstring under the arrow nock.

3-D ROUND - an archery round shoot in which the targets are three dimensional lifelike foam or rubber animal targets and placed at unknown distances to simulate hunting.

3-D TARGET - a lifelike foam shaped animal target, decorated to look like real animals, with ideal kill zones marked.

TIE BREAKER – most X's, most 10's, most 9's, if still tied shoot head to head competition to determine champion. Tied scores only shot off for the championship title.

TIGHT SHOOTER (firm) - that condition which describes the form of an archer using a tight push-pull method of shooting, has a break away or flying follow-through.

TILLERING - the art of properly balancing the bow limbs and bringing about a uniform bend through out the bow, a notched bar to hold the bow as drawn to variety of draw lengths.

TILLER POINT- point on the handle of the bow from which the limbs have been constructed to bend symmetrically.

TIMBER - in field archery a warning which should be called out to give other archers in the shooting area a warning that an arrow is on the fly.

TIMBER HITCH - a kind of knot used to secure the lower end of a single loop bowstring.

TIP - the point attached to the forward end of the arrow.

TITLE – sanctioned tournament designated as a championship by an archery organization; local, state, sectional, national, regional, world and Olympic titles.

TFC – Torque Flight Compensators are adjustable rubber vibration dampeners fitted to a stabilizer rod or rods.

THROWING – the movement of the bow hand at release.

THUMB RING - a ring worn on the thumb in archery by those peoples that use the Mongolian release, a femur cut from a large animal; called sefin by the Persians.

TILLER - measurement comparison perpendicular from the bowstring to the top and bottom of the riser section of the bow. Up to ½ in. on the upper tiller of a recurve or longbow and an even tiller is on a compound bow. To construct the bow limbs by the shaping of an unfinished bow for even bending of the bow limbs allowing for the handle section.

TILLER-POINT – point on the handle of the bow from which the limbs have been constructed to bend symmetrically.

TIMBER HITCH – a kind of knot used to secure the lower end of a single-loop bowstring.

TIP – The extreme ends of the bow and/or the forward extremity of an arrow, point, a term applied to the sharp apex of an arrowhead.

TIP PROTECTOR – Cover over the lower limb string nock on a recurve.

TIP STRING ANGLE (recurve) - the angle between the bowstring and the face of the bow limb immediately adjacent to the bowstring at full draw.

TOLERANCE – a close variation in a dimension or adjustment of archery equipment and personal shot execution. In tuning make adjustment to show correct setting and adjust past acceptable, then come back to the center of corrections.

TORQUE – any rotation or twisting motion of the bow in the horizontal or vertical plane as being shot. There are three axis of torque centered from the pivot point of the bow. A center stabilizer only dampens only two axis of torque an undesirable twisting of the bow. The torque created in the bowstring by the release hand or release aid at the releasing of the bowstring.

TORQUE (negative) - a rotation or twisting action anticlockwise of the bow at release, to the right for a right handed archer.

TORQUE (positive) - a rotation or twisting action of the bow at release, to the left for a right handed archer. There are three axes of torque in the bow as the bowstring is released, a stabilizer (extended weight) can dampen this movement.

TOURNAMENT - organized archery competition.

TOURNAMENT DIRECTOR (DOS) - person in charge of organizing and running a archery tournament.

TOXOLOGY - the study of archery.

TOXOPHILY - the art and craft of archery.

TOXOPHILITE - a devotee or lover of archery.

TOXOPHILUS – A book written by Roger Ascham in the sixteenth century. He was teacher to Queen Elizabeth. The book was the first complete written explanation of English archery.

TOXOPHILITE - the love of archery.

TRADITIONAL – a longbow or recurve shot instinctively, gapping or point of aim with no accessories, no sight and no stabilizers. Some traditional groups do not allow an arrow rest. The IFAA, NAA, NFAA, ASA & IBO have traditional styles of shooting in their competitions.

TRADITIONS – target face colors, used by Henry the 8th. Dress code of wearing white is from the same time period. Western archery came from the English longbow, wood on wood is traditional archery in the US.

TRAINER BOW - a bow designed to shoot without an arrow for training.
5 lb. pull or less for classes, checking a shooter's draw length or use at demo's.

TRAINING MATERIAL – books, videos, CDs, DVDs, brochures and the Internet have equipment knowledge and shooting techniques from which to learn.

TRAJECTORY - the curved path an arrow follows to the target, the curve which as arrow describes in space.

TREE STAND – a hanging platform, a ladder platform and a climbing platform from which to bowhunt.

TRIGGER – a mechanism in a crossbow to release the bowstring. A hand held mechanism in a release aid to release the bowstring.

TROPHY – an award with columns and figurine with date, location and style of shooting on it. All beginners wish to win a large trophy, to prove something. Long time archers wish to compete and win, but the award is irrelevant. American attitude: no one remembers 2nd place, after a month no one remembers 1st place in archery.

T-SQUARE - a device to measure brace height and locating the nocking point and peep sight location on the bowstring.

TUNE - to adjust the arrow rest, nocking point, brace height, tillering of bow, bow draw weight, eccentric timing for adjusting arrow flight to get the best arrow grouping.

TWAC – The World Archery Center foremost archery camp for over 60 yrs, started in the 1930's by the Millers.

TWO WHEEL COMPOUND BOW - a compound bow having one eccentric on each bow limb tip and a cable or string system connecting each eccentric with the axle of the opposite eccentric.

TWENTY PIN – An award for NFAA members that shoot a perfect score on a Field or Hunter target during competition

TWISTED BOW LIMB - the extreme ends of a bow limb that is not in line with the main portion of the bow, caused by improper bracing or storage.

UNDERBOWED – a bow not strong enough to shoot the distance needed in practice or competition, usually a beginner working to build the strength to use a heavier draw bow.

UNDERDRAWN – insufficient drawing back of the bowstring, not reaching full draw or your anchor point before releasing the bowstring, inconsistent power from the bow.

UNDERSTRUNG - a bow with a bowstring that is too long.

UNIFORMITY - description of shot to shot sameness, consistent shot sequence.

UNITED BOWMEN of PHILADELPHIA – archery club founded by Titian Ramsey Peale in 1828.

UNIQUE – every kid who hits their first bulls eye. The tranquility of shooting a perfect shot. The experience of sharing a well run tournament with friends.

UNKNOWN – one phase of archery seems to know little of other phases of archery. Making decisions in archery without knowing all your options; in equipment, styles of shooting, organizations and tournaments available; much less the rules.

USOC – United States Olympic Committee, web Olympic-usa.org.

VALLEY - the point of lowest holding weight on the bowstring reached near full draw on a compound bow.

VANE - a type of fletching (other than feathers) usually made of soft plastic.

VENEER - a thin strip of tough, elastic substance glued to the back of a bow. A coat of silica or urethane to seal and protect the bow.

V BAR – two short stabilizer rods mounted to the riser or center stabilizer, angled back in the form of a "V". Can be used as a counter balance in the system, dampens all three axis of normal torque.

V BAR MOUNT – unit that screws into the riser and holds the v bars in place.

VIBRATION REDAMPENERS – limb savers, cable dampeners, modular stabilizer and stabilizer enhancers, rubber bushings, many new designs dampen vibration and help with torque.

VOLUNTEERS – archery has no states or money, it runs on volunteer help. Instructors, club officers, officials, workers and many more are needed or there would be no archery competition. What you have to be careful of is to only schedule things you wish to help with. Never do something because you feel obligated - you will burn yourself out. If it is important someone will do it, no one is indispensable.

WALL - the region where rapid weight increase on the bowstring is reached when drawing a compound bow beyond the valley.

WAITING LINE – line at which archers wait for the starting signal to shoot and to retire after completing shooting the arrows for that end, generally 5 meters behind the shooting line.

WAND TARGET - a narrow stick of wood used as a target.

WAND ROUND - a three inch strip of masking tape is stuck vertically on the target butt, arrows that pierce the tape get a value. historically, the wand round was a 6" strip of soft wood at a hundred years. Men shoot 90M, women shoot 70M. Shoot 36 arrows in six arrow ends as a wand 5cm wide and 2M high.

WEIGHT ADJUSTMENT BOLT - the bolt placed through the butt end of the bow limb that attaches the bow limb to the handle or riser that controls the peak draw weight of the bow limbs in drawing the bow to full draw.

WEIGHT-IN-HAND – the physical weight of the bow and accessories, not it's power.

WHIPPING (historical) - seizing, serving, wrapping any part of a bow or arrow with cord or sinew regularly laid on its surface.

WHISTLE SIGNALS – 2 blasts, come to the shooting line; 1 blast, start shooting; 3 blasts, retrieve and score arrows; multiple blasts, stop shooting (emergency).

WIDE ARROWS - those arrows shot to the right or left of the mark.

WINDAGE – horizontal adjustment (right to left) of the bow sight to allow for the wind deflecting of the arrow in flight to the target. Cant the upper bow limb into the wind, do not aim off of the center of the target.

WINDLASS – a medieval device to pull the bowstring back on a crossbow.

WOBBLE - the erratic motion of an arrow flying to the target; not stable.

WOOD CORE LIMB - a bow limb constructed of two or more layers of fiberglass or carbon veneer between which a layer of wood laminations are placed.

WOOD ARROWS - arrow shaft of one piece or more (footed) of straight grained wood. many different woods used.

WORKER – archer who helps with the many things needed to be done before anyone can shoot on the range or at a tournament. Many shooters are not workers.

WRIST – the lower part of the forearm, where it joins the hand. The wrist is best relaxed when shooting (low wrist), to allow the pressure from the pivot point of the bow to be transferred into the stub of the arm. Bowarm is relaxed and straight. The wrist can be extended to accept the pressure from the pivot point, pressure must still be transferred into the stub of the arm (high wrist). There is a natural wrist position that can be used (medium wrist).

WRIST SLING - a device of string, leather or other material attached to the bow below the grip or handle to keep from dropping the bow upon releasing the bow and following through to complete the shoot, looped over the archers wrist and looped around two fingers of that bow hand so as not to drop the bow keeping the archers bowhand and fingers relaxed.

X-RING - a small circle at the very center of the bull's-eye, the number of x-rings is often used as a tiebreaker for ties scores in archery competitions.

YARN TASSEL - a large tuft of yarn that is used to clean an arrow.

YEW – the wood of a European evergreen tree (taxus baccata)used for making longbows.

YOUTH – under the age of 18 years of age. With little effort on the youth's part he or she will improve at shooting and gain self confidence and self respect and learn structure they can use in everyday life. Tournament rules and regulations teach discipline and structure.

ZEN - Japanese religious ritual, a thought focused on a single object, emphasizes enlightenment by means of meditation and direct, intuitive insights. In archery you must realize unconsciousness, completely empty and rid of the self, he becomes one with the perfecting of his technical skill, through there is in it something of a quite different order which cannot be attained by any progressive study of today.

Over the centuries archery equipment and terminologically have changed, this is what I have found over the last 65 years in archery, many are terms no longer used anymore.

Index

About the Author

Jake Veit started shooting and competing at the age of 11 as a family sport. He was certified as an archery instructor by the NFAA after starting an Archery Club in Ohio. Was Idaho Field Archery Assoc.'s secretary for 7 years. Served as NFAA National Instructor Chairman in the 1980's. Was Georgia Bowhunter & Archery Assoc. tournament director for 9 years. Won his first National Archery championship in 1973. Won his first World Archery championship in 1988. After shooting and promoting Archery in Ohio, Idaho and Georgia has won over 70 state, over 50 sectional and 6 national Archery Championships

Authors Resume

Elected to be an office with the Ohio Archers, Idaho Field Archers, the Georgia Bowhunters & Archery Assoc. and the Georgia Archery Assoc.

Over 62 State Championships in Ohio, Idaho and Georgia one in Ohio, seven in Idaho and 54 in Georgia

Life Member since 1983 in USAA, NFAA & NRA

Hosted Archery Tournaments mostly NFAA & NAA since 2000, was a USAA (NAA) Judge for 21 years, NAA National Judge in 1994 earned NAA National Coach Level 4 in 1997

Earned the NFAA Master Coach in 1982

Was an Olympic Scoring Judge for Archery in the 1996 Olympic Games and a Scoring Judge in the 1996 Paralympics

Over 38 NFAA Sectional Championships in Idaho & Georgia three in Idaho and 35 in Georgia

USAA National Champ in 1973 and in Masters 2012 (as a judge you can not judge and shoot in USAA)

NFAA National Champ in 1993 Outdoor and 1998 Indoor

Over 25 State Senior Games Champion and National Senior Games placing 2nd three times

Over 30 State Games Championships in Georgia Archery and 1 National State Games Championship in 2013

IFAA North American Champ 1984 Colorado and 2003 Texas

IFAA World Champ in 1988 Outdoor, 1998 and 2001 Indoor

Has earn a National Volunteer Lifetime Achievement Award in 2017 in Georgia

Printed in the United States